WHAT IS PSYCHOTHERAPEUTIC RESEARCH?

WHAT IS PSYCHOTHERAPEUTIC RESEARCH?

Edited on behalf of the United Kingdom Council for
Psychotherapy by

Del Loewenthal and David Winter

KARNAC
LONDON   NEW YORK

First published in 2006 by
H. Karnac (Books) Ltd.
6 Pembroke Buildings, London NW10 6RE

British Library Cataloguing in Publication Data

A C.I.P. for this book is available from the British Library

ISBN 1 85575 301 4

Edited, designed and produced by The Studio Publishing Services Ltd,
www.publishingservicesuk.co.uk
e-mail: studio@publishingservicesuk.co.uk

Printed in Great Britain

10 9 8 7 6 5 4 3 2 1

www.karnacbooks.com

CONTENTS

ABOUT THE CONTRIBUTORS

Dr Talal Al Rubaie is a psychiatrist and psychotherapist. He is interested in the scientific nature of psychotherapy research methodologies. His research questions the so-called scientific method as the only legitimate method of obtaining "scientific" knowledge. He advocates the plurality of research methodologies for the sake of advancement of the theory and practice of psychotherapy. He works currently as consultant psychiatrist a Peterborough District Hospital in the UK.

Dr Andrew R. Arthur is head of Primary Care Psychology & Counselling for West Kent NHS & Social Care Trust. He is a Chartered Clinical and Counselling Psychologist and a psychoanalytic psychotherapist with experience in applying psychological therapies to a wide variety of client groups, including adults with mental health problems, people with learning disabilities, patients with chronic pain, and employees experiencing work-related stress. This research represents an interest in why therapists adopt particular approaches and theories to helping their clients and find it difficult to listen to different therapeutic perspectives.

Professor Mark Aveline, MD, FRCPsych, Hon Fellow, BACP Emeritus Consultant, Nottinghamshire Healthcare NHS Trust Honorary Professor, Institute of Lifelong Learning, University of Leicester. In May 2002, Dr Aveline retired after twenty-seven years as consultant psychotherapist in Nottingham, where he founded a "one-stop" integrated specialist NHS service in psychodynamic and cognitive–behavioural psychotherapy. The service has close links with psychiatry; it is dedicated to providing effective and relevant patient care. He is particularly interested in brief individual therapy, interpersonally orientated group therapy, training, research, and the use of technology in healthcare. In 1981, he co-founded the South Trent Training in Dynamic Psychotherapy, a NHS specialist training which registers its graduates through the Psychoanalytic Section of UKCP. For several years, he was in charge of specialist psychotherapy training in the Royal College of Psychiatrists, served on the Governing Board of the United Kingdom Council for Psychotherapy, and was President of the British Association for Counselling and Psychotherapy. In 2003–2004, he was President of the Society for Psychotherapy Research and was formerly President of the UK Chapter.

Dr Thaddeus Birchard has a BA in Sociology from the University of New Orleans and a postgraduate Diploma in Theology from Nottingham University. He trained at the Whittington Hospital, has an MSc in Psychosexual Therapy from the School of Health and Social Care, London South Bank University, and a Doctorate in Psychotherapy from Middlesex University and the Metanoia Institute. He is accredited for practice by the British Association for Sexual and Relationship Therapy and is registered with the United Kingdom Council for Psychotherapy.

Julia Buckroyd is Professor of Counselling at the University of Hertfordshire and a researcher in the field of eating disorders and obesity. She has published widely in this field and is currently continuing to develop interventions for the treatment of obesity in primary care using psychological strategies.

Dr Jocelyn Catty is a psychodynamic counsellor (Foundation for Psychotherapy and Counselling) working as a school counsellor and with adults in primary care and private practice. She is also a Research Fellow in Social and Community Psychiatry at St George's Hospital Medical School, with research interests in the interface between psychotherapy and psychiatry and in the therapeutic alliance. She has a doctorate in English Literature from Oxford University and has published a book on representations of rape in late sixteenth- and early seventeenth-century literature, as well as numerous papers on mental health services, including home treatment and day care.

Julia Cayne is a lecturer in Psychotherapy and Counselling at the University of Roehampton and practices as a psychotherapist in Hampshire. Her current research interest is in the development of a methodology for investigating the unknown in psychotherapy training and practice.

Dr Deborah Dobson is a psychologist with the Calgary Health Region, Adjunct Associate Professor with the Departments of Psychology and Psychiatry, University of Calgary, and has a private practice. She has conducted research in the areas of severe mental illness, anxiety disorders, and depression. She has supervised practicum students and pre-doctoral interns in clinical psychology, as well as residents in psychiatry. She has served on the Boards of the Psychologists' Association of Alberta, the Potential Place Clubhouse, and the Canadian Mental Health Association—Calgary Division. Current interests include client access to empirically supported treatments, clinical training, consumer advocacy, and cognitive–behaviour therapies.

Dr Keith Dobson is a Professor of Clinical Psychology at the University of Calgary in Canada, and a cognitive therapist. His research interests are in the areas of cognition and depression, as well as cognitive–behavioural therapy. He has published widely, including seven books, the most recent of which is *The Prevention of Anxiety and Depression* (with David Dozois, American Psychological Association Press).

Richard Evans is a registered UKCP psychotherapist, now retired from private practice. He was associated with the early development of the CORE System as the Chair of the Counselling in Primary Care Trust (a joint funder of the development) and as a member of the Society for Psychotherapy Research. In recent years he has acted as an adviser to the CORE System Trust and to CORE Information Management Systems Ltd, while also being Chair of the Artemis Trust, which is providing funding for research on the use of CORE.

Nick Gilbert is a research assistant in the Clinical Psychology department at the Barnet, Enfield and Haringey Mental Health NHS Trust.

Dr Dennis Greenwood is a Lecturer at the Centre for Therapeutic Education, Roehampton University. He has a PhD and his research interests include exploring the possibility of psychotherapy with a person suffering from dementia and the implications of continental philosophy for practice.

Dr Andrew Gumley graduated in clinical psychology from the University of Glasgow in 1993. His first position as a clinical psychologist was within a north Glasgow Community Mental Health Team. In that team he was able to develop his interests in the psychological treatment of individuals with psychosis. He has carried out PhD research into psychological aspects of relapse in schizophrenia. This research involved the implementation of a randomized controlled trial of Cognitive Therapy for relapse and an investigation of the role of cognitive factors in the vulnerability and transition to relapse. Currently he is Senior Lecturer in Clinical Psychology, and Research Tutor for the Doctorate in Clinical Psychology training course at the University of Glasgow. He is Honorary Consultant Clinical Psychologist at ESTEEM: North Glasgow First Episode Psychosis Service.

Dr Tirril Harris has divided her time over the past thirty years between private practice in psychoanalytic psychotherapy and carrying out social psychiatry research in the Socio-Medical Research Group, first at Bedford and Royal Holloway New College, University of London, and latterly in the Health Services Research Department, Institute of Psychiatry, London. In the course of the latter she has worked closely with Professor George Brown, focusing particularly on the role of psychosocial factors in contributing to the onset and remission of depressive and anxiety disorder. Their joint-authored works include *Social Origins of Depression* (1978), *Life Events and Illness* (1989), and *Where Inner and Outer Worlds Meet* (2000), as well as many journal articles.

Colleen Heenan is Senior Lecturer in Psychology at Bolton Institute, UK and adult psychotherapist in private practice. She was a co-founder of the Leeds (UK) Women's Counselling and Therapy Service. Her area of interest and research is gender, psychoanalysis and postmodern thinking, with particular reference to women, bodies, and eating problems, and she has edited a number of special features in the journal *Feminism and Psychology* as well as contributing to other texts and journals on these subjects. Colleen is co-author of two books (with Erica Burman et al.)—*Challenging Women: Psychology's Exclusions, Feminist Possibilities* (Open University Press, 1996) and *Psychology, Discourse, Practice: From Regulation to Resistance* (Taylor and Francis, 1996). She is also co-editor (with Bruna Seu) of *Feminism and Psychotherapy: Reflections on Contemporary Theories and Practices* (Sage, 1998).

Dr Georgia Lepper is a professional member of the Society of Analytical Psychology (now retired from clinical practice) and Lecturer in Psychotherapy at the University of Kent. As co-ordinator of the psychotherapy research programme, she supervises doctoral research students and is an active researcher, specializing in the application of Conversation Analysis to psychotherapeutic interaction. She is author of two introductory textbooks on research methods: *Categories in Text and Talk: A Practical Guide to Categorization Analysis,* and *Psychotherapy Process Research: A Practical Guide to Text-based Methods* (with Nick Riding).

Del Loewenthal is Professor of Psychotherapy and Counselling and Director of the Centre for Therapeutic Education , formerly at the University of Surrey and now at the University of Roehampton, UK. He is an existential–analytic psychotherapist and chartered counselling psychologist. He recently served for many years on the Governing Board of the UKCP, and was Chair of their Research Committee and First Research Conference, which forms the basis of this book. His other publications include: *Case Studies in Relational*

Research (Palgrave), and (with Robert Snell) *Postmodernism for Psychotherapists: A Critical Reader* (Routledge). He is Chair of the University Psychotherapy and Counselling Association and also Editor of the *European Journal of Psychotherapy and Counselling* (Routledge).

Dr Martin Milton is Senior Lecturer at the University of Surrey, where he directs the Practitioner Doctorate in Psychotherapeutic and Counselling Psychology. He is a chartered counselling psychologist and registered psychotherapist, and was formerly Consultant Psychologist in Psychotherapy with North East London Mental Health Trust. Martin is active in the BPS where he is Chair Elect of the Division of Counselling Psychology and a representative to the Register of Psychologists Specialising in Psychotherapy.

Jayne Redmond is a UKCP registered psychotherapist and BACP registered practitioner with twelve years' experience in NHS, Further Education, and private practice. Jayne is currently a visiting lecturer at Roehampton for the Undergraduate and Postgraduate programmes, also supervising trainees and qualified counsellors. Jayne is from a nursing background, specializing in working with adolescents, and has an interest in male suicide from an existential perspective. She has previously been an Associate Editor for the *European Journal for Psychotherapy, Counselling and Health*.

Dr Theresa Rose formerly worked at the Centre for Therapeutic Education at the University of Surrey. She is currently working in the NHS and private practice.

Julie Ryden is a lecturer in Primary Care at Bournemouth University. The research presented in this chapter was undertaken as part of her MSc in Psychotherapy and Counselling as a means to Health in the School of Educational Studies, University of Surrey. Interest in the topic arose from her personal experiences of therapy, where she felt constrained in discussing her own sexuality with one therapist, though not with a subsequent therapist. This prompted an interest in exploring the issue through research with other lesbians.

Dr Christine Stevens, in addition to leading the MA programme in Gestalt Psychotherapy at the Sherwood Institute, is a UKCP registered Gestalt psychotherapist and a clinical supervisor. She has many years' experience working in the statutory and voluntary sectors as well as in private practice. Christine has a PhD in social science and an active interest in psychotherapy research. She is a visiting trainer for the Gestalt Foundation, Greece, and represents SPTI in the European Association for Gestalt Therapy. She lives in Nottingham with her GP husband and two teenage children.

Maureen Taylor is a UKCP registered psychotherapist and a BACP senior registered practitioner working in the NHS and private practice. Her background is in nursing, research, industry, voluntary services, and education. Previously an associate lecturer in the Centre for Therapeutic Education at the University of Surrey, she supervised students on person-centred and psychodynamic counselling diploma courses, and occasionally taught MSc and PhD students. She was an associate editor for the *European Journal of Psychotherapy, Counselling, and Health*. She has published papers in *Psychodynamic Counselling*; *European Journal of Psychotherapy, Counselling and Health*; the *CMS Journal* (BACP) and *The Journal for Existential Analysis*.

Finn Tschudi is a retired Professor of Psychology from the University of Oslo. He has a keen interest in personal construct psychology, on the subject of which he has contributed several book chapters. For several years he has worked to develop programmes for analysing multiple grids in order to study homogeneity/heterogeneity in various groups. The most important current project he is involved with concerns studying how Swedish auditors construe their tasks post Enron and similar scandals. This fits in with his other major interest, which is emotions and conflict transformation. He has introduced a special form of conferencing—elaborated in Australia, which is influenced by the Maoris and other indigenous societies in the Pacific—in Norway. He is involved in further developments in this area in a joint project with Albania.

David Winter is Professor of Clinical Psychology and Course Director of the Doctorate in Clinical Psychology at the University of Hertfordshire. He is Head of Clinical Psychology Services and Coordinator of Research for the Barnet, Enfield and Haringey Mental Health Trust.

Introduction

Del Loewenthal and David Winter

This book may mark an important watershed in the development of psychotherapy in the UK. For many years there have been those with a particular interest in psychotherapeutic research who may or may not have been practitioners. This book has been produced particularly with existing and future practising psychotherapists in mind; and as such suggests that the ability to carry out and use research may indeed also be necessary for practitioners.

While psychotherapy in the UK is seen as being taught at postgraduate level (unlike counselling, which can be seen to be provided more, but not exclusively, at undergraduate level), it is counselling, through, in particular, the work of John McLeod (2003), that has taken a lead in developing practitioner research. This lead, however, is only relative to psychotherapy and is not the case with regard to other professions, including Freud's other "impossible" professions involving management and education. There are those who argue that such so-called professionalism, coupled with what some see as too narrowly defined evidence, is detrimental to the purposes of psychotherapy. In one sense, this is tied to the notion of psychotherapy as a profession. In other disciplines it is expected that practitioners will learn about research as a way of underpinning—and thereby legitimizing—their knowledge. There is also a further complication, with the argument that psychotherapy and counselling can themselves be forms of research.

These are important considerations that have been voiced at least since the time of Plato, when he suggested that while scientific and technical thinking is important, it should be secondary to the resources of the human soul. However, what has developed is a lack of relative knowledge of research in psychotherapy, a history of apparent defensiveness in being evaluated, and a reluctance to work with universities. This situation contrasts to that of psychology, which is well enshrined in research and the university, and where the development of professional-looking counselling psychology is being followed by the British Psychological Society's Psychotherapy Register. All this threatens further marginalization of psychotherapy and, as there are those who consider that the inherent undermining of authority is an essential part of the psychotherapeutic enterprise, a view that this is where it rightly belongs. This book, however, provides examples of how psychotherapeutic research and the abilities to carry this out can help the practising psychotherapist.

We hope that this book is of interest to all psychotherapists who wish to understand, whatever they may make of it, the growing importance of research in our current psychotherapeutic cultural practices. In common with the British tradition and beyond, this book focuses on the empirical aspects of research. The important development of theory outside of this is not covered within this book.

The contents are primarily based on the First UKCP Research Conference (University of Surrey, Centre for Therapeutic Education, 2002). The design of this conference was the responsibility of the UKCP research committee, whose members were: Professor Del Loewenthal (Chair); Professor David Winter; Dr Talal Al Rubaie; Dr Georgia Lepper; Dr Tirril Harris; and Dr Chris Williams. We would like to take this opportunity to thank the other committee members for their contribution to the design of the conference and also record our thanks to Helen McEwan, Rhiannon Thomas, and Andrew Balchin from the Centre for Therapeutic Education, now at Roehampton University, for their assistance in the book's production.

The papers presented were partly invited and partly received through submission and represent a cross-section of current research thinking within UKCP, as well as including international contributions from North America and continental Europe. It is hoped that what is presented will inspire current practitioners and those in training to develop themselves, and hence their practice, through research. (Some of the papers have been published elsewhere: Martin Milton's Chapter Six was first published in *Psychoanalytic Psychotherapy* (2002), *16*(2); and Julie Ryden and Del Loewenthal's Chapter Twelve is drawn from Ryden, J., & Loewenthal, D. (2001). "Psychotherapy for lesbians: the influence of therapist sexuality", *Counselling Research*, *1*(1). Furthermore, Chapters Two to Five have been reprinted from previous issues of *The Psychotherapist*.)

The book has been divided into five parts, with each part focusing on a different area of the research endeavour. In Part I Mark Aveline, who is among the foremost nationally and internationally in developing psychotherapy research, outlines the stages in the research process from research idea through investigation to evidence-based practice, and gives an overview of the features of different research methods. Following this are four chapters originally published in *The Psychotherapist* by members of the UKCP Research Committee in order to start to open up the question "What is psychotherapeutic research". In Chapter Two Talal Al Rubaie opens the debate for case study, challenging the notions of traditional research methods, and in Chapter Three David Winter describes the pressures on psychotherapists to embrace and incorporate formalized research into their normal working week. Del Loewenthal argues in Chapter Four that researching narrow notions of evidence may be dangerous for psychotherapeutic practice. Chapter Five, by Georgia Lepper and Tirril Harris, advocates a pluralist approach to the research endeavour, suggesting that it need not be as problematic as others would have. The section concludes with a chapter by Martin Milton, raising some issues for evidence-based psychotherapy and suggesting that their demystification would allow a more empowered moving forward for the discipline.

The papers in Part II differ from those presented at the conference in that they have been rewritten to provide introductions to quantitative and qualitative methods rather than focusing on particular research findings. Andrew Gumley provides an introduction to quantitative research using single case evidence in routine psychotherapy practice. This is followed by four short chapters that introduce a selection of different qualitative research methods (a more detailed account of these can be found in Loewenthal, 2005). Chapter Eight, by Maureen Taylor, Jayne Redmond, and Del Loewenthal, describes the use of discourse analysis. In Chapter Nine Dennis Greenwood shows the evolution of a case study, echoing issues outlined in the previous section. Chapter Ten, by Julia Cayne and Del Loewenthal, introduces the phenomenological method. In Chapter Eleven, Theresa Rose and Del Loewenthal explore heuristic research. In Chapter Twelve Julie Ryden and Del Loewenthal use postmodern feminist methodology to examine the influences of therapists' sexuality. This is followed in Chapter Thirteen by a report by Thaddeus Birchard on researching sensitive and distressing topics.

Part III focuses on research into the process of psychotherapy. In Chapter Fourteen Christine Stevens investigates brief focused Gestalt therapy in an NHS setting. Colleen Heenan uses discourse analysis to throw light on the creation of meaning in psychotherapy in Chapter Fifteen. In Chapter Sixteen Georgia Lepper explores group cohesion using text- and conversation analysis. In Chapter Seventeen Jocelyn Catty compares different assumptions about the research effort in relation to the therapeutic alliance.

Part IV focuses on research into the outcomes of psychotherapy. Chapter Eighteen, by Richard Evans, highlights the utility of a recently-developed outcome measurement scale. In Chapter Nineteen Tirril Harris discusses the need for an aetiological framework. Keith and Deborah Dobson, in Chapter Twenty, describe a history of the movement towards evidence-based practice, using major depression as a focus for the paper. In Chapter Twenty-one Julia Buckroyd shows how the languages of psychoanalysis and of social sciences research can be synthesized.

The chapters in the final part investigate therapeutic context with regard to the personal preferences of the therapist. Andrew Arthur, in Chapter Twenty-two, shows that therapists' thinking styles differ, which may have implications for the kind of conversation that patients are able to have in their therapy. In the final chapter of the book, Winter, Tschudi, and Gilbert examined differences between therapists of different orientations, allowing investigation of the relationship between personal styles and philosophical beliefs.

We very much hope that this book proves useful for students and practitioners of psychotherapy, as well as those more traditionally engaged in psychotherapeutic research. The Research Committee of UKCP, with Dr Chris Evans and Dr Andrew Gumley replacing Drs Talal Al Rubaie and Chris Williams in those listed above, have produced the reading list given at the end of the book for those who wish to further explore the literature of psychotherapy research.

References

McLeod, J. (2003). *Doing Counselling Research* (2nd edn). London: Sage.

Loewenthal, D. (2005). *Case Studies in Relational Research*. Basingstoke: Palgrave.

PART I

ISSUES IN PSYCHOTHERAPEUTIC RESEARCH

CHAPTER ONE

Psychotherapy research: nature, quality, and relationship to clinical practice

Mark Aveline

Introduction

E very therapist has a keen interest in practising effectively and efficiently. The practitioner wants to know that what she does is at least as helpful in addressing the patient's problems as other forms of help on offer and preferably is better! Although patient motivation can be complex and contradictory, overall the patient has the same interest as do employers, health purchasers and planners, and practice regulators.

But how can the practitioner know that he or she is practising effectively and efficiently?

The time-honoured way is through experience. Therapists learn to be therapists through practice. Each therapy is a form of research. Before I consider this proposition further, consider Jerome Frank's formulation of common therapeutic factors in all effective psychotherapies (Frank, 1973). At the heart of the work is an imaginative encounter between patient and therapist.[1] With the assistance of the therapist, the patient identifies feelings, thoughts, relationships, situations, actions, and dilemmas that are problematic. The patient confides emotionally and intensely. The therapist, often in the role of trusted healthcare professional within that society, engages the patient in addressing the problems and, through the exercise of theory, expert intuition, explanation, interpretation, and interaction, provides a way of understanding the significance of the problems and their origin. A plausible rationale helps the patient feel more hopeful about their situation and counters the demoralization that typifies those seeking help. Finally, therapy can provide success experiences, both inside the consulting room and outside in everyday life, as the patient's problems are grappled with and overcome. These experiences enhance the patient's sense of mastery.

But this generic model of how change comes about in successful psychotherapy is broad-brush. It gives a general direction and identifies fundamental principles, building one on the other, but it does not tell the therapist either how to match or adapt the type of therapy to patient need or how to proceed moment to moment in sessions. It is the answers to these critical questions that differentiate therapy with one person from that with another and guide the therapist towards the Holy Grail of efficiency and effectiveness.

Earlier, I put forward the proposition that each therapy is a form of research. From this perspective, the central event in therapy is a series of interactions. In response to what is occurring, therapists make their best judgement on what to do next; what happens subsequently is reviewed in the light of experience and new judgements are made; the effects of what is then done or not done is reviewed in turn. On a pragmatic level, it is an informal experiment, influenced by feedback and judged against the classical markers of progress, e.g., enhanced alliance, deepened empathy, fuller understanding, problem resolution, and patient satisfaction.

However, the therapist's view of intervention, process, and outcome is always partial. It is profoundly affected by the circumstance of the particular case, including the therapist's position in his or her own life. What may appear obvious in the formulation may lack supporting evidence. What may appear important in the process may actually mask another truly important variable. Beyond the single case, therapists can draw upon their experience of seemingly similar cases. However, even experienced therapists have a relatively small pool of experience from which to draw conclusions that they hope will improve their practice. The range of patients that they have worked with is limited in variety and severity of problem, stage, and life situation. Therapists' ideas on what therapy can achieve may be narrowed by restrictions in type or types of therapy practised and the constraining imperatives of the clinical settings in which they work. Unless their training was broad, or specifically addressed eclectic and integrative approaches, it is likely that their knowledge of alternatives and how therapy can be adapted to patient need will be narrow and prejudiced. Of course, the individual and summative judgements made in particular cases may be well founded, but the raw data will be based on partial evidence and heavily influenced by recent selective experience.

The primary contribution that research can make is to minimize bias. Clinicians, researchers and other stakeholders are enabled to stand to one side of their inevitable bias and take a fresh look at what is revealed; what happened and how and why. Formal research is the systematic investigation of an identified area of incomplete knowledge. The classic paradigm is conducting experiments. To test their significance, elements in the clinical story are held constant or varied, and the different outcomes subjected to detailed scrutiny. By virtue of its structure, research is an essential element in reliable communication between colleagues; it brings to the table the discipline of clear definition, the benefit of transparent methodology, the value of access to the experience of others through shared results and the potential for replication and further testing of conclusions.

Good research has three essential and challenging characteristics:

1. Scrupulous testing of hypotheses by evidence.
2. Openness to public assessment of results.
3. Readiness to revise or abandon theories in the light of new or better data.

Empirical research is often accused of subscribing to an inappropriate positivistic view of the world. The use of objectified methodology, it is said, risks giving false certainty to the external world when the inner world is essentially subjective and idiosyncratic.[2] Certainly, researchers need to guard against reductionism and over-simplification and be modest about the implications of their findings. Basing our understanding of human nature on observable facts only would be an unfortunate over-simplification. Conversely, being explicit about how our constructs are to be measured and confirmed or disconfirmed is a valuable part of the scientific approach (Barker, Pistrang, & Elliott, 1994) These caveats apply equally to clinicians!

What is the level of knowledge that we can derive from either research or clinical intuition? Plato distinguished between *truth*, which is perfect, eternal, and unchanging, and *opinion*, which reflects individual concerns and is local and temporary in nature. According to the standard set by this definition, *truth* is not to be found in human affairs. Our knowledge is more than opinion but lies towards that end of the spectrum rather than the enduring certainty of truth. We deal with probabilities and processes in psychotherapy that are non-linear and where our decisions are essentially heuristic.

This chapter outlines the stages in the research cycle from clinical intuition through investigation to evidence-based practice and describes the features of different types of research. It makes the case for research that is practice-close and sets out criteria for good quality research. It draws on an overview of psychotherapy research in the *Oxford Textbook of Psychotherapy*, a new textbook published by Oxford University Press (Aveline, Strauss, & Stiles, 2005). The reader is referred to the chapter for information on the history of the field and a summary of what is known about process and outcome.

Clinical practice and the research cycle

This Section overviews the cycle and identifies elements and terms that are described later.

In the quest to improve practice, the clinician draws upon experience, her own and the experience of others, through the theory, technique, and supervision internalized during training and extended through continuing professional development (CPD). This traditional resource is now supplemented by three new influences: (1) the product of *evidence-based practice* in the form of

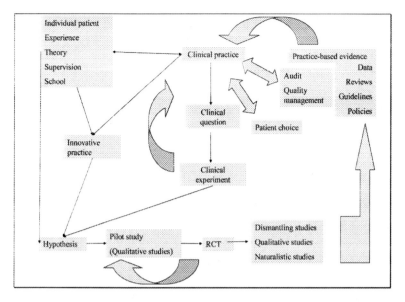

Figure 1.   The research cycle

published data, treatment reviews, therapy guidelines and governmental or purchaser guidelines; (2) feedback on local clinical performance through *audit* and *quality management*; and (3) *patient choice*.[3] Ideally these resources combine to provide the background for a unique and effective engagement with the patient. As I have described above, uncertainties abound in clinical practice and prompt informal mini-experiments in that engagement. Some outcomes lead to the development of *innovative practice* and others to questions whose scope cannot be answered without *systematic enquiry*. These are two of the main entry points to formal research.

Investigators have at their disposal a wide range of methodologies, some well established in classical empirical research in medicine and psychology and some breaking new ground in their exploration of subjectivity and individual meaning. Each has potentials and limitations in providing significant answers. The supporters of the two dominant paradigms of *qualitative* and *quantitative* research sometimes position their approach antagonistically to the other, but increasingly the methods are seen as synergistic. They have complementary roles in the research cycle.

Studying process is the principal subject of *qualitative* research. In focus, it is in the same domain as that considered by a clinician in internal or external supervision; the difference is in degree of systematization. *Quantitative* research provides an empirical, often controlled, means of validating and refining psychotherapy theory and practice.

Here are some pressing clinical questions suitable for *qualitative* investigation.

- What is the effect of making this or that intervention in a session?
- Does the effect persist from one session to the next?
- What is the relationship between sessions that go well or badly to outcome at termination?
- What are the contributory factors and how do they interact?
- In what way do patients, therapists, and significant others perceive sessions or the therapy differently?
- How may a patient's intra-psychic or interpersonal conflicts be formulated? Can this be done reliably? Can such formulations benefit clinical practice?
- How do patients' narratives alter over time, and what relationship does this have to psychotherapy theory?

Here are some suitable for *quantitative* investigation.

- Is this treatment more effective than other treatments?
- How does the efficacy of new therapies conducted under experimental conditions translate into clinical effectiveness in everyday work?
- What extra gain can a patient expect to derive from a therapy that lasts for fifty as opposed to twenty-five sessions?
- Does the gain justify the cost of the larger investment in time and duration?
- Do different forms of gain accrue with different durations of therapy?
- Do different therapies have different effects?
- Which patients with what conditions do best with what therapy?
- What training is necessary to maximize gain or minimize harm from therapy?

Forming a hypothesis is an essential step in the systematic investigation of a clinical question.

In the investigation, the method chosen depends on where one is in the cycle of developing or refining a therapy. A hypothesized therapeutic effect might be evaluated through observational single case studies. Should these generate large *effect sizes* (see Roth & Fonagy, 1996, pp. 379–380), this would indicate that there could be something worthwhile in the innovation. The next step would be small-scale single group designs, i.e., uncontrolled naturalistic studies. A major step up in rigour would be to move to a randomized controlled trial (RCT); this is the acid test of *efficacy* (see below). Results under controlled conditions, however, do not necessarily generalize to everyday clinical practice. *Effectiveness* has to be established through *naturalistic field trials*; these establish *generalizability* (see below and section on implementing evidence into clinical practice). Finally, *dismantling* studies tease out what are the effective ingredients in the practice being studied. *Qualitative* studies at each stage can be a rich source of ideas about the process of change.

Going through the sequence once is not enough. New perspectives arising from the findings at various stages prompt new paths through the cycle; studies need to be repeated to test the robustness of the findings. All this has to be evaluated against a standard of *clinically significant change*, a more stringent and relevant standard than simple statistical significance (Jacobson & Truax, 1991; Ogles, Lunnen, & Bonesteel, 2001). Where the threshold is set in a particular study is determined by clinical judgement. Its prior declaration is part of the transparency and rigour of the scientific method.

The difference between efficacy and effectiveness is crucial in understanding the divergence between research and service planning.

Efficacy versus effectiveness

Outcome studies are commonly divided into studies determining the *efficacy* of a treatment versus studies focusing on a treatment's *effectiveness* (Lambert & Ogles, 2004; Seligman, 1995; Strauss & Kächele, 1998).

Efficacy is determined by (randomized) clinical trials in which as many variables as possible are controlled in order to demonstrate unambiguously the relationship between treatment and outcome, and potentially infer causal relationships from the findings (Strauss & Wittmann, 2005).

Efficacy studies emphasize the *internal validity* of the experimental design through random assignments to treatments, controlling the types of patients included with respect to their diagnosis (commonly excluding patients with co-morbid disorders), through using manualized treatments, pre-training the therapists in the study's clinical practice, and monitoring adherence to the treatment manual. These parameters ensure uniformity of therapy and enable other researchers to replicate the investigation. The price of high *internal validity* is usually poor *external validity;* the nature of the intervention is clear and consistent but unrepresentative of everyday practice and, thus, the findings of the study may not generalize. An example of an important efficacy study is the National Institute of Mental Health (NIMH) Collaborative Depression Study (Elkin, 1994; Krupnick *et al.*, 1996; Ogles, Lunnen, & Bonesteel, 2001) in which patients with major depressive disorder were randomly assigned to four treatments: imipramine plus clinical management, placebo plus clinical management, cognitive behaviour therapy, interpersonal psychotherapy (IPT). One surprising result was that there was little evidence for the superiority of any of the active treatments in contrast to the placebo condition. All interventions were beneficial, with imipramine and cognitive behaviour therapy being particularly helpful for more depressed subjects. However, it should be noted that clinical management in the placebo contained many therapeutic elements and should be considered as a "benchmark" treatment.

Effectiveness studies, on the other hand, focus on clinical situations and the implementation of a treatment in clinical settings. Such studies emphasize the external validity of the experimental design: usually patients are not pre-selected, treatments commonly are not manualized, the duration of the treatment and other setting-related characteristics are not controlled. These *clinically representative* studies show how interventions perform in routine clinical practice (Shadish *et al.*, 1997). Their weakness is the converse of the strength of efficacy studies; it is difficult to know what was done, when, and how. The variability inherent in effectiveness studies makes it much harder to disentangle what were the therapeutic elements and replicate the work in other settings. An example of an effectiveness study is the German multi-site study on inpatient psychotherapy for patients with eating disorders (Kächele, Kordy, Richard, & TR-EAT, 2001). Questions examined in this prospective, naturalistic design included: what is the effectiveness of inpatient psychodynamic therapy for eating disorders?, what factors determine the length of treatment?, how do treatment duration and intensity contribute to effectiveness?, can such effects be attributed to specific patient characteristics?

Naturalistic effectiveness studies are the principal research approach for the assessment of outcome in treatments that are hard to assess within a controlled clinical trial, either because of formal characteristics (e.g., treatment length) or because of ethical reasons (e.g., impracticalities in randomizing subjects to treatments) such as inpatient treatments or long-term psychoanalysis. Examples of representative effectiveness studies from the psychoanalytic field are the Menninger Psychotherapy Research Project (Wallerstein, 1986), the Heidelberg Psychosomatic Clinic Study (Fonagy, 2001) and the Berlin Multicentre Study on psychoanalytic orientated treatments (Rudolf, 1991) (see the "open door review of outcome studies in psychoanalysis" (Fonagy, 2001)).

Research designs and the evaluation of their products

Research began with Freud's case studies but accelerated in the 1930s, when tabulated outcomes started to be collected, and in the 1940s, when tape recordings of sessions for the purpose of process research were introduced. Since then the research literature has grown exponentially and is substantial. This section gives a brief introduction to types of research design and suggests some questions that will help the clinician assess the quality and significance of published results. First, some general questions that apply to all studies.

1. What is the study about? What hypotheses are being tested?
2. What is being "done" between whom and whom? Can you as reader understand the context?
   a. Type, duration, frequency and setting of intervention. Adequacy of the intervention. Degree of standardization

    b.   Real or quasi-patients, diagnosis (type, homogeneity, co-morbidity), severity of disturbance, exclusion and inclusion criteria

    c.   Representative exemplars in quantitative research, informative exemplars in qualitative studies

    d.   Novice or experienced therapists, degree of competence in and commitment to interventions

    e.   Reasons for doing the study.

3.   Are the change measures convincing?

    a.   Relevance

    b.   Validity

    c.   Sensitivity

    d.   Reliability

    e.   Multi-person perspective and dimension

    f.   Multi-time point

    g.   In common usage (allowing comparison with other studies).

4.   Is the research ethical? Have the subjects given informed consent?

5.   Have conflicts of interest been declared?

6.   What is the therapy allegiance of the clinicians(s) and researchers?

Randomized clinical trials (RCTs) control?

RCTs are the most rigorous experimental way of demonstrating causality. The logic of the experimental method is that if all prior conditions except one (the *independent variable*) are held constant (controlled), then any differences in the outcome (the *dependent variable*) must have been caused by the one condition that varied. For example, if one patient is given psychotherapy and another identical patient is not, but is treated identically in all other respects, then any differences in their outcomes must have been caused by the therapy. In order to enhance the consistency of the experimental intervention, researchers have attempted to standardize psychotherapeutic treatments by constructing *treatment manuals* (e.g., Beck, Rush, Shaw, & Emery, 1979; Elliott, Watson, Goldman, & Greenberg, 2003) and by assessing treatment delivery via studies of *adherence* and *competence* (e.g., Shapiro & Startup, 1992; Startup & Shapiro, 1993; Waltz, Addis, Koerner, & Jacobson, 1993).

However, it is difficult to apply the experimental method to study psychotherapy, because no two people are identical and because it is impossible to treat two people identically in all respects except for the theoretically specified treatment (Haaga & Stiles, 2000).

Randomization is an essential element in the design. Rather than comparing single patients, investigators randomly assign patients to groups that are to receive the different treatments, on the assumption that any prior differences that might affect the outcomes will be more or less evenly distributed across the groups. Even though individuals' outcomes might vary within groups (because patients are not identical), any mean differences between groups beyond those due to chance should be attributable to the different treatments. The process minimizes allocation bias.

In passing, it should be noted that even strongly significant results do not predict individual outcome. What is predicted is a quantifiable probability of a particular outcome with some subjects in the cohort doing better and some worse than the average. This is a lot better than not knowing the probability in a defined situation.

Quasi-experimental designs

Quasi-experimental designs refer to comparisons between groups of patients who were not randomly assigned (Cook & Campbell, 1979). For example, groups of patients who seem generally comparable but were assigned to different treatments on some other basis, perhaps because they appeared before or after the introduction of a new programme, or because of scheduling constraints, or because they were treated at different sites. Such designs are often more feasible than strict RCTs; indeed they may appear as *natural experiments*, in which apparently similar groups happen to receive contrasting treatments. In such cases, however, there are always variables that were confounded with the variable of interest, so the evidence of causality is, to some degree, ambiguous.

In evaluating quantitative research, the clinician needs to ask:

1. How well has bias been excluded?
    a. Randomization;
    b. Stratification;
    c. Representiveness;
    d. Blindness;

    e.   Independent raters;

    f.   Practice distortion;

    g.   Practice bias.

2.   Is the study powerful enough to yield significant results? What assumptions for clinically significant effects have been made and do you agree with them? In particular, the size of the sample and the *power analysis* (Cohen, 1977).

3.   Are the results invalidated by attrition? *Intention to treat numbers* should be reported.

4.   Are the statistics valid? Clinically usefully statistics are *relative risk, confidence intervals, clinically significant change*, and *numbers needed to treat* (Altman, 1998; Cook & Sackett, 1995; Jacobson, Roberts, Berns, & McGlinchey, 1999).

Correlational process-outcome studies

Another major genre in psychotherapy research is the process-outcome study, which uses a correlational approach. Correlational studies are those in which two (or more) variables are observed, and the degree to which they co-vary is assessed.

In a widely-cited article, Yeaton and Sechrest (1981) argued that effective psychotherapeutic treatments should contain large amounts of helpful change ingredients (*strength*) and should be delivered in a pure manner (*integrity*). If the theory underlying the treatment is correct, then delivering interventions with strength and integrity should be effective in producing client change. This view of process-outcome relations has been called the *drug metaphor* (Stiles & Shapiro, 1989, 1994). This logic suggests that clients who receive a larger quantity or greater intensity of the helpful ingredients (process variables) should show greater improvement (outcome variables), so that process and outcome should be positively correlated across patients. Much process-outcome research has adopted this drug metaphor and sought to assess the relationship of process ingredients with outcome by correlating the process and outcome measures. It has been assumed that this method would allow researchers to determine which process components are the active ingredients, which should be positively correlated with outcome, and which are merely inert flavours and fillers, uncorrelated with outcome (Orlinsky, Grawe, & Parks, 1994). This reasoning may be misleading (Stiles, 1988, Stiles, Honos-Webb, & Surko, 1998).

Case study

Since psychotherapy began, case studies have been a standard tool for investigating the theory and practice of psychotherapy. Although they are vulnerable to significant bias and distortion, as investigators unintentionally (or intentionally) perceive and report data selectively, case studies have always been a principal source of ideas and theories about psychotherapy.

Theoretically based case studies can be confirmatory as well as exploratory. Interpretive and hypothesis-testing research are alternative strategies for scientific quality control on theory (Stiles, 1993, 2003). In hypothesis-testing research, scientists extract or derive one statement (or a few statements) from a theory and compare this statement with observations. If the observations match the statement (that is, if the scientists' experience of the observed events resembles their experience of the statement), then people's confidence in the statement is substantially increased, and this, in turn, yields a small increment of confidence in the theory as a whole. In case studies, however, investigators compare a large number of observations based on a particular individual with a correspondingly large number of theoretical statements.

Such studies ask, in effect, how well the theory describes the details of a particular case. The increment or decrement in confidence in any one statement may be very small. Nevertheless, because many statements are examined, the increment (or decrement) in people's confidence in the whole theory may be comparable to that stemming from a statistical hypothesis-testing study. A few systematically analysed therapy cases that match a clinical theory in precise or unexpected detail may strongly support a theory, even though each component assertion may remain tentative when considered separately.

Qualitative research

Qualitative research differs from traditional quantitative research on human experience in several ways. Results are typically reported in words rather than primarily in numbers. This may take the form of narratives (e.g., case studies) and typically includes a rich array of descriptive terms, rather than focusing on a few common dimensions or scales. Investigators use their (imperfect) empathic understanding of participants' inner experiences as data. Events are understood and reported in their unique context; theory is generated from data. Materials may be chosen for study because they are good examples rather than because they are representative of some larger population. Sample size and composition may be informed by emerging results, e.g., cases chosen to fill gaps in understanding and data-gathering continued until new cases seem redundant (*saturation*). One well-known form of qualitative research is *grounded theory*, in which the organizing theory arises from the data itself (Glaser & Strauss, 1967). The strength of the approach lies in its immersion in *lived experience*, the constructions of *individual meanings* and the value given to *contextualization* and reflexivity. But the consequence of these characteristics is that the interpretations of the data are always tentative and bound by context (Stiles, 2003); they may be idiosyncratic and insubstantial.

A scientific theory can be understood not as an organized edifice of facts but as an understanding that is shared to varying degrees by those who have propounded it or been exposed to it. In this view, research is cumulative not because each new observation adds a fact to an edifice but because each new observation that enters a theory changes it in some way. The change may be manifested, for example, as a greater or lesser confidence in theoretical assertions, as the introduction or revised meanings of terms, or as differences in the way particular ideas are phrased or introduced. In this view, theory can be considered as the principal product of science and the work of scientists as quality control—ensuring that the theories are good ones by comparing them with observations (Stiles, 2003). If science is understood in this way, theory is just as central in interpretative (qualitative) research as it is in hypothesis-testing research.

Not all qualitative investigators of psychotherapy see quality control on scientific theory as their main activity. Some use instead alternative forms of discourse that can be described as *hermeneutic*, after Hermes, the messenger (e.g., McLeod & Lynch, 2000; Rennie, 1994a,b; Rhodes, Hill, Thompson, & Elliott, 1994). This alternative discourse form represents a distinct sort of intellectual activity, entails different goals and procedures, and yields distinct products. The goal of hermeneutic discourse can be described as *deepening*. The activity consists in understanding what the target material, such as some text or concept, has meant or could mean to other people. The exploration of alternatives is itself the product of the activity rather than a means of developing a particular theory. The understanding achieved is valued for its depth—the richer appreciation—not necessarily because it is more simple or unified.

Specific questions for qualitative research

1. How permeable is the study, i.e., does it show capacity for understanding to be changed by encounters with observations?
2. Validity of an interpretation is always in relation to some person, and criteria for assessing validity depend on whom that person is, e.g., reader, investigator, research participant. Is this explicit?
3. Has sample size and composition been informed by emerging results, e.g., cases chosen to fill gaps and data gathering continued until new cases appear redundant?
4. Are the methods for gathering and analysing observations clearly described to the point where you could replicate them?
5. Is permeability enhanced by:
    a. engagement with material;
    b. grounding;
    c. asking "what", not "why".
6. Can you, as reader, make adjustments for differing forestructure in the author, e.g., initial theories, relevant personal experience, preconceptions, and biases and assess how well the observations permeate the interpretations?
    a. Is there disclosure of investigators' forestructure?
    b. Explication of social and cultural context, e.g., shared assumptions between investigators and participants, relevant cultural values, data-gathering circumstances, meaning of the research to the participants.
    c. Description of investigators' internal processes.
7. Is there convergence across several perspectives and types of validity, i.e., triangulation?
8. In making your own assessment of validity, look for:

a. coherence;
b. uncovering; self-evidence;
c. testimonial validity;
d. catalytic validity.

Implementation of evidence into clinical practice

Clinical effectiveness is only one dimension in planning psychotherapy services. In addition, services need to meet the criteria of being *comprehensive, co-ordinated and user-friendly, safe, and cost-effective* (Parry, 1996). Research evidence is at the centre of the drive by governments and health strategists in many countries to base practice on robust evidence. Optimally, clinicians would routinely and systematically review the research literature and come to conclusions about best practice. This, of course, is a mammoth task. Fortunately, commissioned and individually generated reviews fill the gap. In the UK, the Cochrane database is open to all. The database uses a hierarchy of evidence with RCTs at its pinnacle (www.cochrane.org). The National Institute for Clinical Excellence (NICE) examines the literature and recommends optimal treatments (www.nice.org.uk). *Dr Foster*, a professionally-informed consumer-orientated organization, publishes reviews of performance by various health providers (www.drfoster.co.uk). The *British Medical Journal* (*BMJ*), along with several other journals, has two useful ways of advancing the evidence-based agenda. Articles routinely end with a summary of "What is already known on this topic" and "What this study adds" and POEMS (Patient-Orientated Evidence that Matters), which succinctly review the evidence that can help answer a clinical question (www.infoPOEMs.com).

Another source of summary information is to be found in the aptly named book *What Works for Whom?* (Roth & Fonagy, 1996). Concentrating largely on RCTs, the authors review the evidence for benefit in different diagnostic groups, predominantly Axis I. Each chapter ends with a summary and implications for service delivery and future research. When, as now, RCTs are not fully representative of the range of therapies or types of presentation in clinical practice, it has to be recognized that absence of evidence is not evidence of ineffectiveness (or effectiveness). Furthermore, as previously noted, there is a considerable problem in extrapolating from efficacy studies to clinic practice.

In the USA, there has been a move to favour *empirically supported therapies*.[4] Concentrating on brand names over-emphasizes difference between approach and risks fossilizing the field when there is still much innovation to come. The person of the therapist and their allegiance contribute significantly to outcome, leading some to suggest that we should speak of *empirically supported therapists* (Wampold, 2001)

Empirical research evidence from RCTs tells us what can be achieved under optimal conditions. The evidence is complementary to clinical judgement. For this reason, I welcome the "Guideline" subtitle to the useful Department of Health report on treatment choice in psychological therapies and counselling (Parry, 2001).

Research (can) tells us what to do: audit tells us if we are doing it right (Smith, 1992). Audit is the systematic review of the delivery of healthcare in order to identify deficiencies so that they can be remedied (Crombie, Davies, Abraham, & Florey, 1993). Audit measures performance against standards. It is part of the process of ensuring that evidence-based practice is delivered in practice. Each audit cycle of observing current practice, setting standards of care, comparing practice with the standards, and implementing change initiates the next pass through the cycle (Aveline & Watson, 2000; Fonagy & Higgitt, 1989)

A new paradigm of *practice-based evidence* is well established (Margison *et al.*, 2000). Inferences are drawn from naturalistic unselected clinical populations. The samples may be large, particularly when services pool routinely collected data through locally organized practice–research networks (PTNs). Typically, the clinic work is with complex cases where therapist competence may be more important then therapy adherence. Here the clinician comes out of the planning shadows and is a stakeholder in the form of the service and its delivery. Routine monitoring of outcome is an essential component with performance feedback to the clinicians and the service as a whole. This facilitates *quality management* by charting the expected and actual course of patients in the service with various conditions. *Benchmarks* allow one service to compare and review outcomes with other similar services. Several reliable, relevant, and sensitive psychometric systems for routine use have been developed, of which one of the most promising is CORE (Evans *et al.*, 2002).

Once an individual's dose-response curve has been determined, predictions can be made about likely outcome (Lueger *et al.*, 2001). This is the *patient-focused* outcome paradigm. There is good evidence that outcome can be improved by *signalling* to clinicians that the clinical course of a particular patient is problematic. Typically, a traffic-light metaphor is used; red signalling clinically significant deterioration, yellow being a lesser alert, and green indicating that the therapy is on its expected beneficial course. Clinical decision-making is enhanced and there is an opportunity for timely corrective action (Kordy, Hannover, & Richard, 2001; Lambert, Hansen, & Finch, 2001).

Evidence, audit and quality management are essential complements to clinical judgement (and supervision) in maintaining good practice.

For the clinician, the final step in assessing research evidence is to pose some questions that address the implications for evidence-based practice.

1. Is the author's selection of positive findings and interpretation of the results justified by the evidence? Do you agree with them?
2. How representative is the study of your clinical practice (what is being done between whom and whom)?
3. If the results are sufficiently robust, representative, and significant, what are the implications for your practice?
4. What further evidence do you require before changing or confirming practice?
5. What further questions does the study raise?
6. If you change your practice, how are you going to audit the implementation?

Conclusion

Research can enhance the validity of impression, elucidate processes, and provide evidence to confirm and—more importantly—disconfirm received clinical wisdom. But it is only one element in improving clinical practice. It can never be a total substitute for clinical judgement. I commend the idea of the *scientist–practitioner*, as it embodies an admirable readiness to look for evidence and the preparedness to change direction if the evidence is sufficient and compelling (Shakow, 1976).

While research can shift knowledge along the Platonic continuum from opinion towards truth, most of the answers provided by research are small, sometimes contradictory, increments in knowledge, a few of which add to our understanding of complex issues. Rarely are results definitive; studies generally breed more questions than answers. Grand epiphanous ideas have to be scaled down to what can be achieved in the available time and resource. For good methodological reasons, what is studied may not be representative of everyday clinical practice. Results may take years to arrive and have limited generalizability. Results have to be interpreted in light of clinical and social context, researcher bias and allegiance. Sometimes, however, research can meet the seven desiderata of being *representative, relevant, rigorous, refined, realizable, resourced* and *revelatory* (Aveline, Shapiro, Parry, & Freeman, 1995). Then the rewards can be great for the labour of doing research.

Good quality research gives the best chance of achieving these aims. Quality depends as much on the appropriate choice of method as on the rigour of its application. I look forward to improvements in methodology whereby quantitative researchers are more open to *contextualism* and *reflexivity* in their work and qualitative researchers find ways to enhance the *validity* and *generalizability* of their findings. I welcome the move towards greater acceptance of the value of practice-close research as robust, positive findings in less artificial health contexts are inherently more relevant to everyday clinical practice than results from the controlled but often unrepresentative world of the RCT. I anticipate that we will arrive at a psychotherapy that is much more *integrated* and *eclectic* than our present versions and that gives more weight to *informed patient choice* and *natural capacity for healing* within individuals (Hubble, Duncan, & Miller, 1999).

Society for Psychotherapy Research

Readers wanting to take their interest in research further are encouraged to consider joining SPR. SPR is a non-denominational, multidisciplinary, international organization committed to exchanging information about psychotherapy research. One of its primary functions is to organize scientific meetings on psychotherapy research. International meetings have been held annually since 1970. Regional Chapters are established in North America, South America, Europe, and the United Kingdom, each with their own programme of scientific meetings. Membership includes a subscription to *Psychotherapy Research*, the Society's journal. The journal disseminates research practice and findings to members of the Society and the wider community of researchers, practitioners, providers and commissioners. Four issues are published each year.

More information is available at www.psychotherapyresearch. org.

Notes

1. The word *patient* simply means someone who suffers. In my lexicon, *patient* is an honourable term that in no way implies passivity or subservience. I prefer the word to the common alternatives, the pallid *client* and contextless *customer*.
2. For a critique of *naturalism* and a call for *reflective pragmatism*, see Slife (2004) in M. J. Lambert (Ed.), *Handbook of Psychotherapy and Behavior Change* (pp. 44–83), Wiley, New York.
3. For a discussion of how *discrete choice experiments* might influence the choice of healthcare, see Ryan (2004) *British Medical Journal, 328*: 360–361.
4. For a critique of *empirically supported therapies*, see Special Section of *Psychotherapy Research* (1998) Volume 8, pp. 115–170.

References

Altman, D. G. (1998). Confidence intervals for the number needed to treat. *British Medical Journal, 317*: 1309–1312.

Aveline, M., & Watson, J. (2000). Making a success of your psychotherapy service: the contribution of clinical audit. In: C. J. Mace, B. Roberts, & S. Morey (Eds.), *Evidence in the Psychological Therapies* (pp. 199–210). London: Routledge.

Aveline, M., Shapiro, D. A., Parry, G., & Freeman, C. (1995). Building research foundations for psychotherapy practice. In: M. Aveline & D. A. Shapiro (Eds.), *Research Foundations for Psychotherapy Practice* (pp. 301–322). Chichester: Wiley.

Aveline, M., Strauss, B. M., & Stiles, W. B. (2005). Psychotherapy research. In: G. Gabbard, J. Beck, & J. Holmes (Eds.), *Oxford Textbook of Psychotherapy*. Oxford: Oxford University Press.

Barker, C., Pistrang, N., & Elliott, R. (1994). *Research Methods in Clinical and Counselling Psychology*. New York: Wiley.

Beck, A. T., Rush, A. J., Shaw, B. F., & Emery, G. (1979). *Cognitive Therapy of Depression*. New York: Wiley.

Cohen, J. (1977). *Statistical Power Analysis for the Behavioural Sciences*. Hillsdale, NJ: Erlbaum.

Cook, R. J., & Sackett, D. L. (1995). The number needed to treat: a clinically useful measure of treatment effect. *British Journal of Medicine, 310*: 452–454.

Cook, T. D., & Campbell, D. T. (1979). *Quasi-experimentation: Design and Analysis for Field Settings*. Boston: Houghton-Mifflin.

Crombie, I. K., Davies, H. T. O., Abraham, S. C. S., & Florey, C. d. V. (1993). *The Audit Handbook*. Chicester: John Wiley & Sons.

Elkin, I. (1994). The NIMH Treatment of Depression Collaborative Research Program: Where we began and where we are. In: A. E. Bergin & S. L. Garfield (Eds.), *Handbook of Psychotherapy and Behavior Change* (pp. 114–139). New York: Wiley.

Elliott, R., Watson, J., Goldman, R., & Greenberg, L. S. (2003). *Learning Emotional-focused Therapy: The Process–Experiential Approach to Change*. Washington, DC: American Psychoanalytic Association.

Evans, C., Connell, J., Barkham, M., Margison, F., McGrath, G., Mellor-Clark, J., & Audin, K. (2002). Towards a standardised brief outcome measure: psychometric properties and utility of the CORE–OM. *British Journal of Psychiatry, 180*: 51–60.

Fonagy, P. (Ed.) (2001). *An Open Door Review of Outcome Studies in Psychoanalysis*. London: University College of London Press.

Fonagy, P., & Higgitt, A. (1989). Evaluating the performance of departments of pscyotherapy: a plan for action. *Psychoanalytic Psychotherapy, 4*: 121–153.

Frank, J. D. (1973). *Persuasion and Healing*. Baltimore, MD: Johns Hopkins University Press.

Glaser, B. G., & Strauss, A. L. (1967). *The Discovery of Grounded Theory*. Chicago: Aldine.

Haaga, D. A. F., & Stiles, W. B. (2000). Randomized clinical trials in psychotherapy research: methodology, design, and evaluation. In: C. R. Snyder & R. E. Ingram (Eds.), *Handbook of Psychological Change: Psychotherapy Processes and Practices for the 21st Century* (pp. 14–39). New York: Wiley.

Hubble, M. A., Duncan, B. L., & Miller, S. D. (1999). *The Heart and Soul of Change: What Works in Therapy.* Washington, DC: American Psychological Association.

Jacobson, N. S., & Truax, P. (1991). Clinical significance: a statistical approach to defining meaningful change in psychotherapy research. *Journal of Consulting and Clinical Psychology, 59*, 12–19.

Jacobson, N. S., Roberts, L. J., Berns, S. B., & McGlinchey, J. B. (1999). Methods for defining and determining the clinical significance of treatment effects: description, aplication, and alternatives. *Journal of Consulting & Clinical Psychology, 67*: 300–307.

Kächele, H., Kordy, H., Richard, M., & TR-EAT (2001). Therapy amount and outcome of inpatient psychodynamic treatment of eating disorders in Germany: data from a multicenter study. *Psychotherapy Research, 11*: 239–258.

Kordy, H., Hannover, W., & Richard, M. (2001). Computer-assisted feedback-drive quality management for psychotherapy: The Stuttgart–Heidelberg Model. *Journal of Consulting & Clinical Psychology, 69*(2): 173–183.

Krupnick, J. L., Sotsky, S. M., Simmens, S., Moyer, J., Elkin, I., Watkins, J., & Pilkonis, P. A. (1996). The role of therapeutic alliance in psychotherapy and pharmacotherapy outcome: findings in the National Institute of Mental Health Treatment of Depression Collaborative Research Program. *Journal of Consulting and Clinical Psychology, 64*(3): 532–539.

Lambert, M. J., & Ogles, B. M. (2004). The efficacy and effectiveness of psychotherapy. In: M. J. Lambert (Ed.), *Bergin and Garfiield's Handbook of Psychotherapy and Behavior Change* (5th edn) (pp. 139–193). New York: Wiley.

Lambert, M., Hansen, N. B., & Finch, A. E. (2001). Patient-focused research: using patient outcome data to enhance treatment effects. *Journal of Consulting & Clinical Psychology, 69*: 159–172.

Lueger, R. J., Howard, K. I., Martinovitch, Z., Lutz, W., Anderson, E. A., & Grissom, G. (2001). Assessing treatment progress of individual patients with expected treatment response models. *Journal of Consulting & Clinical Psychology, 69*: 150–158.

Margison, F., Barkham, M., Evans, C., McGrath, G., Mellor-Clark, J., Audin, K., & Connell, J. (2000). Measurement and psychotherapy: evidence based practice and practice-based evidence. *British Journal of Psychiatry*, *177*: 123–130.

McLeod, J., & Lynch, G. (2000). "This is our life": strong evaluation in psychotherapy narrative. *European Journal of Psychotherapy, Counselling, and Health*, *3*(3): 389–406.

Ogles, B. M., Lunnen, K. M., & Bonesteel, K. (2001). Clinical significance: history, application, and current practice. *Clinical Psychology Review*, *21*, 421–426.

Orlinsky, D. E., Grawe, K., & Parks, B. K. (1994). Process and outcome in psychotherapy —Noch einmal. In: A. E. Bergin & S. L. Garfield (Eds.), *Handbook of Psychotherapy and Behavior Change* (4th edn) (pp. 270–376). New York: Wiley.

Parry, G. (1996). *NHS Psychotherapy Services in England Review of Strategic Policy*. London: HMSO.

Parry, G. (2001). *Treatment Choice in Psychological Therapies and Counselling: Evidence Based Clinical Practice Guideline*. London: HMSO.

Rennie, D. L. (1994a). Clients' accounts of resistance: a qualitative analysis. *Canadian Journal of Counselling*, *28*: 43–57.

Rennie, D. L. (1994b). Clients' deference in psychotherapy. *Journal of Counseling Psychology*, *41*: 427–437.

Rhodes, R., Hill, C. E., Thompson, B. J., & Elliott, R. (1994). Client retrospective recall of resolved and unresolved misunderstanding events. *Journal of Counseling Psychology*, *41*: 473–483.

Roth, A., & Fonagy, P. (1996). *What Works for Whom? A Critical Review of Psychotherapy Research*. New York: Guilford.

Rudolf, G. (1991). *Die therapeutische Arbeitsbeziehung*. Heidelberg: Springer.

Ryan, M. (2004). Discrete choice experiments in health care (editorial). *British Medical Journal*, *328*: 360–361.

Seligman, M. E. P. (1995). The effectiveness of psychotherapy: The Consumer Reports study. *American Psychologist*, *50*, 965–974.

Shadish, W. R., Matt, G. E., Navarro, A. M., Siegle, G., Crits-Christoph, P., Hazelrigg, M. D., Jorm, A. F., Lyons, L. C., Nietzl, M. T., Prout, H. T., Robinson, L., Smith, M. L., Svartberg, M., & Weiss, B. (1997). Evidence that therapy works in clinically representative conditions. *Journal of Consulting and Clinical Psychology*, *65*(3): 355–365.

Shakow, D. (1976). What is clinical psychology? *American Psychologist*, *31*: 553–560.

Shapiro, D. A., & Startup, M. J. (1992). Measuring therapist adherence in exploratory psychotherapy. *Psychotherapy Research, 2*, 193–203.

Slife, B. D. (2004). Theoretical challenges to therapy practice and research: the constraint of naturalism. In: M. J. Lambert (Ed.), *Bergin and Garfield's Handbook of Psychotherapy and Behavior Change* (5th edn) (pp. 44–83). New York: Wiley.

Smith, R. (1992). Audit and research. *British Medical Journal, 305*: 905–906.

Startup, M. J., & Shapiro, D. A. (1993). Therapist treatment fidelity in prescriptive vs. exploratory psychotherapy. *British Journal of Clinical Psychology, 32*: 443–456.

Stiles, W. B. (1988). Psychotherapy process-outcome correlations may be misleading. *Psychotherapy, 25*: 27–35.

Stiles, W. B. (1993). Quality control in qualitative research. *Clinical Psychology Review, 13*: 593–618.

Stiles, W. B. (2003). Qualitative research: evaluating the process and the product. In: S. P. Llewelyn & P. Kennedy (Eds.), *Handbook of Clinical Health Psychology* (pp. 477–499). London: Wiley.

Stiles, W. B., & Shapiro, D. A. (1989). Abuse of the drug metaphor in psychotherapy process-outcome research. *Clinical Psychology Review, 9*: 521–543.

Stiles, W. B., & Shapiro, D. A. (1994). Disabuse of the drug metaphor: psychotherapy process-outcome correlations. *Journal of Consulting and Clinical Psychology, 62*: 942–948.

Stiles, W. B., Honos-Webb, L., & Surko, M. (1998). Responsiveness in psychotherapy. *Clinical Psychology: Science and Practice, 5*: 439–458.

Strauss, B., & Kächele, H. (1998). The writing on the wall—comments on the current discussion about empirically validated treatments in Germany. *Psychotherapy Research, 8*: 158–170.

Strauss, B., & Wittmann, W. W. (1999). Psycotherapieforschung: Grundlagen und Ergebnisse. In: W. Senf & M. Broda (Eds.), *Praxis der Psychotherapie* (3.; völlig neu bearbeitete Auflage) (pp. 760–781). Stuttgart: Thieme.

Wallerstein, R. S. (1986). *Forty-two Lives in Treatment: A Study of Psychoanalysis and Psychotherapy*. New York: Guilford.

Waltz, J., Addis, M., Koerner, K., & Jacobson, N. S. (1993). Testing the integrity of a psychotherapy protocol: assessing therapist adherence and competence. *Journal of Consulting and Clinical Psychology, 61*: 620–630.

Wampold, B. E. (2001). *The Great Psychotherapy Debate: Models, Methods, and Findings*. Mahwah, NJ: Lawrence Erlbaum.

Yeaton, W. H., & Sechrest, L. (1981). Critical dimensions in the choice and maintenance of successful treatments: strength, integrity, and effectiveness. *Journal of Consulting and Clinical Psychology, 49*: 156–167.

Further reading

Aveline, M., & Shapiro, D. A. (Eds.) (1995). *Research Foundations for Psychotherapy Practice*. Chichester: Wiley.

Barker, C., Pistrang, N., & Elliott, R. (1994). *Research Methods in Clinical and Counselling Psychology*. New York: Wiley.

Holloway, I. (1997). *Basic Concepts for Qualitative Research*. Oxford: Blackwell.

Lambert, M. J. (Ed.) (2004). *Handbook of Psychotherapy and Behavior Change*, 5th edn. New York: Wiley.

Parry, G., & Watts, F. N. (Eds.) (1996). *Behavioural and Mental Health Research: A Handbook of Skills and Methods*, 2nd edn. Hove: Lawence Erlbaum Associates.

Murphy, E., Dingwall, R. *et al.* (1998). Qualitative research methods in health technology assessment: a review of the literature. Southampton, Health Technology Assessment, NHS R&D HTA Programme: 276.

CHAPTER TWO

Case study revisited

Talal Al Rubaie

This brief article is written in the light of the recent establishment of the Research Committee (RC) within the UKCP and the continuing discussion about what constitutes (scientific) evidence in respect of psychotherapy and its effectiveness. Also, one aim is to stimulate further, relevant discussion. The views expressed here are my own and not necessarily shared by other members of the RC. Owing to different philosophical and political reasons, there are several strands of research philosophy that challenge the traditional, quantitative ("positive" "scientific", "hypothetico-deductive", or "modern") approach that psychology/ psychotherapy developed largely under the influence of advances in "hard sciences", particularly classical physics. The challenges come from some qualitative researchers known collectively as "new paradigm" or "postmodern".

Quantitative data commonly use statistics and the research results are analysed and evaluated in terms of statistical significance. Qualitative data are generally content analysed and evaluated subjectively, often in terms of themes, categories, or new concepts. This article focuses mainly on case study as a special form of qualitative research.

Many traditional researchers discount the results obtained by case studies, claiming, for example, that these studies are anecdotal, lacking generalizability and fraught with placebo effect or therapist bias. Hence, they are considered non-scientific and their results unreliable. These claims are based on misconceptions that I will seek to dissipate here. But, let us first examine the significance of case study in the context of clinical (non-experimental) research; i.e., the real-life research.

Real-life research case-study is defined as an in-depth study of a person (usually) or a group. It is usually (not always) qualitative in nature. This method can be used to investigate outstanding cases, contradict a theory, collect data, and enhance our overall psychological knowledge without necessarily testing a specific hypothesis (Coolican, 1996). It encourages researchers to focus on the entire context and to be open to multiple, interacting influences. Researchers are permitted to be more spontaneous and flexible. In contrast, quantitative data are criticised for diminishing the psychological richness of human experience by focusing on overt behaviour or by limiting responses to pre-selected categories. Process researchers (Rice & Greenberg, 1984) and discovery-orientated researchers (e.g., Mahrer, 1988) have also called for qualitative, new paradigm research.

In keeping with Weber's (1947) "Verstehen" tradition, qualitative methods are well suited to understanding of meanings, interpretations, and subjective experiences of individuals, couples, and families. Araoz (1982) notes that group experimental research would tell us nothing about a particular individual, thus becoming rather useless to the clinician. Indeed, this information may even become damaging if the clinician treats the individual who does not respond according to the research results as deviant or abnormal. Our quandary as psychotherapists is that there is no such thing as exactly the same kind of psychological problem or disorder. Subtle and often undetectable cognitive, emotional, and behavioural differences within the same disorder may actually be the determining factor (Wolberg, 1988). Bromley (1990) argues for a clinical case study approach to evaluation, which allows for the "scientific study of the individual without recourse to experimental and quantitative investigation" (p. 299).

Van Kaam (1969) notes that irrelevant empirical research has been produced by "neutral" spectators of behaviour who are indifferent to the relationship between abstract games and life situations. Contrariwise, relevant research, van Kaam stresses, is that which explores, describes, and empirically investigates human behaviour while preserving a "lived" relationship with it in the reality of life.

As Todd and Stanton (1983) note, "life and research are inevitably messy" (p. 14). Research is especially "messy" in a field like couple/family therapy, which is concerned with complex systemic changes in human beings. Qualitative research designs can provide a systemic scientific way of approaching therapy holistically, with all its "messiness" intact (Moon, Dillon, & Sprenkle, 1990). Consistent with the current movement in family sociology challenging monolithic presentations of couple and family structures and reality (Eichler, 1988), the versatility of qualitative methods is a good match for examining the diversity of couple/family forms and experiences.

Modernism versus postmodernism

The features characterizing modern and postmodern thought, can be presented schematically as follows (Efran, Lukens, & Lukens, 1990; Laurence, 1994).

The modern approach:

1. General laws and truths may be attained by way of reason, science or technology.
2. There is determinancy of meaning in any text or event, i.e., the objective nature of reality.
3. The subject itself has an ontological essential status.

The postmodern approach:

1. Natural/universal laws or truths are rejected, and so the idea of progress, in favour of local, unique, personal, contextual "truths"
2. There is indeterminacy, or a plurality, of meaning in texts/ events. Attempts, however, have been made to define objectivity without adopting universalism (Bernstein, 1983).

3. The ontological status of the self is denied. Instead, the self is considered a socio-historical construct that is linguistically mediated.

Defining qualitative research, Goetz and LeCompte (1984) describe four continua that underlie all social science research:

Constructive	Enumerative
Generative	Verificative
Inductive	Deductive
Subjective	Objective

These continua imply different views of reality and how reality is known: different epistemologies. Qualitative or postmodern research is usually located closer to the constructive, generative, inductive, and subjective poles of these continua. Experimental–modern research is typically located nearer to the enumerative, verificative, deductive, and objective poles. These continua, useful for didactic purposes, are somewhat artificial, since the line demarcating the dichotomy "modernism–postmodernism" in respect of psychotherapy cannot be rigidly drawn. Freud, for example, can be considered a modern psychotherapist because he advocated universal principles governing the psyche, whereas his methodology was qualitative and hence more in keeping with the postmodern approach.

Some researchers suggest that the quantitative and qualitative paradigms are incompatible because they make different assumptions about the nature of knowledge and reality and have different research objectives. Pragmatists, on the other hand, are concerned with answering their research questions using the most suitable methods possible. Synthesists attempt to resolve this debate by stating that the two methodologies are neither incompatible nor compatible: they are complementary (Moon, Dillon, & Sprenkle, 1990).

Placebo: a misleading notion

The definition of placebo and the problems associated with the use of controls in group experimental psychotherapy research are notoriously difficult and perplexing. The usual practice of using clients on the waiting list as controls is difficult to justify ethically, because this might deny clients a therapy which could be potentially useful. Experimental researchers, as indicated above, frequently dismiss case studies, allegedly because their results are greatly attributable to placebo effects. Thus, the improvements attained are sometimes referred to as non-specific. This attribution is misleading, as Grunbaum (1989) indicates, because the effect itself may be highly specific: it usually mimics the expected effects of the treatment and can produce considerable mental and physical change. For example, placebos in drugs research have been shown to produce side effects and even to be addictive when substituted for drugs that are known to have these properties (Shapiro & Morris, 1978; Vinar, 1969). When we call a change a placebo effect, what we usually mean is that it is brought about by some means other than that intended in a particular treatment.

The use of intentional placebo to test the efficacy of psychotherapy, however, is an example of the misapplication of drug trial methods (Stiles & Shapiro, 1988). Critelli and Neuman (1984) indicate that most of the innate procedures that have so far been adopted as psychotherapy placebo controls would not fool anyone. In their own words:

> At a minimum, placebo controls should be equivalent to test procedures on all major recognised common factors. These might include induced expectancy of improvement: credibility of rationale; credibility of procedures; demand for improvement; and therapist attention, enthusiasm, effort, perceived belief in treatment procedures, and commitment to client improvement. [p. 38]

The inescapable conclusion is that once one has achieved all that, one has created a new psychotherapy.

An additional difficulty is that one cannot have an adequate control group in an outpatient psychotherapy study, because clients who are suffering and are refused help will usually look elsewhere for assistance. They will go to friends, neighbours, or practitioners of various sorts (Wolberg, 1988).

Reliability, validity, generalizability, and sampling

Broadly speaking, reliability of data reflects whether or not similar findings would be obtained at different times, in different contexts, or with different researchers. Validity refers to whether or not the methods used to study a phenomenon actually do assess that phenomenon. These concepts are key issues in most quantitative methods and are given a very high priority in such research.

These concepts, however, are more problematic in the domain of qualitative research (Henwood & Pidgeon, 1995). Those adopting qualitative research suggest that if they were to adopt criteria of reliability and validity, then this would suggest that there is some truth or reality waiting to be discovered, a notion inconsistent with postmodern thought.

Wells (1987) notes that, while individual cases cannot be generalized, samples of traditional research are also not universally representative due to geographical and historical specifics. Lincoln and Guba (1985) prefer to replace previous measures of generalizability with the notion of "transferability". This reflects concern that responses may vary in different contexts and assesses how consistent findings are in similar contexts, but not necessarily across contexts. Yin (1994) argues that both case studies and samples in traditional experiments can be generalized analytically to theory. From this perspective, the well conducted case study can generate hypotheses and research questions. Interpretations made on the basis of one case study can be tested against evidence from subsequent case studies, so several possible perspectives can be viewed in the process.

Science, empiricism and method

Traditional researchers maintain that the "scientific method" is the sole guarantor of "truth" and the attainment of reliable evidence. Yet, Feyerabend (1994), one of the most distinguished philosophers of science in the last century, has espoused what he refers to as an "anarchist epistemology". In his view, there are no absolute judgements and fixed method or theory of rationality. His arguments are based on the consideration of the history of science, which shows it to be complex and unpredictable and entails the necessity of pluralistic methodology for the growth of knowledge. Walters (1990), too, has argued convincingly that "There is no predictable blueprint that regulates the pattern of discovery" (p. 461).

Traditional researchers erroneously equate data with facts, empirical generalizations with natural/universal laws, and systematic empiricism with science (Bortoft, 1996; Willer & Willer, 1973). Striving to model psychotherapy on natural sciences, quantitative researchers are oblivious of the fact that even natural sciences, such as astronomy and geology, use case study as a major research method.

Consistent with what Grant (1998) calls "postmodern sciences", the philosophy underlying new paradigm research questions the traditional distinction between overt (outer) behaviour and covert (inner) awareness, fact and value, the observable and the unobservable, and even the distinction between scientific knowledge and non-scientific knowledge (e.g., Fulford, 1989; Margolis, 1987). Further, many distinguished natural scientists (e.g., Hayward, 1993; Maturana & Varela, 1987) concur that there is no universal methodology that can lead to the kind of certainty that many once hoped the positive, empirical approach to science would give us.

Butz, Chamberlain, and McCown (1997) indicate that measuring changes in therapy can be properly understood in the "phrase phase" (i.e., changes occurring through exchange of thoughts as a basic assumption of psychotherapy), which does not lend itself to static descriptions that have so long underestimated the complexity of therapeutic interactions.

Despite the poignancy of the arguments disrupting the validity of positive science and its methodology, it is important to remind ourselves that the popularity or persistence of a particular concept, category, or method depends on its utility (particularly its usefulness for social influence and control), rather than on its validity.

The narrative/democratic approach to psychotherapy

Traditional science is usually concerned with the so-called "objective" definition of "the truth", a requirement considered *sine qua non* of the experimental design and its underlying philosophy, logical positivism. Contrariwise, in the narrative approach to psychotherapy, a truth is not regarded as a verifiable fact; it is rather a narrative construction, a negotiable given (Al Rubaie, 1999; Holstein & Gubrium, 2000). In line with this approach, psychotherapy aims at helping clients to gain a sense of "being their own expert". Such an approach is conducive to the democratization of the psychotherapeutic encounter by virtue of enabling clients to author their own narratives that are based upon their experiences, thoughts, and feelings, rather than upon definitions of "normality" or "abnormality" that are dictated by an external agency, scientific or otherwise. Added to that, this approach ensures that participants, client and therapist, have an equal say in determining the process and outcome of therapy. Thus, the modern doctrine, "knowledge is power" (Foucault, 1980), which inescapably allocates disproportionate power to the therapist/expert/professional at the expense of the client, is undermined.

The desired democratization of psychotherapy is manifested in the continuing shift in behavioural medicine towards more individualized designs, which allow the individual client to select and/or tailor interventions within the overall treatment frame (Brown & Fromm, 1987).

Atkinson and Heath (1991) argue that although the insights generated through qualitative research need to be scrutinized and evaluated, the trustworthiness of explanations and insights cannot be established by individual researchers, irrespective of the method they use. Rather, the legitimization of knowledge requires the judgement of an entire community of observers and is most appropriately a democratic process in which all stakeholders can have equal input.

Many feminist researchers (e.g., Henwood & Pidgeon, 1995; McHugh, Koeske, & Frieze, 1986) rightly note that the traditional paradigm is biased against women, since it perpetuates unchallenged views of "women's character". Because the qualitative paradigm emphasizes social and holistic contexts, it may help to answer the feminist call for a greater appreciation for contextual and social structures (Denzin & Lincoln, 1994; Taggart, 1985).

Conclusion

Recognizing that many thoughtful individuals in our field do not share the (postmodern) assumptions about the nature of knowledge I prefer, I have argued above, in an abridged fashion due to space limitation, that the case study is a valid research method and that it is consistent with contemporary change in philosophy and science.

But the points I have made are inseparable from the question: can we say that psychotherapy is cost-effective and that its benefits justify the expenditure of effort, time or money? This question, understandably, is related to concern with the rising costs of health care that has focused the spotlight on the safety and cost-effectiveness of psychotherapy. However, if we agree with Wolberg (1988) that "What makes a procedure unsafe and ineffective is not the technique itself, but how it is applied" (p. 102), then the answer to this question would greatly depend on how we rate the tangible and intangible costs of emotional problems and how much monetary value we put on human suffering and the misfortunes psychological disorders foist on the community.

References

Al Rubaie, T. (1999). NLP therapy of sex and relationship problems. *NLP World*, 6(1): 17–31.

Araoz, D. L. (1982). *Hypnosis and Sex Therapy*. New York: Brunner/Mazel.

Atkinson, B., & Heath, A. (1991). Qualitative research and the legitimization of knowledge. *Journal of Marital and Family Therapy*, 17: 161–165.

Bernstein, R. (1983). *Beyond Objectivity and Relativism*. Philadelphia: University of Pennsylvania Press.

Bortoft, H. (1996). *The Wholeness of Nature*. Edinburgh: Cambridge University Press.

Bromley, D. B. (1990). Academic contributions to psychological counselling. 1: A philosophy of science for the study of individual cases. *Counselling Psychology Quarterly*, 3: 299–308.

Brown, D. P., & Fromm, E. (1987). *Hypnosis and Behavioural Medicine*. Hillsdale, NJ: Erlbaum.

Butz, M. R., Chamberlain, L. L., & McCown, W. G. (1997). *Strange Attractors: Chaos, Complexity and the Art of Family Therapy*. New York: Wiley.

Coolican, H. (1996). *Introduction to Research Methods and Statistics in Psychology*. London: Hodder and Stoughton.

Critelli, J. W., & Neuman, K. F. (1984). The placebo: a conceptual analysis of a concept in transition. *American Psychologist, 39*: 32–39.

Denzin, N. K., & Lincoln, Y. S. (Eds.) (1994). *Handbook of Qualitative Research*. London: Sage.

Efran, J. S., Lukens, M. D., & Lukens, R. J. (1990). *Language, Structure and Change: Frameworks of Meaning in Psychotherapy*. New York: W. W. Norton.

Eichler, M. (1988). *Families in Canada Today*. Toronto: Gage.

Feyerabend, P. (1994). *Against Method*. London: Verso.

Foucault, M. (1980). *Power/Knowledge*. New York: Pantheon.

Fulford, K. W. M. (1989). *Moral Theory and Medical Practice*. Cambridge: Cambridge University Press.

Goetz, J. P., & LeCompte, M. D. (1984). *Ethnography and Qualitative Design in Educational Research*. San Diego: Academic Press.

Grant, L. H. (1998). Postmodern science and technology. In: S. Sim (Ed.), *The Icon Dictionary of Post-modern Thought*. London: Icon Books.

Grunbaum, A. (1989). The placebo concept in medicine and psychiatry. In: L. M. Shapiro & N. Sartorius (Eds.), *Non-specific Aspects of Treatment*. Toronto: Hans Huber.

Hayward, J. (1993). *Perceiving Ordinary Magic: Science and Intuitive Wisdom*. Boston: New Science Library.

Henwood, K., & Pidgeon, M. (1995). Remaking the link: qualitative research and feminist standpoint theory. *Feminism and Psychology, 5*: 7–30.

Holstein, J. A., & Gubrium, J. F. (2000). *The Self We Live By: Narrative identity in a Postmodern World*. Oxford: Oxford University Press.

Laurence, S. (1994). *Psycho "Therapy", Theory, Practice, Modern and Postmodern Influences*. London: Praeger.

Lincoln, Y. S., & Guba, E. G. (1985). *Naturalistic Inquiry*. Thousand Oaks, CA: Sage.

Mahrer, A. R. (1988). Discovery-oriented psychotherapy research. *American Psychologist, 43*: 694–702.

Margolis, J. (1987). *Texts without References: Reconciling Science and Narrative*. Oxford: Basil Blackwell.

Maturana, H., & Varela, F. (1987). *The Tree of Knowledge*. Boston: New Science Library.

McHugh, M. D., Koeske, R. D., & Frieze, I. H. (1986). Issues to consider in conducting non-sexist psychological research: a guide for researchers. *American Psychologist, 41*: 879–890.

Moon, S. M., Dillon, D. R., & Sprenkle, D. H. (1990). Family therapy and qualitative research. *Journal of Marital and Family Therapy, 16*: 357–373.

Rice, L. M., & Greenberg, L. S. (1984). The new research paradigm. In: L. M. Rice & L. S. Greenberg (Eds.), *Patterns of Change: Intensive Analysis of Psychotherapy Process*. New York: Guilford.

Shapiro, A. K., & Morris, L. A. (1978). The placebo effect in medical and psychological therapies. In: S. L. Garfield, & A. E. Bergin (Eds.), *Handbook of Psychotherapy and Behaviour Change*. New York: Wiley.

Stiles, W. B., & Shapiro, D. A. (1988). Abuse of drug metaphor in psychotherapy process-outcome research. *Clinical Psychology Review, 58*: 352–359.

Taggart, M. (1985). The feminist critique in epistemological perspective. *Journal of Marital and Family Therapy, 11*: 113–126.

Todd, T., & Stanton, M. D. (1983). Research on marital and family therapy: answers, issues and recommendations for the future. In: B. Wolman & G. Striker (Eds.), *Handbook of Family Marital Therapy*. New York: Plenum.

Van Kamm, A. (1969). *Existential Foundations of Psychology*. New York: Doubleday.

Vinar, O. (1969). Dependence on placebo: a case report. *British Journal of Psychiatry, 115*: 1189–1190.

Walkers, K. (1990). Critical thinking, rationality and the vulcanization of students. *Journal of Higher Education, 61*: 448–467.

Weber, M. (1947). *The Theory of Social and Economic Organisation*. New York: The Free Press.

Willer, D., & Willer, J. (1973). *Systematic Empiricism: Critique of a Pseudoscience*. Englewood Cliffs, NJ: Prentice-Hall.

Wolberg, L. R. (1988). *The Technique of Psychothrapy*. New York: Grune & Stratton.

Yin, R. (1994). *Case Study Research*. Thousand Oaks, CA: Sage.

CHAPTER THREE

Avoiding the fate of the Dodo bird: the challenge of evidence-based practice

David Winter

A quarter of a century ago, Luborsky, Singer, and Luborsky (1975), reviewing comparative outcome studies of different therapies, concluded with the verdict of the dodo bird from *Alice in Wonderland* that "everybody has won and all must have prizes". However, despite the fact that more recent meta-analyses (Grissom, 1996) have generally supported this conclusion, it is unlikely that in the new millennium our judges will be as benign and generous as was the dodo bird, and even if they were it is unlikely that there would be sufficient prizes to share between the burgeoning number of different forms of psychotherapy. At the last count the literature contained references to nearly 500 of these (Karasu, 1986), and the number is growing, with philosophers recently getting in on the act with the growth of philosophical consultancy (Boele, 1999).

A specific demand with which we are increasingly faced, particularly by commissioners and purchasers of health care, is for clinical practice to be "evidence-based" (National Health Service Executive, 1996), or "empirically validated", to use the terminology of the American Psychological Association (Task Force on Promotion and Dissemination of Psychological Procedures, 1995). We are confronted with the spectre, already apparent in the USA and likely to gain ground elsewhere, of managed health care systems requiring evidence of the efficacy of particular treatment approaches before agreeing to fund them, and of insurance companies prescribing what form, and how many sessions, of therapy a client should receive. Indeed, arguably health insurance companies are becoming more in touch with the therapy outcome literature than are many clinicians.

This literature includes papers with such titles as "Clients deserve empirically supported treatments, not romanticism" (Perez, 1999), and there are even catalogues advertising empirically validated treatment programmes (e.g., Therapy Works, 1997) and books, such as *The Complete Adult Psychotherapy Treatment Planner* (Jongsma & Peterson, 2003), designed to enable you to create "treatment plans that satisfy all of the demands of managed care companies". In this book you may find, for example, a seven-page, thirty-six-point treatment plan for borderline personality disorder, while psychoticism can be disposed of in a mere twenty-five steps. Also included are a thirty-point plan for the relief of financial stress, and a twenty-four-point plan to resolve spiritual confusion.

Although the situation in the UK, as in most other countries (e.g., Strauss & Kächele, 1998), allows clinicians a little more freedom than in the USA, four years ago the Department of Health published a review of its policy concerning psychotherapy services in England that included the statement that

> it is unacceptable . . . to continue to provide therapies which decline to subject themselves to research evaluation. Practitioners and researchers alike must accept the challenge of evidence-based practice, one result of which is that treatments which are shown to be ineffective are discontinued. [Parry & Richardson, 1996, p. 43]

Concurrently with the production of this document, the Department commissioned a review of psychotherapy research, entitled *What Works for Whom* (Roth & Fonagy, 1996), an aim of which was to consider whether there is research evidence that would help health care purchasers decide on the appropriate therapies for their populations. There is, then, a real danger that readers of *What Works for Whom* may conclude, on not finding a particular form of psychotherapy in its index, that this therapy works for no one. If those readers are purchasers of health care, they may well decide to channel their funding elsewhere; towards therapies that do have an accepted evidence base.

Despite such dangers, many psychotherapists have been resistant to engaging in empirical research. For example, Bobart, O'Hara, and Leftner (1998) argue that empirical validation, at least as it is espoused by the American Psychological Association, may lead to "empirically violated treatments". In their view, with which therapists of some other orientations will doubtless concur, the apparent emphases on manualization of treatments, on studying therapies targeted for specific disorders, and on natural science methodology are incompatible with the assumptions of humanistic or constructivist psychotherapies. While, as a constructivist and therefore not a believer in knowable realities, I have some sympathy with these arguments, I do not agree with the conclusion that we should withdraw from the empirical validation arena unless its rules are on our own terms (Winter, 2000).

If the results of an outcome study will only be considered if the therapy studied is manualized, then we should manualize, being mindful that a treatment manual need not be written in the prescriptive style of *The Complete Psychotherapy Treatment Planner* but rather in terms of more superordinate principles guiding the therapist's choice of alternative courses of action. In regard to specifying the clients treated in a research study, perhaps in terms of their particular disorders, this can be viewed as no more than an exercise in speaking the language of the reviewer or reader of our research papers, including health purchasers, rather than necessarily implying that the therapy itself has been focused on disorders construed in this way. A similar point can be made in regard to objections which have been raised to the use of symptom-focused outcome measures and natural science methodologies. Several forms of psychotherapy, including that which I practise, are technically eclectic, borrowing techniques from other models without necessarily accepting the attendant theoretical and metatheoretical trappings of these techniques. Surely psychotherapy research can display a similar methodological pluralism, employing not only methods rooted in the assumptions of the therapies concerned but also more traditional methods, which may provide results which are more meaningful to a wider audience.

To distance ourselves from demands for empirical validation is, in my view, similar to Kelly's (1961) description of the form of suicide to which he referred as a dedicated act, in which death is chosen in preference to an anticipated relinquishing of some core belief. What we are likely to be killing in this case, rendering as extinct as Luborsky, Singer, and Luborsky's dodo bird (to borrow Watson's (1998) extension of this metaphor), is not ourselves but our favoured model of psychotherapy. Thus, while we may well feel more righteous if we do not dirty our hands with such issues as effect sizes, I would suggest that this will be of no benefit to our clients if as a result many of them may be denied access to an approach that is able to combine humanity with effectiveness. A further research area that, in my view, we ignore at our clients' peril, is that of adverse effects of therapy. While therapies may still be broadly equally effective, I have argued elsewhere (Winter, 1997) that if the dodo bird were to hand out booby prizes on the basis of whether therapies produce casualties, not all would receive these.

In view of these considerations, the Research Subcommittee of the Experiential Constructivist Therapies Section of UKCP is producing documents setting out the evidence base for some of the forms of therapy represented in the Section. The document on personal construct psychotherapy is already available and may be obtained from the author on request. Workshops have also been held for experiential constructivist psychotherapists, in which they have been invited to collect outcome data routinely on their clients (Watson & Winter, 2000). The principal method employed is the CORE system of standardized audit and evaluation measures (CORE System Group, 1998).

In addition, to provide a more individualized outcome measure, clients rate the severity of their self-defined problems pre- and post-therapy and at follow-up, and therapists also collect data by any methods that they consider to be more consistent with their favoured models and with their view of what constitutes "evidence". Scoring and analysis of the measures is being carried out centrally, with the aim of creating a databank on the outcome of experiential constructivist psychotherapies, the data from which can be compared with that from similar banks on other approaches; for example, the data from over 100 services that is being collected by the CORE System Group.

References

Boele, D. (1999). The art of living: philosophical contributions to psychotherapy. *Psychotherapy Section Newsletter: British Psychological Society*, 25: 25–33.

Bobart, A. C., O'Hara, M., & Leftner, L. M. (1998). Empirically violated treatments—disenfranchisement of humanistic and other psychotherapies. *Psychotherapy Research*, 8: 141–157.

CORE System Group (1998). *The CORE System Information Management Handbook*. Leeds: Core System Group.

Grissom, R. (1996). The magical number .7 ± .2: Meta-meta analysis of the probability of superior outcome in comparisons involving therapy, placebo, and control. *Journal of Consulting and Clinical Psychology*, 6(5): 973–982.

Jongsma, A. E. Jr., & Peterson, L. M. (2003). *The Complete Adult Psychotherapy Treatment Planner* (3rd edn). New York: Wiley.

Karasu, T. B. (1986). The psychotherapies. benefits and Urnitations. *American Journal of Psychotherapy*, 40: 324–343.

Kelly, G. A. (1961). Theory and therapy in suicide: the personal constrict point of view. In: M. Farbarow & E. Shneidman (Eds.), *The Cry for Help*. New York: McGraw-Hill.

Luborsky, L., Singer, B., & Luborsky, L. (1975). Comparative studies of psychotherapies: is it true that everyone has won and all must have prizes? *Archives of General Psychiatry*, 32: 995–1008.

National Health Service Executive (1996). *Promoting Clinical Effectiveness: A Framework for Action in and through the NHS*. London: NHS Executive.

Parry, G., & Richardson, A. (1996). *NHS Psychotherapy Services in England: Review of Strategic Policy*. London: NHS Executive.

Perez, J. E. (1999). Clients deserve empirically supported treatments, not romanticism. *American Psychologist*, 54: 205–206.

Roth, A., & Fonagy, P. (1996). *What Works for Whom? A Critical Review of Psychotherapy Research*. New York: Guilford.

Strauss, B. M., & Kächele, H. (1998). The writing on the wall: comments on the current discussion about empirically validated treatments in Germany. *Psychotherapy Research*, 8: 158–170.

Task Force on Promotion and Dissemination of Psychological Procedures (1995). Training in and dissemination of empirically validated psychological treatments. Report and recommendations. *The Clinical Psychologist*, 48: 3–23.

Therapy Works (1997). *Empirically Supported Treatment Programs*. San Antonio: The Psychological Corporation.

Watson, S. B. (1998). A process and outcome study of personal construct, cognitive, and psychodynamic therapies in a NHS setting. Unpublished PhD thesis, University of Hertfordshire.

Watson, S. B., & Winter, D. (2000). Towards an evidence base for personal construct psychotherapy. Paper presented at the Fifth Conference of European Personal Construct Association, Mafta.

Winter, D. J. L. (1997). Everybody has still won but what about the booby prizes? *Psychological Society Psychotherapy Section Newsletter, 21*, 1–15.

Winter, D. (2000). Can personal construct therapy succeed in competition with other therapies? In: J. W. Scheer (Ed.), *The Person in Society: Challenges to a Constructivist Theory*. Giessen: Psychosozial-Verlag.

CHAPTER FOUR

Questioning psychotherapeutic "evidence" (and research)

Del Loewenthal

H eaton (2001) argues that much that is important to psychotherapy (tradition, custom, intuition, and love) is ignored in evidence-based medicine. He concludes, "evidence-based medicine has little relevance to psychotherapy and counselling". While sympathetic to this argument I do not entirely agree with the conclusion, regarding it important for practitioners to be at least familiar with current fashions in research methods in a similar way to those such as Freud and Rogers, who put their case using the dominant recent methods of their day. However, the ability to use such approaches as CORE (Mellor-Clark, Connell, Barkham, & Cummins, 2001), which many practitioners appear to have found useful in legitimizing their work, does not mean that we should just replace thoughtfulness by such tools, otherwise the measurement system determines the approach rather than what is natural to, the phusus, of psychotherapy.

In contrast to Heaton, Baker and Firth-Cozens (1998) argue that psychologists should take advantage of this trend as "The increasing emphasis on evidence-based care is world-wide and represents a huge shift in the ways we deliver services, make decisions, involve patients and manage outcomes". American notions of evidence-based approaches to psychotherapy would indeed appear to be having a radical effect on the provision of publicly funded health service psychotherapy services in Europe as well as on the training of therapists. For example, the *Review of Strategic Policy of Psychotherapy Services in England* (Parry, 1996) states:

> Psychotherapies carried out incompetently can be harmful to patients. The possibility of gross misapplication of techniques and serious error in therapy can be reduced by ensuring that people offering psychotherapy are appropriately qualified and supervised, and that they demonstrate a *commitment* to evidence based practice. [p. 6, my italics]

Is such a commitment good practice? What is meant by "evidence"? So often it would appear that evidence must be based on research and that this research must be scientific—which means that it should be objective—and this in turn ideally assumes a quantitative approach. Furthermore, anything worthwhile that is subjective is covered by qualitative approaches, which might be included if they can prove they are scientific. But what about some European thinking that might seriously challenge these assumptions? For example, Kierkegaard, in his *Concluding Unscientific Postscript*, wrote:

> While objective thought is indifferent to the thinking subject and his existence, the subjective thinker is as an existing individual essentially interested in his own thinking, existing as he does in his thought. His thinking has therefore a different type of reflection, namely the reflection of inwardness, of possession, by virtue of which it belongs to the thinking subject and to no one else. While objective thought translates everything into results, and helps all mankind to cheat, by copying these off and reciting them by rote, subjective thought puts everything in process and omits the result: partly because this belongs to him who has the way, and partly because as an existing individual he is constantly in process of coming to be, which holds true of every human being who has not permitted himself to be deceived into becoming objective. [Kierkegaard, 1941, p. 67]

Thus, psychotherapy here can be seen to be not about goals or notions of objective reality, but more about how patients/clients view their world in their striving for existence. For Kierkegaard, "objective thought translates everything into results, and helps all mankind to cheat". Yet "results" appears as a key word in evidence-based practice, a concept which currently predominates in the management of healthcare and is having a significant effect on the provision of psychotherapy. For example, it is recommended that in evidence-based medicine the following questions need to be asked: "Are the results valid?" (qualified by, for instance, "Is the assignment of patients to treatment randomized?"); "What are the results?" (giving rise to questions such as "How large was the treatment effect?") (Rosenberg & Donald, 1995). In much of the literature there is a common debate that qualitative research results need also to be considered as evidence, even though it does not have the rigour of randomized control trials. Yet an examination of such qualitative literature shows that the language of results again predominates; for example, "Are the results trustworthy?", "What were the results?" (Rosenberg & Donald, 1995). This is still to do with attempts at objective thought.

Thus, it is argued here that in terms of evidence the quantitative versus qualitative debate, while of some interest, takes us away from questions of truth and justice. Foucault (1970) argues that

> in medicine . . . within a period of about 25 years there arose a completely new way of speaking and seeing . . . There is a whole new regime of discourse which makes possible separation not of the true from the false, but of what may be characterised as scientific from what may not be characterised as scientific. [Sarup, 1993, p. 64]

But what of evidence and this "speaking and seeing"? The focus on behavioural approaches can prevent us hearing our patients/ clients and as a society make us deaf to their and our problems. In fact, the growth of e-mail for communication means that we see people less, and the growth of evidence-based approaches can mean that we hear our patients less and, most importantly, think less. If, therefore, we are moving even more into a "regime" where we cannot hear, see, think, or indeed feel, how can we come to our senses?

With a few exceptions, psychologists in the United Kingdom, as previously stated, are being advised that evidence-based medicine is an important opportunity for them: "Through its focus on the study of behaviour change, psychology has the potential to take on a much greater role in the development of clinical governance" (Baker & Firth-Cozens, 1998). But if by evidence (as a key aspect of clinical governance) is meant randomized control trials, or even qualitative research look-alikes, then it will further encourage measurable, observable therapies where more added value apparently can be easily demonstrated to managers. It is not being suggested here that behaviourally based therapies are not important; they are, and they can be very helpful to some patients. Furthermore, they can be less expensive to carry out and train therapists in, which is particularly important in a world that is increasingly concerned with cost effectiveness. However, there are also horrendous dangers if other modalities are swamped through the implications of an increasingly dominant discourse of such evidence as science.

We are in an era where those psychotherapeutic approaches and services for which an evidence-based approach is regarded as inconclusive can be cut. Furthermore, the temptation will be to fund research in those areas where the research tools already appear to provide objective evidence.

Some in psychology and psychiatry are now voicing their concerns: Marzillier (2004) argues that the outcome research of evidence-based psychotherapy ". . . does justice neither to the complexity of people's psychology nor to the intricacies of psychotherapy." He cites Bentall's work (2003), showing how psychiatric diagnostic distinctions are fundamentally flawed, yet ". . . psychotherapists, anxious to prove that what they do works, have bought into a medicalised way of defining psychological experience" to the detriment of a focus on personal relationships. I am not disputing that psychotherapy needs to be evaluated, that science is important, and that this, together with questions of value for money, are areas that counsellors, psychologists, psychotherapists, and psychoanalysts need to be open to and haven't always been.

It is, though, interesting that while postmodernism is attacking some of the current scientific foundations of research (for example, questioning whether replication and triangulation are feasible and opening up such linguistic problematics, as the messages sent by the researched are not the ones received by the researcher), scientific notions of evidence appear to try not to leave a gap for any other readings. If, however, therapy can also be seen, for example, in terms of a practice of thoughtfulness rather than necessarily a science, then this questions how "evidence" is currently being used and draws attention to the danger that such a limited understanding can continue to provide a conceptual smoke-screen for reductions in standards.

References

Baker, R. & Firth-Cozens, J. (1998). Evidence, quality of care and the role of psychology. *The Psychotherapist*, September, 430–432.

Bentall, R. (2003). *Madness Explained: Psychosis and Human Nature.* London: Allen Lane.

Foucault, M. (1970). *The Order of Things.* London: Tavistock.

Heaton, J. (2001). Evidence and psychotherapy. *European Journal of Psychotherapy, Counselling and Health*, 4(2): 237–248.

Kierkegaard, S. (1941). *Concluding Unscientific Postscript.* Princeton, NJ: Princeton University Press.

Marzillier, J. (2004). The myth of evidence-based psychotherapy. *The Psychologist*, 17(7): 392–395.

Mellor-Clark, J., Connell, J., Barkham, M., & Cummins, P. (2001). Counselling outcomes in primary health care: a CORE system data profile. *European Journal of Psychotherapy, Counselling and Health*, 2(1): 65–86.

Parry, G. (1996). *NHS Psychotherapy Services in England, Review of Strategic Policy.* London: NHS Executive.

Rosenberg, W., & Donald, A. (1995). Evidence-based medicine: an approach to clinical problem solving. *British Medical Journal*, 310: 1122–1126.

Sarup, M. (1993). *An Introductory Guide to Post-stucturalism and Postmodernism.* Hemel Hempstead: Harvester Wheatsheaf.

CHAPTER FIVE

Towards a collaborative approach to clinical psychotherapy research

Georgia Lepper and Tirril Harris

I n the Spring 2001 issue of *The Psychotherapist*, our UKCP Research Committee colleague David Winter put a compelling case for therapists to meet the challenge of evidence-based practice and become involved in empirical validation of their work. In echoing his call we would like to suggest that psychotherapy research, far from being the dehumanizing and difficult toil that has sometimes been suggested, can help clinicians to humanize their practice by collecting and responding to evidence.

Previous articles in this series have argued the case for the merits of one or other of the different research approaches available to us, as if, for example, by undertaking quantitative analyses with samples of many patients we would automatically prevent ourselves from using the insights that can be obtained from qualitative analysis such as emerges in the single case history. In this article, we hope to make the case for a pluralistic approach to research that would increase understanding along several fronts simultaneously.

We argue that certain conceptual polarizations—between "subjective" and "objective" truth, between "art" and "science'— are neither real nor productive in the complex task of studying the multi-dimensional process of psychotherapy: for example, we believe that an intersubjective response is part of that process, and that the art of such responding can ultimately be mapped scientifically. Likewise, we argue that the size of the perceived gulf between the tasks of researcher and clinician has also been exaggerated. We consider, from the perspective of our experience, the relationship between the procedures of psychotherapy research and its outcomes. Then we explore how these procedures relate to the psychotherapy process that we know as clinicians. In this way we hope to show how growing scientific understanding of the psychotherapy process—achieved through a variety of methods and approaches—can make a direct contribution to the work of the clinician; and how, in parallel, clinicians can make a contribution to research.

There are many conceptual and practical tools that are used in scientific research to gather and map knowledge. Among those are, first and foremost, the development of accurate, unbiased, and reliable measurements of the phenomena to be studied—that is, measures which can be used with the same definitional thresholds by different research workers regardless of the hypotheses each holds—and second, the use of the well-known tools of statistics. We have no more robust methods for ordering large quantities of information in order to build a generalized picture of a phenomenon. Many are discouraged by the idea of the first, believing it entails jargon, or sterilized and, thus, almost meaningless checklists that distance us from what is really happening to the human beings involved.

However, one of the most important discoveries of recent years is the so-called "theory of mind hypothesis", which suggests that in order to develop into a relating person, each child must successfully reach an understanding that the point of view of other people is different from their own, and that in order to communicate (and to lie!) we need to take the other person's point of view into account. This suggests that the concepts of "objectivity" and "subjectivity" are not abstract philosophical concepts, but everyday psychological realities that we must all make use of in assessing the world around us and communicating with others. In ordinary relating, we observe and make inferences about the subjective reactions of others—their feelings, wishes, desires, and motives—in order to communicate; and we observe our own subjective reactions in deciding what to do next. As clinicians and as researchers, we have the same information to go on. And it is perfectly possible to develop procedures for measuring such phenomena by consensus and enshrine these rules in detailed scientific manuals to ensure they are always used in a comparable manner. In other words, scientific measurement does not have to be difficult and different from ordinary language commentary, though it must be carefully monitored to ensure this comparable usage of the "language" and, thus, prevent bias.

Thus, a markedly stressful loss experience can be reliably distinguished from a mild humiliation—though some experiences may be both of these simultaneously (Brown, Harris, & Hepworth, 1995); a dismissive style of relating reliably distinguished from an enmeshed style (Cassidy & Shaver, 1999); and a markedly supportive response to a request for help distinguished from a moderately or mildly supportive one, as well as a markedly undermining one (Veiel & Baumann, 1992).

Similarly, how the participants in a therapeutic dialogue react to each other is never available to us exactly as it is to them, but how they interact with each other can be studied from the same point of view—of a consensus of outside observers. Suppose we imagined that what the researcher does is not so different from what a clinician does, or what we all do in relating to the world and others. Suppose we thought of psychotherapy research as a way of slowing down observation of the process of relating through the use of a variety of methods, so that we can discover more deliberately and consciously what is happening. Would that be so different from what the clinician does?

Turning to the second research tool mentioned above, thanks to statistics, we can argue, with confidence, that psychotherapy is, overall, effective (Bergin & Garfield, 1994). To some extent, such methods have begun to shed some light on who benefits from psychotherapy, and to provide some indicators of what kind of treatment may be beneficial in a particular case. We learn that there isn't much difference in outcome between the different kinds of therapies, such as interpersonal, cognitive-behavioural, psychodynamic, or client-centred counselling, but that there are common factors that are reliably present in therapies of all types that result in good outcomes (Hubble, Duncan, & Miller, 1999).

This is a surprising result; researchers, like clinicians, are fond of thinking that the particular concepts from their own theoretical schools have strong explanatory power. The evidence points to factors that are far less doctrinaire, and far closer to the "art" of therapy. The major factor contributing to good outcome appears to be the "therapeutic alliance" or empathy (Burns & Nolen-Hoeksema, 1997; Horvath & Symonds, 1991; Orlinsky & Howard, 1986; Piper, Azim, Joyce, & McCallum, 1991). Also important are personality factors in both therapist and patient, as well as the effects of events and people in the patients' life outside the therapy itself. Conceptual understanding—and our theories—do play a part, but only a part.

If, as it appears, relationship factors provide an important element in the processes of psychotherapy, another aspect of the process of psychotherapy comes into focus. It is one clinicians are aware of, but it leaves us with the question: what is a "therapeutic working alliance", and how can we find out more about it? In the past decade research workers have developed several measures of the alliance [Penn Helping Alliance Questionnaire (HAQ), Morgan, Luborsky, Crits-Christoph, Curtis, & Solomon (1982); Working Alliance Inventory (WAI), Horvath & Greenberg (1989); California Psychotherapy Alliance Scale (CALPAS), Marmar, Weiss, & Gaston (1989); Agnew Relationship Measure (ARM), Agnew-Davies, Stiles, Hardy, Barkham, & Shapiro (1998)] but there is still definitely a need to make these more subtle. How can the clinician build a good therapeutic alliance, and what can research tell us about it?

By going into more detail about this one out of many research questions, we may be able to convey more fully our message that research workers need clinicians as much as the latter need the former. A robust area of research here is that of Attachment Style, based on Bowlby's general theory of attachment as the basis of human development. Various effective measures of this have been developed, but perhaps the best known is a research instrument called the Adult Attachment Interview (AAI), elaborated by Mary Main, Mary Ainsworth and their co-workers (Ainsworth, Blehar, Waters, & Wall, 1978; George, Kaplan, & Main, 1985).

The AAI work uses a combination of interview techniques (with adults, often pregnant) along with another instrument, the Strange Situation Test observation (of children later born to those pregnant adults), combined with coding and statistical methods to build a sound empirical basis for the study of development and psychopathology from childhood into adulthood. Their research has demonstrated that there are three very different patterns of engagement with the world and with others, which arise as a response to early experience with others. They have been termed "securely attached"; "dismissive"; and "anxiously ambivalent" or "preoccupied/enmeshed"; in addition, some infants may be classified "disorganized".

Securely attached individuals have the capacity to describe and relate to their experiences—both good and bad—with a capacity for self-reflection and a willingness to engage with others about their meaning. "Detached", or "dismissive" individuals seem not to be able or willing to do this. They find it difficult to remember, or to recount, their experiences of the world of their childhood. A third term—the "pre-occupied'—describes people who cannot recount their experiences of others in their childhood in a coherent way. The stories they tell are chaotic and confused. These very different ways of relating present us with very different problems in the consulting room.

These findings suggest that for the clinician, struggling to understand the patient in the early phases of the therapy, different approaches to building a relationship may be crucial to the outcome of the work. Patients with a dismissive style of relating may need to be helped to express themselves through the active engagement of the therapist (Dozier, Lomax, Tyrrell, & Lee, 2001); while preoccupied patients may need much help in structuring their overwhelming thoughts and feelings in order to find a way to relate successfully. Clinician style must be responsive to these very different patterns of relating and need. But what can researchers tell us about what adjustments need to be made? We need yet further tools to unpack the here and now processes of the session. Some are already beginning to be used (see, for example, Hardy et al., 1999; Mergenthaler, 1996; Ogrodniezuk, Piper, Joyce, & McCallum, 1999), but we have a long way to go before all the issues will be clarified. On the other hand, there is more prospect of these advances than ever before as groups who formerly identified each other as operating in different worlds come to learn how to communicate. For, just as quantitative research workers are increasingly coming to appreciate and adopt the techniques of qualitative research in combination with their usual approaches, so let us hope the gap between clinicians and research workers of all kinds will increasingly be bridged as each realize how easy and essential such communication could be.

It is our impression that, with the recent evolution and simplification of research methodologies and the rapprochements taking place throughout UKCP, what has long been seen as a difficult linguistic hurdle, with each profession struggling with each other's terminology, may become no more than a mere difference in dialects as each seek to improve psychotherapy outcomes.

References

Agnew-Davies, R., Stiles, W. B., Hardy, G. E., Barkham, M., & Shapiro, D. A. (1998). Alliance structure assessed by the Agnew relationship measure. *British Journal of Clinical Psychology*, 37: 155–172.

Ainsworth, M. D., Blehar, M. C., Waters, E., & Wall, S. (1978). *Patterns of Attachment: A Psychological Study of the Strange Situation*. Hillsdale, NJ: Erlbaum.

Bergin, A. E., & Garfield, S. L. (1994). *Handbook of Psychotherapy and Behavior Change*. New York: John Wiley & Sons.

Brown, G. W., Harris, T. O., & Hepworth, C. (1995). Loss, humiliation and entrapment among women developing depression: a patient and non-patient comparison. *Psychological Medicine*, 25: 7–21.

Burns, D., & Nolen-Hoeksema, S. (1997). Therapeutic empathy and recovery from depression in cognitive-behavioural therapy. A structural equation model. *Journal of Consulting & Clinical Psychology*, 60, 441–449.

Cassidy, J., & Shaver, P. R. (1999). *Handbook of Attachment Theory. Research and Clinical Applications*. New York: Guilford.

Dozier, M., Lomax, L., Tyrrell, C. L., & Lee, S. W. (2001). The challenge of treatment for clients with dismissing states of mind. *Attachment and Human Development*, 3: 62–76.

George, C., Kaplan, N., & Main, M. (1985). Adult Attachment Interview (2nd edn). Unpublished manuscript. University of California at Berkeley.

Hardy, G., Aldridge, J., Davidson, O., Rowe, C., Reilly, S., & Shapiro, D. (1999). Therapist responsiveness to client attachment and issues observed in client-identified significant events in psycho-dynamic–interpersonal therapy. *Psychotherapy Research, 9*: 38–53.

Horvath, A. O., & Symonds, B. D. (1991). Relation between working alliance and outcome in psychotherapy: a meta-analysis. *Journal of Counselling Psychology, 38*: 139–149.

Horvath, A. O., & Greenberg, L. S. (1989). The working alliance inventory. *Journal of Counseling Psychology, 36*, 223–233.

Hubble, M., Duncan, B., & Miller, S. (1999). *The Heart and Soul of Change: What Works in Therapy?* Washington, DC: American Psychological Association.

Marmar, C. R., Weiss, D. S., & Gaston, I. (1989). Towards the validation of the California Psychotherapeutic Alliance Rating System. *Psychological Assessment, 1*: 46–52.

Mergenthaler, E. (1996). Emotion–abstraction patterns in verbatim protocols. A new way of decoding psychotherapeutic processes. *Journal of Consulting & Clinical Psychology, 64*(1): 306–315.

Morgan, R., Luborsky, L., Crits-Christoph, P., Curtis, H., & Solomon, J. (1982). Predicting the outcomes of psychotherapy by the Penn Helping Alliance rating method. *Archives of General Psychiatry, 39*: 397–402.

Ogrodniezuk, J. S., Piper, W. E., Joyce, A. S., & McCallum, M. (1999). Transference interpretations in short-term dynamic psychotherapy. *Journal of Nervous & Mental Disease, 187*: 572–579.

Orlinsky D. E., & Howard, K. I. (1986). Process and outcome in psychotherapy. In: S. L. Garfield & A. E. Bergin (Eds.), *Handbook of Psychotherapy and Behavior Change* (pp. 344–347). New York: Wiley.

Piper, W. E., Azim, H. F. A., Joyce, A. S., & McCallum, M. (1991). Transference interpretations, therapeutic alliance and outcome in short-term individual psychotherapy. *Archives of General Psychiatry, 48*: 946–953.

Veiel, H. O. F., & Baumann, U. (Eds.) (1992). *The Meaning and Measurement of Social Support*. Washington, DC: Hemisphere Publishing.

Winter, D. (2001). Avoiding the fate of the dodo bird: the challenge of evidence-based practice. *The Psychotherapist, 16*, 39–41.

CHAPTER SIX

Evidence-based practice: issues for psychotherapy[*]

Martin Milton

Summary

This paper attempts to review both the frequently discussed "objective" factors in evidence-based practice as well as the more subjective factors facing psychotherapists engaged in this debate. The contention is that greater familiarity with the issues will allow us to inform and structure this debate in a more appropriate manner than if we allow those from other disciplines to structure it for us.

Introduction

Readers of this journal will be familiar with the attention that is currently being paid to the concept of evidence-based practice (EBP). Readers are also likely to have views on the strengths and limitations of this approach and on what constitutes "evidence".

---

[*] This chapter previously appeared in: Milton, M. (2002), *Psychoanalytic Psychotherapy* , 16(2): 160–172.

These positions are also evident in the literature (Owen, 2001; Roth & Fonagy, 1996,)

While the concept of EBP addresses some of the desires that psychotherapists have for their patients' best interests, it is also one that requires thorough consideration, as the notion of "evidence" is not a straightforward, unambiguous, clear notion (Newnes, 2001; Spinelli, 2001). This dimension of the evidence-based debate therefore often fosters a level of anxiety, confusion, and ambivalence that is not well attended to in the literature or in health service policy.

This paper reflects on the current literature about evidence-based practice and attempts to include attention to the impact of this organizational discourse on the profession of psychotherapy and its practices, and on psychotherapists themselves.

The meaning of research

EBP has clear links to a scientist–practitioner model of practice, as well as calls to accountability. A simplified and well-intentioned understanding of the term draws our attention to the notion that where there is research evidence for a given therapy, this approach should be used first (Department of Health, 2001b). This is a concept many psychotherapists will have sympathy for, and they will feel that this ethos is embedded within their everyday practice. However, it is in the attempts to operationalize this term, in calls to develop "lists" of empirically validated therapies, that some psychotherapists experience the greatest anxiety. It seems that part of this anxiety is in relation to "Research" and how decisions are made with regard to what is valid and what is not. At the centre of this confusion is the concept of "evidence". It is interesting to note that while this may be experienced as a contemporary "threat" to psychotherapy, it has a long history. Indeed, Jones drew our attention to this very issue almost half a century ago when he wrote:

> Mediocre spirits demand of science a kind of certainty which it cannot give, a sort of religious satisfaction. Only the real, rare, true scientific minds can endure doubts which are attached to all our knowledge. I always envy the physicists and mathematicians who can stand on firm grounds. I hover, so to speak, in thin air. Mental events seem to be immeasurable and probably always will be so. [Jones, 1957, p. 418]

At this point in time, it is not only mathematicians and physicists who seek certainty; it is a current socio-cultural preoccupation and pervades all aspects of our lives, including health service policy. At times, this seems to be completely at odds with the awareness that the psychotherapists has, from day to day, moment to moment, experience of the fluid, moving nature of personal meaning in the therapeutic encounter. The juxtaposition of these two perspectives draws our attention to the chasm that still exists between human reality and empirical certainty.

This conundrum is central to the EBP debate and the role of research. While health service documents outline the usefulness of a hierarchy of evidence with the randomized controlled trial (RCT) as the "gold standard" (Department of Health 1996, 2001a, b; Roth and Fonagy 1996) when thinking at a populations level, the psychotherapist has a different focus. Ours is the consideration of what this "evidence" means for the client we sit with session after session and the psychotherapeutic project that has been engaged in. As well as an ethical discourse about appropriate therapy for particular patients, this chasm also results in dilemmas with regard to organising services that meet the demands of EBP, yet are still relevant to the unique and very personal psychotherapeutic journeys that are undertaken by "mere" individuals. The impact of this on services and psychotherapists will be considered later in this paper.

Rather than just applying science to practice within a politically set schedule, a true call to EBP is a rather more complex (and, might I add, exciting) issue. At epistemological and service levels, the call to EBP requires us to reconsider the research that we have undertaken and to consider a range of evidence and research methodologies to ensure that they are relevant and appropriate to the task before us (Department of Health, 1996; Milton, 2001; Sandler, Sandler, & Davies, 2000).

The usefulness of RCTs is not an issue here, as RCTs enlighten psychotherapy with respect to epidemiology and a degree of response to "treatment." What is worth considering is the predominance that such an approach should have, as it cannot account for individual experience and the evolving and continuing co-construction of meaning. Despite the best efforts of some of our technocrats, we may never be able to technologize existence and to develop complete certainty. Another interesting and related question is the relationship that traditional, quantitative methodologies based on modernist assumptions can have on other research findings—formal research such as that undertaken by qualitative researchers (Dennis, Fetterman, & Sechrest, 1994; Howe, 1996) as well as those which are informal yet highly educative and more sociological (Newnes, 2001); for example, biography and literature.

This raises the question of what these other forms of research would look like and what sort of evidence they would generate. It is also interesting to consider the impact that other research methods and questions might have on psychotherapists' abilities to warm to and focus on empirical research.

Appropriate methodologies and "How to do it"

To jump models briefly—it is self-evident that structural engineering and chemistry will generate different research questions and require different forms of inquiry. It is also, of course, evident that the materials used in an engineering project will have a chemical composition and the chemist will eventually be required to attend to the structural implications of their compounds. The point of invoking such a metaphor has, as its intention, the aim to clarify a point by way of novel and different meaning. In terms of psychotherapy, the appropriateness of research and the evidence it generates is dependent upon a understanding of the nature of the relevant discipline and the aim of the research. Thus, psychotherapists (like engineers) are right to be cautious about adopting research methodologies directly from medicine or elsewhere before critically evaluating their ability to remain true to the psychotherapeutic aim and ethos. One of the particular concerns is the difficulty in developing models of research and human science that recognize an appropriately attuned exploration (Spinelli, 2001).

As with schools of engineering and chemistry, different psychotherapies are based on different assumptions and practices and may therefore require different approaches to research. A definition of psychoanalysis (PA) that limits PA to the intrapsychic (Green, 2000) will offer different views on the nature of appropriate research as opposed to another understanding that might privilege the internal or intersubjective. Yet both, of course, are relevant to the work of most psychotherapists when engaged in psychotherapeutic work with the complex personalities humans are blessed with (or burdened by).

Another way of thinking about this is to examine current Department of Health policy. Those within psychotherapy recognize the difficulties in finding appropriate methodologies with which to explore the effects of interpretative and insight-oriented psychotherapies. Indeed, this difficulty has led to a lack of research in some areas. Despite the fact that this is a difficulty for psychoanalytic and systemic therapies in particular, it should not be taken to suggest that there is evidence against the usefulness of these psychotherapies. The Department of Health recognizes this, and its publication is littered with comments such as "Other psychotherapeutic approaches have not been systematically reviewed/evaluated" (Department of Health, 2001a, p. 24).

This awareness has implications for our stance to evidence and requires us to be cautious about the definitions of science, research, and evidence that we adopt. Much research undertaken in the health services is seen to be "quick and dirty" research in order quickly to explore a question and offer information to stakeholders. While at times this is useful, psychotherapists have learnt that "quick and dirty" may not do service to science or to psychotherapy. As a corollary, we should also recognize that, as in psychotherapy, a difficulty may not need an extensive analysis when a concise, time-limited response will suffice; the issue of deciding which approach to take requires consideration of the question, anticipated outcome, and contextual realities.

One issue to note when considering appropriate research strategies is the distinction between hypothesis generation and hypothesis proving. RCTs are often useful in illuminating, supporting, and challenging our assumptions about the general impact of our work. However, in order for psychotherapy to be in a position to undertake such efforts at validation, we require attention to the hypothesis-generation phase of any research project. This is captured in the concepts of "innovative practice", "case series evaluation", and "theory development"—all of which have legitimate positions within the cycle of research recognized by the Department of Health (1996).

While attending to some slightly different issues, Fonagy addresses the complexity of this situation when he notes the place of clinical work:

> The empirical basis of psychoanalysis is the clinical situation. The laboratory does not provide its empirical base and as the theory is not based on laboratory findings it cannot be either disproved or validated by them. [Fonagy, 1982, p. 127]

Fonagy's point is important as it again notes the chasm that can occur between academic research and clinical practice. If these two highly important domains are to usefully inform each other and generate fruitful dialogue (rather than deny or attack) we need some kind of bridging potential. Wallerstein outlines the qualities of what such a bridge might look like when he states:

> Research that is simultaneously faithful both to the highly subjectivistic and complex data of the psychoanalytic consulting room and the so-called objective canons of the empirical scientific enquiry. That should be, after all, the heart of what we call psychoanalytic research. [Wallerstein, 2000, p. 28]

The notion of "psychoanalytic research" is important here, as by invoking such terms and working to include these in the EBP debate we may be in a position to clarify questions that will enlighten our therapeutic practices, and to give thought to the methods we might develop to explore them—without having to fall into the narrow confines of traditional and rather static quantitative methodologies, pre- and post-therapy explorations, and the like. The advantages, of course, are that by having both a research and a practice eye, both endeavours may be enriched. This is a point made in the literature.

> There is room for a form of psychodynamic research that is more systematic than what we presently do, and more rigorous, but which is not based on, as it were, extra-psychoanalytic data. [Sandler, Sandler, & Davies, 2000, p. 34]

These thoughts bring us to the crucial issue—if psychotherapy recognizes the limitations of some of the more orthodox approaches to research, what alternatives can it suggest? Some responses to this question seem to argue the case for alternative methods to be used. Other responses have challenged the focus of the whole EBP debate and suggested alternative foci.

Alternative methodologies suggested include that mainstay of psychoanalytic and psychotherapeutic research—case study methodologies (Sandler, Sandler, & Davies, 2000). In some respects these have a clear place in official EBP as a manifestation of innovative practice and case-study evaluation. (Department of Health, 1996) As well as health targets on a population level, health service policies also support the psychotherapist in a personalized approach to psychotherapy through the activities of personalized assessment and decision-making on the specifics of each individual's need (Department of Health, 2001a,b). As case studies are so individually responsive to particular therapies, they have the potential to be used to illuminate factors in the therapeutic process as well as client characteristics. As with RCT methodologies, they also have limitations—one being that by taking a case-study approach the psychotherapist is not able to take a stance that their findings are generalizable at a population level and, of course, the presence of the author's subjectivity has both great advantages and its own difficulties.

In addition to their legitimacy as a research enterprise in their own right, case studies can also be used in other qualitative methodologies as the data for further and alternative analyses (Milton, 2001; Mitchell & Brownescombe Heller, 1999). Methodologies such as discourse analysis (DA), grounded theory, thematic content analysis, and interpretative phenomenological analysis, can all use a single case study or series of case studies to explore issues relevant to psychotherapy and the questions that EBP asks us to consider. Diamond (2001) uses DA on stored transcripts from the Psychological Therapies Research Centre to review the "to-and-fro" of therapeutic sessions in order to explore the manner in which unconscious mechanisms manifest themselves in psychodynamic work and the issues that this raises for psychotherapy practice and provision.

Other methodologies can, of course, be used independently of case study work. Of course, the methods outlined above will all be able to offer interesting and unique perspectives on the question of useful and ethical practice and be tailored to consider particular models of psychotherapy, specific population groups, and issues related to therapist practices.

As mentioned above, those involved in the EBP debate have often thought critically and creatively about the issues involved, and a complementary position has been recognized. This is the notion of practice-based evidence (PBE) (Barkham & Mellor-Clark, 2000; Carroll & Tholstrup, 2001). As well as EBP making demands on those in the clinic, PBE attends to how research might be tailored to meet explicitly the agenda of those involved in the therapeutic enterprise. This approach has only recently been invoked in the psychotherapy literature and therefore requires further development, including the development of guidelines and criteria for what PBE would look like. In principle, it uses the evidence of the psychotherapeutic process itself to assist clinicians and service providers to evaluate the service. Such a stance values local and idiographic evidence as well as nomothetic evidence available from RCT research.

As well as recognizing the efforts of those in the clinic and those in the academy, it is very useful when those charged with policy development collaborate in this debate, as contextual factors are important. While clinicians and researchers are aware of what Target calls "feasible research" (1998, p. 79) it is important for this to be discussed with all the "stakeholders" so that the value of what is possible is recognized and the desire for unrealistic answers is recognized and worked through by all involved. It is also important to locate research within systems that have the required support. It is not possible for heads of psychotherapy departments to undertake research of the RCT type and thus it is appropriate to leave such large-scale research within government-sponsored academic departments with access to multi-site samples.

This type of research needs well resourced posts with adequate support. It would also be appropriate to consider the type of work that can occur in single-handed practices, local psychological therapies services, and poorly-resourced psychotherapy services. In these services, clinicians often undertake their own literature reviews (for in-house consumption or to add to published literature in more accessible journals and newsletters) and of course case studies are obviously relatively easy to undertake. In addition, honorary therapists very often need to undertake service-related research for their training. Also, Trust requirements for audit can be useful in examining the relationship between practice and the literature.

Possible gains

If it is possible to protect (or limit) psychotherapy from the problems of the rational/traditional empiricist assumptions of a knowable truth—and if it is possible to enrich science with a respect for what psychotherapy can do—what does psychotherapy gain? How does psychotherapy as a discipline and its practitioners and clients benefit from this effort?

In this respect, the arguments are many and varied. Some have suggested that properly targeted and executed research has the potential to enrich our therapeutic work and in particular make the psychotherapeutic enterprise more relevant to contemporary existence. In addition, where psychotherapy takes advantage of a range of research methodologies, we are able to ensure that we explore questions from a range of perspectives and may thereby avoid some instances of the "false causal connection which may be read into a case history or in the story of a therapeutic intervention" (Target, 1998, p. 81). As well as the "in-session" benefits that may accrue when we undertake and use appropriately-targeted research, there are also advantages to be gained for the relationship between those within psychotherapy and those on the outside.

One benefit that is immediately apparent is to confirm to others—service commissioners and, of course, patients—that our efforts to assist people result in benefit rather than harm. There is also a body of evidence that we can draw upon to assert this, but the greater our body of evidence is the more useful it can become. For useful references see Fonagy (1999) and Milton (1996). In psychoanalysis, we might refer to work with:

- adults (Bateman & Fonagy, 2001; Wallerstein, 1989; Weber, Bachrach, & Solomon, 1985a,b);
- couples (Heller & Gore. 1995);
- groups (Ganzarain & Buchele, 1990; Sigrell, 1992);

- children and adolescents (Fonagy &Target, 1994, 1996; Lush, Boston, & Grainger, 1991, Moran & Fonagy, 1987, Moran, Fonagy, Kurtz, Bolton, & Brook, 1991);
- short- and long-term work (Mitchell & Brownescombe Heller, 1999).

There is also evidence that dynamic psychotherapy is useful for:

- Personality disorders (Waldinger & Gunderson, 1984; Woody, McLellan, Luborsky, & O'Brien, 1985);
- Depression (Barkham *et al.*, 1994; Shapiro *et al.*, 1994);
- Eating disorders (Garner, Rokert, Davies, & Garner, 1993);
- Anxiety disorders *if* there is comorbidity, particularly personality disorder "where evidence for the use of dynamic techniques exists." (Roth & Fonagy, 1996, p. 144).

As well as such broad recognition of the benefits of psychotherapy, there is also evidence of the nature of the benefit experienced by patients in psychotherapy. Authors in the field note that there are broad benefits from psychoanalytically orientated work and suggest that these take the form of:

> reduced somatic symptoms or problems, more satisfying and loving relationships, greater capacity to cope with life and its problems, less use of medication, fewer GP visits, fewer episodes of violence or self-harm, less offending behaviour and more time spent in employment and fewer difficulties at work. [Mitchell & Brownescombe Heller, 1999, p. 40]

In addition to these, it is also apparent that effective psychotherapy can provide economic benefits as well—after working through difficult issues and gaining insight into their concerns many people use fewer Health Service resources in terms of fewer trips to Accident and Emergency departments, lower reliance on medication and visits to GPs, etc. (Mitchell & Brownescombe Heller, 1999).

Anxiety about attack

So far, this paper has addressed some of the issues in the literature with regard to psychotherapy and evidence-based practice. At this point, I want to return to the point made in the opening section and give voice to some of the more dynamic aspects of the EBP debate.

It is interesting to note that many practitioners across the psychotherapeutic professions are (at best) sceptical about the role of formal research in psychotherapy. In fact, there seems to be a reluctance to undertake research once core training is complete (Milton, 2001) and even to read up-to-date research reports regularly. In this climate of research awareness it might be interesting to consider this in line with notions of avoidance and denial.

Where therapists do engage in the EBP debate, there is often a degree of anxiety evident about it (Milton, 2001). Some have gone further than expressing scepticism or anxiety, and construct the call to EBP as an attack on themselves and their profession as is witnessed in the language of the following comment:

> Overvaluation of "Research" often goes together with an under-valuation or devaluation, of the research with which we engage in our psycho-analytic work. And if this Research (with a capital R) is privileged within psychoanalysis, we will, in order to placate and propitiate our enemies from without, succeed in destroying psychoanalysis from within. I believe this to be a "real" not (just a fantasized) danger! [Brenman Pick, 2000, p. 109]

These anxieties may develop for a number of reasons. Some initial possibilities include a lack of familiarity with research and its potential and a lack of research training (Milton, 2001; Target, 1998). The limitations of research methodologies that confine their attention to symptom checklists and the "manualisation of treatment" may also influence this (Target, 1998). As indicated by Brenman Pick (2000), it may also be related to a realistic appraisal of the power and function of what Foucault termed the "psy-complex" (Foucault, 1995). In Foucauldian terms, the mental health systems and professions, such as psychiatry, psychology, and psychotherapy, function as regulators of social interactions and, thus, he draws our attention to their joint powers. The EBP agenda is just one manifestation of this system, with benefits and dangers.

As well as an "objective" reading of the EBP literature, it is interesting to note a tone of moral superiority that is woven through it. This tone attempts to discredit the psychotherapeutic project and/or individual practitioners who are not able to quote indices of behavioural change. This is evident in the government rhetoric about "unqualified/bad practitioners", "bad apples", and "do-gooders with no training". It is interesting that a tone such as this seems to ignore the high quality of work that does occur, the level of skill that exists, and also the goodwill that the NHS relies on.

These dynamics need our attention, as left unattended they threaten to spoil the potential for creative thought that originally drew so many psychotherapists into the field. Reflection on this issue is not just a task for psychotherapists on their own—if EBP is going to reach its potential to assist the profession of psychotherapy in creating fruitful and ethical therapeutic encounters, it needs to be an inclusive debate. Without this, there is potential for splitting at all sorts of levels—research from practice and commissioners from providers with all the disruptive and destructive potential that this has.

Conclusions

This paper has noted both objective and subjective issues involved in the current evidence-based practice debate that is central to the provision of public-sector health care. As is often quoted in our literature, this issue is filled with uncertainty and lower limits of knowability than may be the case in other areas. The challenge facing those that provide such services is again a similar one—to engage with what we do know and what we do not know in a thoughtful and ethical manner, with the best interests of our clients in mind. This aim may infuse both our stance to the practice of psychotherapy as well as research and service development. The challenge also requires us to generalize what we know from psychotherapy (e.g., about staying with uncertainty and aiming for collaborative, engaged, and attuned discussions) to our relationships outside the consulting room with colleagues at all levels of service organization.

Statements such as this, "noble" as they may be, do little to assist clarification of how we might proceed in the dual (and challenging) task of the evidence-based project, at the same time as providing the services already so stretched. My own thoughts are that the curiosity that often drives us as psychotherapists is something that can easily be turned to the research endeavour. However, clinicians and researchers alike have to challenge the prevailing rhetoric about the only useful or informative research being RCT-type approaches. As outlined above, this is, of course, a useful strategy, but local services are simply not equipped or resourced to undertake this type of research. Much more feasible (and to many, much more interesting) approaches to research are those that draw on the well-honed skills used by psychotherapists every day: collaborative, qualitative approaches that value the attunement to the client's world of meaning. Grounded theory research of clients' understanding of specific difficulties, discourse analytic research as to the presence of socio-political material in clients' narratives and its relationship to distress and recovery, are just some projects that come to mind and may be feasible within most psychotherapy services with nothing more than some time available from the continuing professional development "allowance".

Whatever strategies services take, and these will be different depending on local demographics, level of resource, and interest of those involved, the skills of psychotherapists should be capitalized upon to help us take our disciplines forward as broadly and as richly as is possible in an effort to help those we seek to help. An additional outcome might be that therapists could be revitalized in their passion for their chosen fields.

References

Barkham, M., & Mellor-Clark, J. (2000). Rigour and relevance: the role of practice-based evidence in the psychological therapies. In: N. Rowland & S. Goss (Eds.), *Evidence-Based Counselling and Psychological Therapies: Research and Applications*. London: Routledge.

Barkham, M., Rees, A., Shapiro, D. A., Agnew, R. M., Halstead, J., & Culverwell, A. (1994). Effects of treatment method and duration and severity of depression on the effectiveness of psychotherapy: extending the Second Sheffield Psychotherapy project to NHS settings. Sheffield University, *SAPU Memo 1480*.

Bateman, A., & Fonagy, P. (2001). Treatment of borderline personality disorder with psychoanalytically oriented partial hospitalization: an 18 month follow up. *American Journal of Psychiatry, 158*(1): 36–42.

Brenman Pick, I. (2000). Discussion (III) In: J. Sandler, A.M. Sandler, & R. Davies (Eds.), *Clinical and Observational Psychoanalytic Research: Roots of a Controversy: Andre Green and Daniel Stern*. London: Monograph Series of the Psychoanalysis Unit of University College London and the Anna Freud Centre London.

Carroll, M., & Tholstrup, M. (2001). *Integrative Approaches to Supervision*. London: Jessica Kingsley.

Dennis, M., Fetterman, D. M., & Sechrest, L. (1994). Integrating qualitative and quantitative evaluation methods in substance abuse research. *Evaluation and Program Planning, 17*: 419–427.

Department of Health (1996). *NHS Psychotherapy Services in England: Review of Strategic Policy*. Wetherby: NHS Executive.

Department of Health (2001a). *Treatment Choice in Psychological Therapies and Counselling Evidence Based Clinical Practice Guidelines*. Wetherby: NHS Executive.

Department of Health (2001b). *Treatment Choice in Psychological Therapies and Counselling Evidence Based Clinical Practice Guidelines— Brief Version*. Wetherby: NHS Executive.

Diamond, D. (20001). How rude can you get? The dialogic unconscious in therapy. Unpublished PsychD portfolio: University of Surrey.

Fonagy, P. (1982). The integration of psychoanalysis and experimental science: a review. *International Journal of Psycho-Analysis, 9*: 125–145.

Fonagy, P. (1999). *An Open Door Review of Outcome Studies in Psychoanalysis. Report of the Research Committee of the Institute of Psychoanalysis*. London: University College/Institute of Psychoanalysis.

Fonagy, P., & Target, M. (1994). The efficacy of psychoanalysis for children with disruptive disorders. *Journal of the American Academy of Child and Adolescent Psychiatry, 33*: 45–55.

Fonagy, P., & Target, M. (1996). Predictors of outcome in child psychoanalysis: a retrospective study of 763 cases at the Anna Freud Centre. *Journal of the American Psychoanalytic Association, 44*: 27–77.

Foucault, M. (1995). *Madness and Civilisation: A History of Insanity in the Age of Reason*. London: Routledge.

Ganzarain, R., & Buchele, B. J. (1990). Incest perpetration in group therapy: a psychodynamic perspective. *Bulletin of the Menninger Clinic, 54*: 295–310.

Garner, D. M., Rokert, W., Davies, R., & Garner, M. D. (1993). A comparison between CBT and supportive expressive therapy for bulimia nervosa. *American Journal of Psychiatry, 150*, 37–46.

Green, A. (2000). Science and science fiction in infant research. In: J. Sandler, A. M. Sandler, & R. Davies (Eds.), *Clinical and Observational Psychoanalytic Research: Roots of a Controversy: Andre Green and Daniel Stern*. London: Monograph Series of the Psychoanalysis Unit of University College London and the Anna Freud Centre London.

Heller, M. B., & Gore, V. (1995). A tale of two mothers. *Sexual and Marital Therapy*, 10: 83–94.

Howe, D. (1996). Client experiences of counseling and treatment interventions: a qualitative study of family views of family therapy. *British Journal of Guidance and Counselling*, 24: 367–376.

Jones, E. (1957). *Sigmund Freud: Life and Work. Volume 2*. London: Hogarth Press.

Lush, D., Boston, M. & Grainger, E. (1991). Evaluations of psychoanalytic psychotherapy with children: therapists' assessments and predictions. *Psychoanalytic Psychotherapy*, 5: 191–234.

Milton, J. (1996). *Presenting the Case for Psychoanalytic Psychotherapy Services: An Annotated Bibliography* (3rd edn). Jointly sponsored by The Association for Psychoanalytic Psychotherapy in the NHS and The Tavistock Clinic, supported by the Psychotherapy Section of the Royal College of Psychiatrists.

Milton, M. (2001). Supervision: researching therapeutic practice. In: M. Carroll & M. Tholstrup (Eds.), *Intergrative Approaches to Supervision*. London: Jessica Kingsley.

Mitchell, S., & Brownescombe Heller, M. (1999). Why purchase psychoanalytic psychotherapy on the NHS? A set of guidelines. *Clinical Psychology Forum*, 134:, 36–40.

Moran, G. S., & Fonagy, P. (1987). Psychoanalysis and diabetic control: a single-case study. *British Journal of Medical Psychology*, 60: 357–372.

Moran, G. S., Fonagy, P., Kurtz, A., Bolton, A., & Brook, C. (1991). A controlled study of the psychoanalytic treatment of brittle diabetes. *Journal of the American Academy of Child and Adolescent Psychiatry*, 30: 926–935.

Newnes, C. (2001). On evidence. *Clinical Psychology*, 1(1): 6–12.

Owen, I. (2001). Treatments of choice, quality and integration. *Counselling Psychology Review*, 16 (4): 16–25.

Roth, A., & Fonagy, P. (1996). *What Works for Whom: A Critical Review of the Psychotherapy Outcome Literature*. London: Guilford Press.

Sandler, J., Sandler, A. M., & Davies, R. (2000). *Clinical and Observational Psychoanalytic Research: Roots of a Controversy: Andre Green and Daniel Stern*. London: Monograph Series of the Psychoanalysis Unit of University College London and the Anna Freud Centre London.

Shapiro, D. A., Barkham, M., Rees, A., Hardy, G. E., Reynolds, S., & Startup, M. (1994). Effects of treatment duration and severity of depression on the effectiveness of cognitive/behavioural and psychodynamic/interpersonal psychotherapy. *Journal of Consulting and Clinical Psychology, 62*: 522–534.

Sigrell, B. (1992). The long-term effects of group psychotherapy: a 13-year follow-up study. *Group Analysis, 25*: 333–352.

Spinelli, E. (2001). Turning the obvious into the problematic: the issue of evidence from a human science perspective. Presentation to the Round Table Discussion Evidence Based Research Group—*Qualitative or Quantitative: Pros and Cons*. UKCP NHS Forum Conference on Psychotherapy and Evidence Based Practice for the NHS, Regents College, London 11th July.

Target, M. (1998). Approaches to evaluation. *European Journal of Psychotherapy, Counselling and Health, 1*(1): 79–92.

Waldinger, R. J., & Gunderson, J. G. (1984). Completed therapies with borderline patients. *American Journal of Psychotherapy, 38*: 190–202.

Wallerstein, R. S. (1989). The psychotherapy research of the Menninger Foundation: an overview. *Journal of Consulting and Clinical Psychology, 57*: 195–205.

Wallerstein, R. S. (2000). Psychoanalytic research: where do we disagree? In: J. Sandler, A. M. Sandler, & R. Davies (Eds.), *Clinical and Observational Psychoanalytic Research: Roots of a Controversy: Andre Green and Daniel Stern*. London: Monograph Series of the Psychoanalysis Unit of University College London and the Anna Freud Centre London.

Weber, J., Bachrach, H., & Solomon, M. (1985a). Factors associated with the outcome of psychoanalysis: Report on the Columbia Psychoanalytic Center Research Project (III). *International Journal of Psychoanalysis, 12*: 127–141.

Weber, J., Bachrach, H., & Solomon, M. (1985b). Factors associated with the outcome of psychoanalysis: Report on the Columbia Psychoanalytic Center Research Project (III). *International Journal of Psychoanalysis, 12*: 251–262.

Woody, G. E., McLellan, T., Luborsky, L., & O'Brien, C. P. (1985). Sociopathy and psychotherapy outcome. *Archives of General Psychiatry, 179*: 188–193.

PART II
GETTING STARTED AND EXPLORING METHOD

Quantitative approaches to psychotherapy research: using single case evidence in routine psychotherapy practice

Andrew Gumley

Introduction

P sychotherapy has benefited from a range of research methodologies that are based on quantitative approaches. For example, randomized controlled trial methodology has enabled the development of a robust evidence base for a number of psychotherapeutic approaches to alleviating emotional distress (Roth & Fonagy, 1996). In addition, experimental approaches to psychopathology have enabled researchers and psychotherapists to test, evaluate, revise and update clinical theory and practice. Furthermore, quantitative approaches are necessary to develop of reliable and valid measures used by researchers and psychotherapists alike. To cover the breadth and depth of this approach to research methodology is impossible in a single chapter. Therefore, this chapter aims to help readers to incorporate aspects of quantitative approaches to psychotherapy research into their day-to-day clinical practice. In particular this chapter emphasizes the value of using single case methodology as a rigorous procedure to evaluate outcomes in routine care and as a means of elucidating important processes involved in the process of psychotherapy.

Background

Single case methodology has otherwise been referred to as *single case experimental design* (SCED), *N = 1* research, or *single subject design*. Single case design has its origins in the case study approach to psychotherapy research pioneered by psychoanalytical psychotherapists such as Freud and others. While single case designs have been strongly associated with a range of psychotherapy research (Barlow & Hersen, 1984; Barlow, Hayes, & Nelson, 1984; Kazdin, 1982), the methodology developed strongly within the theoretical frameworks of operant conditioning, applied behavioural analysis, behavioural and cognitive psychotherapies. The feature that distinguishes these designs from other common research methodologies is the capacity for conducting experimental research with a single case or a series of single cases (Kazdin, 1982). Single case designs emphasize repeating specific measures over time. This can help psychotherapists evidence their accountability in day to day psychotherapy practice by providing a structured methodology for systematically defining, recording, and interpreting clinical data. As with any research methodology, single case designs have their strengths and weaknesses. Single case design lacks the generalizability that is gained by using randomized controlled trial methodology to evaluate outcomes, and lacks the methodological rigour offered by well devised and conducted randomized controlled clinical trials of psychotherapy. However, single case design does allow a more fine-grained analysis of individual change during psychotherapy. Indeed, single case design embraces client individuality, enabling the development of tailored approaches to psychotherapy while retaining the rigour required by experimental hypothesis testing. Single case design offers the opportunity for psychotherapists to determine the effectiveness of components of therapy within a single case, thereby facilitating the understanding of potential mechanisms of change during therapy. Single case design may also help psychotherapists develop novel theory or techniques or indeed provide an aid to therapy decision-making and planning (Barlow, Hayes, & Nelson, 1984; Kazdin, 1982; Petermann & Muller, 2001). Petermann and Muller (2001) further suggest that this methodology also provides a means of improving treatment by measuring problems and the integrity of treatment in relation to those problems (quality assurance).

From case formulation to single case design

Case formulation provides a conceptual framework to represent individuals' psychological difficulties and provides the basis for assessment and therapy planning. Persons (1989) conceptualizes psychological problems as occurring at two levels: the *overt difficulties* and *underlying psychological mechanisms*. *Overt difficulties* are the problems that clients present with, such as depression, interpersonal problems, procrastination, social anxiety, or body image. Overt difficulties can be broken down into their component parts, including specific emotions (e.g., embarrassment, fear, and shame), behaviours (e.g., pleasing others, avoidance, passivity), and thoughts (e.g., views of self, others, world, and future). *Underlying psychological mechanisms* are the hypothesized psychological structures, processes, or difficulties that underlie and cause overt difficulties. For example, a cognitive psychotherapist may hypothesize that underlying beliefs often expressed in terms of "if–then" (e.g., If people like me then I am a worthwhile person) statements represent the mechanisms behind psychological problems (e.g., depressed mood and feelings of worthlessness).

Psychotherapists from other backgrounds may well hypothesize other important underlying psychological mechanisms. For the purposes of single case design *overt difficulties* and *underlying psychological mechanisms* can be conceptualized as *dependent* and *independent variables*. Independent and dependent variables refer to hypothetical relationships, where deliberately producing change in one variable (the independent variable) leads to change in another variable (the dependent variable). In planning a single case design the first step is to select a measure, or measures, that can be repeated frequently. These measures might be observer rated (e.g., staff ratings of a client's behaviour as an in-patient) or the client's own ratings from their self-monitoring. Measures that can be repeated frequently are often brief and easily completed. Measures are perhaps best developed in collaboration with the client, thus enabling the therapist and client to clearly define relevant terms, their idiosyncratic meaning, and measurement. Having chosen a measure, the next step is to select an appropriate frequency of measurement; for example, daily or hourly, depending on the object of measurement. All single case designs start with a baseline measurement phase that enables the client and psychotherapist to evaluate the impact of subsequent interventions. An example of using case formulation to plan a simple single case design is given below.

Case example

Jenny, a twenty-year-old female recovering from a first episode of psychosis, was referred for cognitive behavioural psychotherapy. Following the resolution of her acute psychotic episode, Jenny had experienced persisting depressed mood characterized by low self-esteem, and feelings of guilt, shame, and humiliation. She also found it difficult to gather enough energy during the day and was unable to experience pleasurable or positive feelings. She experienced anxiety when in the company of others. She imagined that she looked and behaved oddly. The meaning of this was that other people would think that she was mentally ill and/or defective, thus making her unlovable. Further exploration of these beliefs revealed further important meanings, including the belief that mentally ill people are unacceptable, never have partners, and are unemployable. These beliefs were given further credence after she and her family had been informed that she had a diagnosis of schizophrenia. The family felt devastated by Jenny's psychosis and experienced intense feelings of loss in relation to the loss of their own aspirations for their daughter. These feelings of loss were further compounded by the frustration they experienced when they were unable to encourage their daughter to return to some of her previous hobbies, interests, and friendships. This had led to heightened feelings of tension and criticism at home. Jenny dealt with this problematic interpersonal atmosphere by further withdrawing into her own room. There, Jenny tended to ruminate critically on her own past. Prior to developing her psychosis, Jenny had been planning to go to college to study social sciences. She had a number of close friends from school with whom she regularly socialized. She and her family also reported being close and mutually supportive during her development. Prior to her acute episode, Jenny gradually became more withdrawn over the course of approximately one year. During this year Jenny's relationships with others had become more and more vexed and problematic. Events came to a head when Jenny dropped out of college. She stated that there had been a conspiracy to undermine her by a variety of organizations. Their purpose had been to prevent her from making contact with a number of special beings known to only a few people. She believed herself to be part of a special group that was responsible for ensuring the safety and well-being of people around the world.

Therefore the initial case formulation was that Jenny's depressed mood was maintained by a number of cognitive behavioural factors, including negative beliefs about self (e.g., I am defective), others (e.g., people will see I'm defective), the future (e.g., nobody will ever accept me), and problematic interpersonal coping strategies, including withdrawal and avoidance.

An initial course of therapy proceeded well; collaboration and therapeutic alliance were good, there was good initial recovery in terms of reduced depressed mood, suicidal thinking, and hopelessness. However, therapeutic progress became blocked when attempting to work together on dealing with social situations and making contact with friends. It became apparent over two sessions that Jenny was experiencing recurring intrusive, unwanted, sexual images that led to strong feelings of disgust, embarrassment, and shame. Socratic questioning revealed a number of meanings attached to these images including "I'm mixed up", "I'm mentally ill", and "The devil is implanting thoughts in my head". Of these three meanings Jenny identified her belief in being mentally ill as the most salient and distressing. For her, the meaning attached to being mentally ill was that she would always be alone and was unlovable. The content of these images confirmed these beliefs. The case formulation is illustrated in Figure 1 below.

Problematic aspects of these images were explored. Jenny identified a number of dimensions that were relevant to her individual experience, including the frequency of images, their intrusiveness (some images were more intrusive than others), the amount of time spent dwelling on imagery, and the emotional distress arising from the imagery. A single case design was employed to test the hypothesis that Jenny's conviction in her belief that she was mentally ill (*independent variable*) was linked to greater frequency, intrusiveness, dwelling and distress arising from recurring sexual imagery (*dependent variables*). These dimensions were operationalized on a scale of 0 through to 10, with 10 being worse. Over a four-week period Jenny made daily ratings along these dimensions, including rating her level of conviction in her belief that these images meant that she was mentally ill (scale 0 to 10). At the following session, after reviewing the self-monitoring, Jenny and her therapist generated alternative explanations of recurring intrusive sexual images. The work of Rachman (2003) and Salkovskis and Harrison (1984) was reviewed, identifying that intrusive imagery is a

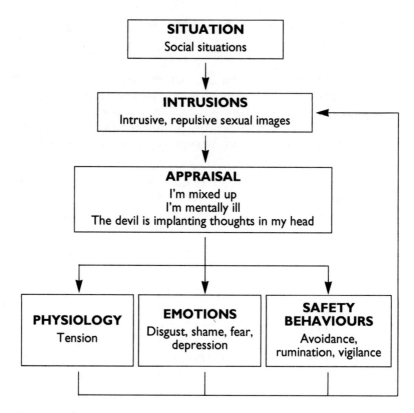

Figure 1.   Idiosyncratic case conceptualization of intrusions.

normal psychological experience that becomes problematic when the image is (mis)interpreted as meaning one is responsible for intrusions, that thoughts and behaviour are the same, or that thoughts mean oneself is in someway defective. Jenny generated an alternative explanatory and compassionate model of her experiences, which allowed her to reflect upon and accept (a) the difficult period of her life that she was recovering from, (b) the importance of not blaming herself for her psychosis, and (c) the normality of intrusive and unwanted imagery. These responses were written down on a small card, so that she was able to carry this alternative explanatory model with her. Jenny and her therapist agreed that it might be useful to test out whether reminding herself of this narrative would reduce the frequency, intrusiveness, distress, and dwelling associated the occurrence of these images. The results of this intervention are illustrated in Figures 2 to 6 below.

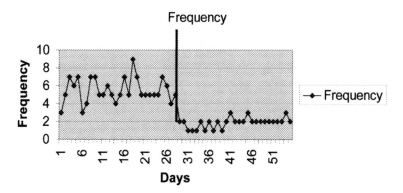

Figure 2.   Frequency of intrusive images.

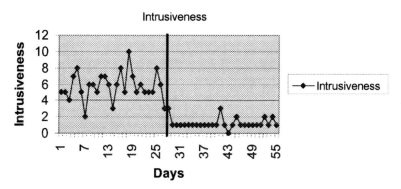

Figure 3.   Intrusiveness of images.

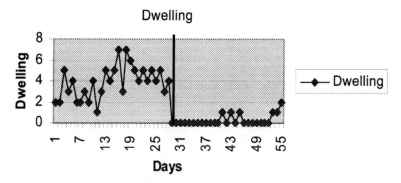

Figure 4.   Amount of time dwelling on images.

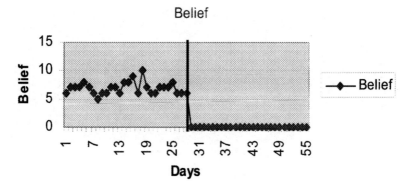

Figure 5.   Conviction in belief "I am mentally ill".

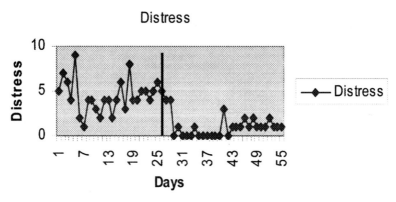

Figure 6.   Distress associated with intrusions.

As can be seen, Jenny's conviction in her belief that these images were a sign that she was mentally ill reduced to 0. As hypothesized, this change of conviction in her belief about being mentally ill was associated with reduced frequency and intrusiveness of imagery. In addition, she spent less time dwelling on the images and experienced less emotional distress arising from re-experiencing imagery. While the design of this single case doesn't allow one to interpret causality easily, i.e., it could have been that Jenny spending less time dwelling on the meaning of her imagery allowed her to defuse the intrusive images (e.g., Hayes, Strosahl, & Wilson, 1999), it did allow a difficult point in therapy to become unblocked. This enabled Jenny to go on to discuss other issues that were linked to distressing emotional experiences, including shame and humiliation.

Options for single N design methodology

The case example above used a single case design called AB, where A represents the baseline phase and B the intervention phase. One of the main problems with an AB design is that it only gives weak evidence for the causal influence of the independent variable (underlying psychological mechanism) over the dependent variable(s) (overt problems). It also suffers from other difficulties related to the validity of the experimental effect; for example, something else could have happened by chance to influence the impact of the therapeutic intervention. Therefore, more complex and elaborate single case designs have been developed to attempt to overcome the limitations of the basic AB design. For a full review of design options Kazdin (1982) is an excellent resource. However, some of the designs most relevant to psychotherapy research include, among others, multiple baseline and single case series designs.

Multiple baseline design

Multiple baseline designs are used where there are more than one independent *overt problem* or *dependent variable*. For example, Chadwick and Trower (1996) investigated the use of cognitive therapy for punishment paranoia. Over twelve therapy sessions three specific beliefs: "I am totally bad and perverted"; "People can read my mind and are planning to attack me"; and "I am been punished by God" were sequentially addressed within therapy. All beliefs were rated in terms of conviction (0 to 100) and preoccupation (0 to 100). Preoccupation did not change over the course of cognitive therapy. Conviction scores for one belief (punishment by God) were unstable throughout treatment. Therefore, the therapeutic efficacy of cognitive psychotherapy could not be established for this belief. However, the other two beliefs changed in terms of ratings of conviction at the point of the respective intervention for each belief. This enabled these changes in belief conviction to be attributed with more confidence to the effects of therapy than if using a simple AB design.

Single case series

A single case series involves replication of a single case design across multiple individuals. For example, Davidson and Tyrer (1996) evaluated the efficacy of a brief cognitive–behavioural treatment for individuals diagnosed with either antisocial or borderline personality disorders. The treatment explored the possibility of changing long-standing maladaptive or problematic behavioural and cognitive patterns in a very brief ten-week course of therapy among twelve individuals. Davidson and Tyrer found that important clinical changes in maladaptive behaviours and beliefs could be achieved with short-term cognitive therapy. Replicating the therapeutic effects of a psychotherapeutic approach across individuals is another way of increasing certainty that the effects observed are due to the interventions as opposed to other factors that are not measured.

However, these descriptions are in no way exhaustive or comprehensive, rather the aim here is to give a brief overview of potential approaches to single case design and to highlight the importance of the relationship between design and therapeutic confidence in effects of treatment.

Analysis of data

Visual inspection is frequently used in analysing the outcomes of single case design. Indeed, graphing data for visual analysis is a useful way of helping clients monitor their progress through therapy. However, visual analysis has been criticized on the grounds that visually analysing data is unreliable and prone to Type I error (that is, concluding there is a significant effect for a treatment when there is actually no effect, or an erroneous inference of a significant difference between phases). Visual analysis is difficult when (i) the baseline phase (A) is unstable; (ii) the baseline phase is too short or has too few observations; (iii) the expected therapy effects cannot be well predicted; or (iv) when statistical control is required for extraneous factors (Kazdin, 1982). Statistical analysis can also be helpful if the effects of a therapeutic intervention are less clear-cut.

For therapists interested in discovering more about statistical analysis of single case data there are a number of useful reference sources (Crosbie, 1993; Morley & Adams, 1989; Parker & Drossart, 2003). These statistical tests allow psychotherapists and researchers to calculate the probability that there is a statistically significant difference between adjacent therapy phases.

Ethical issues

Prior to conducting single case design psychotherapists need to consider carefully any potential ethical issues involved. For example, where the single case design involves a significant departure from accepted conduct of therapy, the trial of a new psychotherapeutic technique, withholding other forms of techniques or psychotherapy from the client, or introducing technique(s) in an unconventional way (e.g., randomizing interventions over time), psychotherapists must seek advice from an appropriate ethics committee as well as their supervisor.

Conclusions

This chapter has aimed to support readers to incorporate aspects of quantitative approaches to psychotherapy research into their day-to-day clinical practice. In particular, this chapter has emphasized the potential value of using single case methodology as a rigorous procedure to evaluate outcomes in routine care and as a means of elucidating important processes involved in the delivery of psychotherapy. A salient feature of single case design is that it offers the opportunity for psychotherapists to (a) determine the effectiveness of components of therapy within a single case; (b) develop and refine novel theory or technique; (c) provide an aid to therapy decision-making and planning; and (d) provide a means of improving quality assurance. An important element involved in planning single case design is the incorporation of individualized case conceptualization that marries the particular *overt problems* that a client is seeking help for with the *underlying psychological mechanisms* that are often derived from the psychotherapist's own particular theoretical and clinical orientation. Single case design requires the transformation of overt problems and underlying mechanisms into specific, measurable constructs that can enable the systematic recording of clinical data over time. The approach provides an important clinical framework to enable psychotherapists and their clients to collaborate on the development and testing of theoretically informed, clinically relevant, tailored hypotheses.

References

Barlow, D. H., Hayes, S. C., & Nelson, R. O. (1984). *The Scientist Practitioner*. New York: Pergamon Press.

Barlow, D. H., & Hersen, M. (1984). *Single Case Experimental Designs: Strategies for Studying Behavior Change* (2nd edn). New York: Pergamon Press.

Chadwick, P., & Trower, P. (1996). Cognitive therapy for punishment paranoia: a single case experiment. *Behaviour Research and Therapy*, 34(4): 351–356.

Crosbie, J. (1993). Interrupted time series analysis with brief single-subject data. *Journal of Consulting and Clinical Psychology*, 61(6): 996–974.

Davidson, K. M., & Tyrer, P. (1996). Cognitive therapy for antisocial and borderline personality disorders: single case study series. *British Journal of Clinical Psychology*, 35(3): 413–429.

Hayes, S. C., Strosahl, K. D., & Wilson, K. G. (1999). *Acceptance and Commitment Therapy: An Experiential Approach to Behaviour Change*. New York: Guilford Press.

Kazdin, A. E. (1982). Single-case Research Designs: Methods for Clinical and Applied Settings. New York: Oxford University Press.

Morley, S., & Adams, M. (1989). Some simple statistical tests for exploring single case time series data. *British Journal of Clinical Psychology*, 28: 1–18.

Parker, R. I., & Drossart, D. F. (2003). Evaluating single case research data: a comparison of seven statistical methods. *Behaviour Therapy*, 34: 189–211.

Persons, J. B. (1989). *Cognitive Therapy in Practice: A Case Formulation Approach*. New York: W. W. Norton.

Petermann, F., & Muller, J. M. (2001). *Clinical Psychology and Single Case Evidence: A Practical Approach to Treatment Planning and Evaluation*. Chichester: John Wiley & Sons.

Rachman, S. (2003). *The Treatment of Obsessions*. Oxford: Oxford University Press.

Roth, A., & Fonagy, P. (1996). *What Works for Whom? A Critical Review of Psychotherapy Research*. New York: Guilford Press.

Salkovskis, P. M., & Harrison, J. (1984). Abnormal and abnormal obsessions: a replication. *Behaviour Research and Therapy, 27*: 549–552.

CHAPTER EIGHT

The use of discourse analysis as a way of psychotherapists thinking about their practice

Maureen Taylor, Jayne Redmond, and Del Loewenthal

Introduction

This chapter reviews elements of two studies utilizing differing approaches to discourse analysis when researching young people's perceptions, preconceptions, and experiences of therapy. In study A, none of the participants had experienced therapy; whereas all participants in study B were in therapy at the time. Similarities found in these studies support findings reported by other studies in the literature. Some considerations of using this and some other approaches will be offered.

Discourse analysis

Discourse analysis comes closest to a postmodern approach to research in that it challenges and critiques traditional research methodology, where proof and certainty are sought (Taylor & Loewenthal, 2001). It offers a radical approach to research that is likely to be of interest to therapists who are interested in words and what they allude to. Evolving from linguistics, cognitive psychology, sociolinguistics, and poststructuralism, it has been widely used to enhance understanding of human experience and how this is described through language.

Freud (in Symington, 1986) claims language, as shown by free association, slips of the tongue, jokes, and dreams is a sign of unconscious desire: one thing representing/meaning another. Sarup (1988, p. 47) explains that Lacan viewed the unconscious as being structured like language, where the unconscious speaks through a chain of changing but interconnected meanings (often expressed as metaphor). This challenged structural linguistic claims that meaning was clear and fixed. Hollway (1989) applied these concepts to her research into subjectivity, believing people's accounts are always subject to time available, relationships, context, power, defences, and regimes of truth. For Heidegger (1962), meaning is found in the ways people are embedded and structure their world and everyday language. Society is linked with the place from which one speaks, thus ethnomethodological research requires immersion in that society/culture (Garfinkel, 1967).

Potter and Wetherell's (1987) ten stages in the analysis of discourse are: Stage 1: research questions; stage two: sample selection; stage three: collection of records and documents; stage four: interviews; stage five: transcription, intermission; stage six: coding; stage seven: analysis; stage eight: validation—(a) coherence; (b) participant's orientation; (c) new problems (d) fruitfulness; stage nine: the report; stage ten: application. Importantly, these stages are not sequential, they are varying and merging phases.

Potter and Wetherell (*ibid.*) are interested in the structure and functions of everyday language. They aim to identify how people construct their way of speaking and why; to learn how language orders perception and makes things happen. Their approach is through an interest in unusual phenomena that may be dismissed by traditional research. Rather than knowledge, belief, and assumption, the researcher needs to develop craft skills and tacit knowledge through openness to ideas and experience emerging through language (*ibid.*).

Postmodern research and language

Postmodernism questions the basis for all knowledge and expertise and asks us to challenge our assumptions and beliefs. Ideologies of objective knowledge, truth, the all knowing expert, and assertions that clients have a centre and can be whole, are challenged (Taylor & Loewenthal, 2001). Such views are considered to be based within powerful and biased cultures that place the other at a disadvantage and where the other becomes an understudy to another's play (Hollway, 1989; Loewenthal, 1996; Scheurich, 1997). Postmodernism requires an ethical response that puts the other first (Gans, 1989; Levinas, 1989).

Derrida (1987), in asking if the message sent out can be received, highlights the importance of the analysis of language to therapists. If we are subject to the inherently fragmentary nature of experience where nothing is definite; language is constantly constructed and deconstructed; where one thing indicates something else that changes and meanings emerge dependent on factors such as when, where, who and what; how can we conduct research in a post-modern world and what value can it have?

Study A

The aim of the research was to explore young people's perceptions of therapy/counselling and where they felt they would be able to access it. The "Health of the Nation" paper (Department of Health, 1993) was targeting mental health and suicide, focusing on prevention and primary care support. Did young people perceive that the medical route was where they could obtain support? A questionnaire, previously applied in a health care setting, was used in a College of Further Education. Then, a student facilitated a debate with a cross-section of fellow students, randomly selected, who had never had counselling. They were asked "What is counselling?" "Where would you go to get it?" This debate was videoed and the resulting transcript compared responses from the first study and repeated questionnaire. Analysing only similar responses to the questionnaire omitted differences; at this point the researcher as therapist comes into play. The video debate enabled the individuals to be heard; the jokes, slips, and everyday language were present. Looking specifically at the slips and jokes revealed that one student spoke more than others, what was she really (unconsciously) saying? Was it about counselling or is all discourse solely subjective? Having knowledge of the student, her input was then analysed as if she were a client. This analysis was presented to her and her response to it became, with consent, part of the research. Applying therapeutic training to discourse and attempting analysis acknowledges the subjectivity of the researcher in what was "coming to mind" in a free associative way. What was it about this student that "spoke" to the researcher? This factor was also part of the research. To omit this is to imply that all messages sent are received and that I can perceive the other's truth and my own. Discourse analysis recognizes this as illusory, because the researcher cuts/edits/sets the scene in terms of how the research is presented. The discourse from student F9 was researched with the approach briefly described below.

Hollway (1989) explains how the theories of repression in psychoanalytic terms and personal experience of interpreting group process lead to the development of what she termed "interpretive discourse analysis (*ibid.*, p. 32). The "face" value of what was said given limited credence . . . "this is the definition of meaning that psychological analysis should get away from" (*ibid.*, p. 49).

F9 said, "I wouldn't want to see a counsellor."

The meaning would seem clear. However the use of the word *want* may be seen to be indicative of desire. She hasn't said *might not*; or *probably not*; but, *would not want*. This may be seen as a signal that the repressed is attempting to break through and the converse "*I want*" may be the unconscious being turned back, repressed. In analytic terms, through condensation and displacement, it should return again. Lacan believed the repressed presented in a signifying chain of metaphor (condensation) and metonymy. "Lacan views metonymy as the same as displacement, the unconscious process whereby something of significance in an idea is detached and passed on to another image" (*ibid.*, p. 52).

F9 went on to say, "I wouldn't, I wouldn't tell anyone. I'd just go to my bed and cry."

The description of going to her bed to cry and she wouldn't tell anyone, seemed significant, a signifier in which repressed feelings may be hidden. So what was hidden?

Signifier . . . *I wouldn't want to see a counsellor* . . . describes (metaphor) *I'd go to my bed and cry*
links to (metonomy) . . . *I would be alone.*

What unconscious desire is being thwarted to make her speak of going to her bed to cry? If she would not speak to a counsellor then whom would she speak to? The next statement would seem to be the conscious/unconscious desire;

F9 "I'd talk to my Mum. My Mum's cool."

At first it was difficult to relate to the unconscious desire (if that was what it was) being voiced, until, looking in an ethnographical way not at what was thought she had said, but what was actually said:

"*I'd* (meaning I would) *talk to my Mum*." She had not said, "*I talked to my Mum*". Is this a "slip", or does this indicate her desire to talk? If she could, what was stopping her from talking to the person she would talk to—her mother? It was only when the session was complete and with information we had about F9 that we attempted to analyse this discourse.

Assuming talking to her mother is the unconscious desire, the signified now comes into place. F9 would rather take to her bed and cry than talk to "*anybody*". The symbolic representation of the bed as the womb may be seen as the desire for mother, but her metaphor gives a picture of being alone and crying.

Signifier . . . *I wouldn't want to see a counsellor* (metonymic axis) . . . *I'd go to my bed and cry alone*

Signified . . . I want to talk to my Mum . . . can't . . . I'd go to my bed and cry alone.

The placing of *I'd go to my bed and cry* can be seen to move between the two places. It is in the last part that the signified (unconscious desire) is heard when the facilitator asks each student to say what a counsellor is.

F9: "*It's just someone who has time to listen and doesn't have to go off and do their shopping in the middle of a deep and meaningful conversation. Just someone who has got time to listen and maybe understand.*"

The "*someone*" she would speak to she identified earlier as her mother. Has the repressed returned by speaking of one thing and "meaning" another?

F9 also provided a joke during the session: speaking of help-lines as a counselling resource, she felt they would be as useful as ringing "Domino's pizza", suggesting that there should be a line you could call and hurl as much abuse as possible. Speaking after the session, we asked about the joke (which all students seemed to understand). The explanation was that you never get what you order from Domino pizza and can never understand what they say to you or you to them as their employees speak very little English. This was a place where a metaphor was again in play for F9: I ask for a pizza . . . can't understand or be understood . . . am angry and frustrated. Could the unconscious desire to be heard/understood/ listened to by her mother be re-presenting itself? F9 was shown the analysis of what she had said and how we had attempted to "hear" what she was saying on a conscious level about counselling and what we felt her subjective position was in her own life at that time. She agreed with the analysis and was surprised at what was "revealed". To look again at what might be influencing her speech at that time was based on the theories as outlined and specifically on knowledge of F9. By being present in the research we were acknowledging subjective views.

Difficulties in transcription

A student I never met altered words and left some out of the typed transcript. Swearing was edited and some unfavourable responses to counsellors were omitted. It transpired that I had counselled her friend, and the typist felt positive towards me and towards counselling. Also, the facilitator was asked what he thought of counselling; his response was, "I'd rather speak to my cat. . . . don't worry, Jayne, I'll edit that out." I was pleased he acknowledged that I had never asked his view, but the idea of editing out comments, even by my facilitator, made me question his perception that all research is "edited". Subjectivity is not exclusive to the researcher.

Study B

Potter and Wetherell's (1987) ten stages guided the conduct of the study (Taylor, 1996). Clients in therapy were invited to volunteer to be interviewed about their experiences of therapy. Ten volunteered and eight interviewed. Young people are rarely asked for their opinions, so enabling them to say what they wanted to say and explore what they meant seemed appropriate. A semi-structured interview was designed, piloted, refined, then used as a guide (Feaviour, 1994; Lawton, 1984).

The aim was to ensure, as much as one is able before an event, that each volunteer would be informed about, comfortable with, and involved in the study only if they wished to be so (Taylor, 1996). No volunteer withdrew from the study having arrived for the interview. Volunteers were invited to say something about themselves and then to speak of their experiences of therapy. Conversational use of comments such as: "Could you say more about that?"; "Has that happened before?"; "And what effect did that have?"; "How did you feel about ...?"; "What did you think about ...?"; "Could you suggest ...?"; "I'm not sure I fully understand", were used. No enquiry was made about clinical issues or therapists by the researcher (Taylor & Loewenthal, 2001).

Transcribing was a painstaking process, taking an average 6.5 hours for each one-hour interview. Pauses and hesitations are shown as a "." for every ½ second (approximate). A raised voice or increased emphasis on a word or phrase is shown in CAPital letters. Where a section of transcript was repetitive the substance is retained and omissions shown as [ ]. Participants were offered and received transcripts and follow-up interviews as requested (*ibid.*).

Themes emerging included preconceptions; beginning; the need to speak and be heard; counselling has helped; and unhelpful aspects (Taylor, 1996). A tentative analysis of a brief fragment of transcript referring to preconceptions of counselling is offered as an alternative approach to discourse analysis.
"Amanda" said

> Everybody says oh, kind of therapy is ... if you're mad or something. [ ] It isn't connected with me because I haven't told them but I can disagree with them because I know that is wrong. [ ] but because I know that's the view of a lot of people, it makes me wary about telling people.

Amanda had been looking down and she raised her head slightly. She looked at the researcher carefully and guardedly, as if waiting to see the reaction, how she might be received, before saying "*it makes me wary.*" The way she spoke seemed to be asking for this to be acceptable, and this goes beyond Potter and Wetherell, who place total reliance upon the text.

One reading of how Amanda constructs or negotiates her position from this fragment of discourse might be:

"*everybody says*" = justifies her version;

"*It isn't connected with me*" = excuses her version;

"*I know that is wrong*" = defends against negative response;
"*it makes me wary*" = appeals for acceptance.

Amanda appears to shift her position in relation to the event until something emerges to justify the position she takes up. She seems to have negotiated a position of not being overwhelmed, of being accepted and acceptable.

She appears to make sense of the situation in which she finds herself by:

- drawing upon different versions of what she knows;
- testing out imaginary views of herself;
- creating a more comfortable position;
- conceivably, gaining a sense of relief.

Maybe, having constructed a version that she finds both personally, and socially acceptable, she can stop. Perhaps it is a position of compromise between conflicting demands that is safer and more comfortable, so she can rest for a while having gained some relief. If the analysis is correct, this manoeuvring can be seen to be highly skilful and elusive. She may be saying that the value of therapy is being able to be open about things that have been hidden away and kept secret. Maybe these things can then be seen for what they really are rather than her preconceptions of them. Amanda does not tell us that the therapist does something to her. She does tell us that she is doing this for herself. The value and power of therapy seems to be in the ability of the therapist to be there, facilitating this without the need to do something.

Amanda indicates this by attending her sessions, speaking her truth; no one told her what to say. By speaking to the therapist she has made a public declaration using her own words.

Taking up the invitation to enter therapy meant that even before she started seeing her therapist she changed, for she no longer says, *I can't do that; it's not for me; I don't need counselling because I feel silly and denying I had a problem.* By choosing to be herself, acknowledging her difficulties and her depression, she moved from inactivity to activity. Taking responsibility and control means she can ask for help. She is not leading such an invalid existence as previously. She came with considerable insight and it is unclear if this increased since commencing therapy. Therapy provided a place where she can speak, where she is listened to respectfully, where nothing is "done" to her. Therapy focused on her language and, clearly, she is less depressed not because of insight, but because she has spoken her own words to another.

Brief comparison

Both studies explore perceptions, preconceptions, and experiences of therapy with young people. In Study A, F9 reflected that people who went for counselling would be viewed in the following ways.

"It means admitting you have a problem."
"Oh they must really be in the head or they need help."
"People might think you have mental problems."
"There is too much stigma attached."

In Study B, Amanada expressed similar perceptions. It appears significant that both young women, in separate studies, were aware of social implications of entering therapy. Despite Amanda's preconceptions she did attend her sessions. F9 had an understanding of a counsellor's role as someone who has time to listen, which was affirmed by Amanda's experience of counselling. Both participants challenge the social perceptions of therapy in differing ways. Discourse analysis presents an opportunity for the pariticpants to speak themselves.

Conclusion

Selecting fragments of discourse to analyse recognizes that subjective choices and value judgements are involved. This is not easy;

something is always lost as well as gained. Given different days or places, the views of the participants might have differed, just as the researchers may have chosen, read, and analysed differently.

These studies support findings in other studies in the literature. However, readers will give meaning to these accounts based on their own preconceptions and expectations, their own history and culture. We can never come to the end of the meaning of a text, as there will always be a new perspective on it (Taylor & Loewenthal, 2001). Although both researchers attempted to conduct their studies with rigour, there are clear illustrations of the need to challenge the traditional notion that objectivity provides proof in research.

Readings here are tentative. Differing understandings emerged than were apparent from the text alone. This approach helped us see how dynamic, skilful, and elusive language can be. Whether, as therapists, we attempt understanding through metaphor, signs, signifiers, structures, functions, or something other, discourse analysis may advance the understanding of events and processes associated with clinical research, supervision, and the development of theory.

References

Department of Health (1993). *The Health of the Nation: A Strategy for Health in England*. London: HMSO.

Derrida, J. (1987). *The Post Card: From Socrates to Freud and Beyond*. A. Bass (Trans.). Chicago: University of Chicago Press.

Feaviour, K. (1994). Who's really listening? Youth Access: Loughborough, December.

Gans, S. (1989). *The Play of Difference: Lacan versus Derrida on Poe*. In: R. Cooper (Ed.), *Thresholds Between Philosophy and Psychoanalysis*, London: Free Association Books

Garfinkel, H. (1967). *Studies in Ethnomethodology*. Englewood Cliffs, NJ: Prentice Hall.

Heidegger, M. (1962). *Being and Time*. Oxford: Blackwell.

Hollway, W. (1989). *Subjectivity and Method in Psychology*. London: Sage.

Lawton, A. (1984). *Youth Counselling Matters*. NAYPCAS (National Youth Agency) & Gulbenkian Foundation.

Levinas, E. (1989). *The Levinas Reader*. S. Hand (Ed.). Oxford: Blackwell.

Loewenthal, D. (1996). The postmodern counsellor: some implications for practice theory, research and professionalism. *Counselling Psychology Quarterly*, 9(4): 373–381.

Potter, J., & Wetherell, M. (1987). *Discourse and Social Psychology: Beyond Attitudes and Behaviour*. London: Sage.

Redmond, J. (1994). An ethnomethodological exploration of perception of counselling in primary health care. MSc Dissertation, University of Surrey.

Sarup, M. (1988). *An Introductory Guide to Post-Structuralism and Postmodernism*. Hemel Hempstead: Harvester Wheatsheaf.

Scheurich, J. J. (1997). *Research Method in the Postmodern*. London: The Falmer Press.

Symington, N. (1986). *The Analytic Experience. Lectures from the Tavistock*. London: Free Association.

Taylor, M. (1996). An evaluation of youth counselling: a pilot study. MSc Dissertation, University of Surrey.

Taylor, M., & Loewenthal, D. (2001). Researching a client's experience of preconceptions of therapy: a discourse analysis. *Psychodynamic Counselling*, 7(1): 63–82.

CHAPTER NINE

An exploration of case study method through an examination of psychotherapy with a person with dementia

Dennis Greenwood and Del Loewenthal

Introduction

This paper starts by exploring some of the literature on case study (Bromley, 1986; Hamel, 1993; Hammersley & Gomm, 2000; Kazdin, 1982; Merriam, 1998; Meyer, 2001; Platt, 1988; Stake, 1995; Yin, 1984) in order to provide a basis for conceptualizing it as a method for psychotherapeutic research. A great deal of the literature focuses on describing the basic principles of a case study approach, with the specifics associated with defining a research method being assimilated in the presentation of the research findings. Yin (1984) outlines a broad method for designing case study research, which can be applied to qualitative and quantitative studies. A small qualitative case study of psychotherapy is presented that was structured by interpreting Yin's (1984) approach. The findings of this study are presented and effectiveness of the approach is discussed.

What is case study?

The term case study originates from that of a case history (Hamel,

1993, p. 1) and so has a tradition in the clinical setting of medicine and psychology. Kazdin (1982, pp. 3–6) states that research using a few subjects has a tradition in experimental psychology, e.g., Wundt, Pavlov, Thorndike and Ebbinghhaus, particularly at the beginning of the 1900s through to the 1920s and 1930s.

Merriam (1998, p. 27) identifies a typical factor in case study research:

> The single most defining characteristic of case study research lies in delimiting the object of study, the case . . . a thing, a single entity, a unit around which there are boundaries. I can "fence in" what I am going to study. The case then, could be a person such as a student, a teacher, a principal; a program; a group such as a class, a school, a community; a specific policy.

Kazdin (1982) states that within the experimental research tradition the identification of a single or few cases was seen as an effective way of being able to identify the independent variables which are those factors that could influence potential results or findings of the study. This is something that can create potential difficulties in some areas of study, such as psychotherapy, as it is difficult to conceive of all likely influences on the findings.

Platt (1988, p. 2) describes a "case study" as:

> One where more than one case may be used, but if more than one is used the individuality of each case is retained and/or the number of cases falling into a given category is not treated as if significant . . . The unit case may be a person, a small group, a community, an event or an episode.

Stake (1995, p. 2) gives the following qualification:

> Custom has it that not everything is a case. A child may be a case. A teacher may be a case. But her teaching lacks the specificity, the boundedness, to be called a case . . . the case is a specific, a complex, functioning thing.

Stake (1995) suggests that the real business of case study is not the formulation of generalizations, as other methods could be seen as more effective in achieving this; but rather the case study endeavours to modify existing theory. He goes on to state:

We take a particular case and come to know it well, not primarily as how it is. There is an emphasis on uniqueness, and that implies knowledge of others that the case is different from, but the first emphasis is on understanding the case itself. [Stake 1995, p. 4]

Hammersley & Gomm (2000) quote Bromley (1986), who refers to case study as a clinical science "in which the aim is not just to develop knowledge but also to search for a remedy to some problem present in the case" (Hammersley & Gomm, 2000, p. 1). They also suggest that:

The existence of close links between case study and various forms of occupational practice has sometimes been regarded as weakness, as indicating the less-than-scientific or even unscientific character of this kind of research. However, such criticism has become less common, and less widely accepted, in recent years. One reason for this has been growing public suspicion of science, and increasing doubts about the possibility or desirability of a science of social life. [*ibid.*, p. 2]

These authors highlight the difference that distinguishes experimental research from case study, the fact that the direct variables are controlled with the experiment and also "the researcher *creates* the case(s) studied, whereas case study researchers construct cases out of naturally occurring social situations" (Hammersley & Gomm, 2000, p. 3).

Case study does not specify one form of data collection in preference to another, the research can be quantitative or qualitative and possibly a combination of both, the definitive feature is the focus of the specific study. This is evident from the experimental and anthropological approaches to focusing on a case. The different approaches raise important issues concerning the place for psychotherapy within a conception of case study research. There is no uniformity in the means of processing or analysing the data, and this often depends simply on the area being studied and/or the researcher's views on the concept of "reality".

Meyer (2001) states that there are virtually no specific requirements guiding case research. However, Yin (1984) describes an approach to case study that attempts to be sensitive to the different types of data that can be produced as a consequence of human observation, so the data can be descriptive or quantitative. Yin's (1984) approach was used to design the method used for the study presented in this paper.

A case study method

Yin (1984, p. 17) begins with the research question and the need to categorize it in terms of: "who", "where", "what", "how", and "why".

The "who" and "where" type questions are associated by Yin (1984 p. 18) with "how many" and "how much", for which he recommends survey and archival search strategies. These types of categories did not reflect the researcher's interpretation of a research question.

Yin (1984, p. 19) goes on to state:

In general, "what" questions may either be exploratory (in which case any strategy could be used) or about prevalence (in which surveys or analysis of archival records would be favoured). "How" and "why" questions favour the use of case studies, experiments, or histories.

The research question in this study is concerned with examining *the possibility of psychotherapy with a person diagnosed with dementia*. The "what" in this question would appear to be the psychotherapy. The difficulty in providing an accurate description of "what" psychotherapy might be suggests that this "what" remains an active part of any research into psychotherapy. This leaves "how" and "why", which would appear closely linked to an assessment of "possibility". The "how" and "why" of psychotherapy with a person suffering from dementia could be seen as integral parts of deciding on "possibility".

Associating the research question with aspects of "what", "how", and "why" identifies case study as an appropriate research method according to Yin (1984)

The next category to consider in relation to case study, according to Yin, is the control that the researcher has over the events being studied.

> The case study is preferred in examining contemporary events, but when the relevant behaviours cannot be manipulated. Thus, the case study relies on many of the same techniques as a history, but it adds sources of evidence not usually included in the historian's repertoire: direct observation and systematic interviewing. [Yin, 1984, p. 19]

Psychotherapy cannot be described in terms of systematic interviewing. However, it is clear that the therapy develops on from a "history" that the therapist and the client bring into the relationship. The account maintained by the therapist reports on the history of the relationship from his perspective. So, direct observation and recording a history are relevant to the process being carried out by the trainee therapist in this study thus making it complicit with Yin's description above.

After identifying the possible boundaries for case study method, Yin (1984, p. 14) describes a strategy for "designing and analysing case studies". Yin maintains that:

> For case studies, five components of a research design are specifically important:
>
> (1) A study's question;
> (2) Its proposition, if any;
> (3) Its unit of analysis;
> (4) The logic linking the data to the proposition; and
> (5) The criteria for interpreting the findings. [Yin, 1984, p. 29]

The researcher conceived it possible to design this study using the framework outlined by Yin:

(1) The question for this research design has already been identified.
(2) The "proposition" relates to areas that might be appropriate to study. This could be interpreted as the testing of hypotheses (Yin, 1984). The underlying hypothesis could be—whether it is or isn't possible to enter into therapy with someone with dementia.
(3) The psychotherapy.
(4) The data that is generated has a direct link to possible propositions described since the trainee therapist and the researcher is the same person.

(5)   The criteria for interpreting the findings are dependent on the therapist's account of the psychotherapy and this provokes issues of bias and unreliability of data that are discussed later.

The application of an established case study design, as described by Yin (1984), provides the study with a structure that could form the basis for the presentation of the subsequent findings. However, even though the approach described by Yin does not dictate the criteria for analysing the data, there is clear indication that it is aimed at providing a basis for generalizing to the external world. Yin states the following:

> . . . case study contributes uniquely to our knowledge of individual, organizational, social, and political phenomena . . . the distinct need for case studies arises out of the desire to understand complex social phenomena. [*ibid.*, p. 14]

The case study example

The study described in this paper examined a case of short-term (ten sessions) psychotherapy with an older person diagnosed with dementia with the purpose of considering *the possibility of psychotherapy with an older person diagnosed with dementia.*

The researcher identified "psychotherapy" as the unit of analysis by examining the theoretical orientation of the therapist's approach to providing therapy to a person diagnosed with dementia. The approach to the psychotherapy needed to encompass the possibility of working with someone who had a diagnosis of dementia and would subsequently be affected by some of the debilitating symptoms associated with this condition. The study concluded that approaches that were dependent on the client/patient's ability to use language were not potentially ideally suited to working with a person diagnosed with dementia. The unit of analysis was acknowledged to be dependent on the therapist's approach or orientation to therapy and this was acknowledged to be influenced by the continental philosophy of Emmanual Levinas and that this approach was subject to issues associated with working with a person with dementia.

The subject of the case study was an elderly man who was resident in a nursing home that specialised in the care of people with dementia. The researcher asked Des (a pseudonym) whether he would like to meet on a weekly basis, over a ten-week period, for psychotherapy. He appeared to consent to this suggestion but the symptoms of dementia made it difficult to assess whether this was an informed decision. Consequently, the researcher asked for permission from Des' family to proceed with the ten-week programme of psychotherapy. Although this appeared the most appropriate way to ensure that Des' interests were being considered, it did highlight how differently he was being treated as a consequence of his diagnosis.

Immediately after each of the ten meetings the therapist, who was also the researcher, wrote notes that represented the data for the case study. Examples of extracts from the notes are included here.

The first example is taken from the first session; the meeting took place in Des' bedroom and when the session began he was looking at the cover of a magazine that was on a table in front of him.

Therapist. Look, you open up the cover and inside is an attractive girl lying on the bed.

Des. Oh yes (smile).

He closed the magazine.

Therapist. Is it difficult opening up the cover and looking on the inside?

Des rubbed the cover and said "Gently".

A thought came to mind . . . the cover might mean his outward appearance, the way he seems on the surface, and the "gently" was about taking time to find the attractive person that is beneath this outward appearance.

The above example does show how hard the therapist is working to provide a meaning to what is going on between them. There was very little conversation and so the therapist was left trying to "understand" what was happening during the session.

In the following few sessions the therapist continued to work hard in discovering meaning in the fragments of conversation that were taking place and made the sessions particularly demanding for him. However, he noted that Des did appear to be having the same experience. He appeared relaxed and smiled regularly.

Extract from session seven

He was looking at a magazine again and reading the headline out aloud.

Des: "It's a Hard Life!"

He turned to me and laughed. He repeated this a few times.

Des: "This chap he has a tray in front of him."

He was pointing at a picture, which could have been interpreted that way.

Therapist: "Is this how you see the picture?"

Des: "Oh yes."

Short silence.

Des: "My wife was here yesterday."

Therapist: "Your wife came to see you yesterday?"

Des: "Yes."

There was a long silence, where breaking it with a question or observation would have felt inappropriate or perhaps motivated by the need to confirm and validate the usefulness of the therapy rather than reacting to Des.

Extract from session eight

Des continued to smile; he was looking into the mirror and appeared to be focusing on something in particular and then smiling. There was a silence and then the therapist spoke.

Therapist: "Are you looking at something in particular, Des?"

Des looked at me with a broad smile.

Des: "Oh yes, I am pleased to see you, of course I am."

This was a very important moment, as it seemed to be associated with feelings that were around in the session. It felt difficult to consider exploring what Des had said at this time since it was possible that he would confirm any type of interpretation that was given. What seemed to emerge was the need to respond to Des without striving for meanings, which would have felt like closing down something rather than attempting to be helpful.

During this session a member of staff walked in and apologized to me and not to Des, even though it was his room.

A theme that emerged from this case study, which is illustrated in the above extracts, was how the therapist was engaged at times in an attempt to prove the value of the therapy. This may well have been associated with the research question that was so much part of the meetings. However, it may well represent the difficulty of just being with a person in what Levinas describes as the "non-intentional" or the moments before an understanding is posited on an experience that would represent the "intentional". The period before the imposition of a meaning, according to Levinas, represents a fleeting moment of human contact that disappears when meanings replace the immediacy of the possibilities associated with being with another person. The significant finding from this study were that Des appeared better able to value and stay with the non-intentional than the therapist, he appeared to be free from the need to posit meanings and understandings and more in touch with a willingness to enjoy in the immediacy of a relationship.

Discussion

The case study approach was designed using Yin's (1984) approach, as highlighted previously. The study generated a set of findings, of which a summary has been outlined. The intention behind the approach advocated by Yin (1984, p. 14) was to "understand complex social phenomena", so the success of a study is determined by the level of understanding generated by the findings. Yin (1984) argues that this level of understanding is likely to be higher if the study is designed to produce quantitative data rather than descriptive accounts. Descriptive data is considered a less persuasive in conveying understanding than quantitative data emerging from an experimentally designed case study. Kazdin (1982) suggests that

dependence on the subjective account of the therapist makes estab-
lishing validity and reliability of the findings of a research report,
such as is described in the study, extremely problematic. The degree
of understanding associated with the findings of this study are
compromised, according to Kazdin's (1982) argument, by the
dependence on the subjective data produced by a therapist's
account of what went on in this case study. Kazdin suggests that the
problems are insurmountable, that this case approach would never
be able to achieve the validity associated with a truly scientific
approach. Yin (1984) and Kazdin (1982) state that studies that are
dependent on descriptive data have a preliminary research status,
so that findings could not claim to illustrate understanding until
verified by a scientifically designed research study.

The positioning of the descriptive approach to case study in a
preliminary and inferior position to more quantitative and scientifically designed approaches assumes that research is focused on
producing understandings that can be applied to the world around
us (Kazdin, 1982; Yin, 1984). The claim that it is possible to identify
understandings that can be applied to the external world is not
unanimously accepted. Crotty (1998) maintains that a picture of
scientists actively constructing scientific knowledge is replacing the
image of science being built on a process of controlled observation
of the world. Crotty's (1998) critique of the scientific or positivists'
position identifies the impossibility of ever "knowing" what is
independent of consciousness when the only way to know this is
through consciousness.

If the outcome of a scientific approach is measured by the
success in producing understandings and this process is challenged
as nothing more than a subjective exercise in observation, what is
there left to achieve in research? Donmoyer (2000, p. 60) suggests
that perhaps what is left is the diversity of experience, "when diversity is dramatic, the knower is confronted by all sorts of novelty,
which stimulates accommodation". Research should be seen more
in terms of divergent experience that enriches a potential observation.

Donmoyer (2000, p. 63) concurs with Stake's (2000) comments
"that case study can provide vicarious experiences", that is, experiences that can act as substitutive illustrations that enhance understanding, and suggests three advantages that case study can offer.

First, they provide the opportunity to benefit from a description of an experience that is unlikely to be open to most observers. Second, they can provide a different viewpoint or perspective of seeing a set of experiences; this might be a feminist, Marxist perspective or other minority discourses. But, most importantly for Donmoyer, the case study should be depicted emphasizing its novelty and uniqueness rather than from some sense of a need to explain the observation in the light of what is "known". Consequently, judged from this perspective, the findings of the study outlined in this paper do not take up an inferior position to a more scientifically orientated approach, they provide a unique perspective on what has been observed that can add and enhance understanding rather than making a claim for definition and truth.

References

Crotty, M. (1998). *The Foundations of Social Research*. London: Sage.

Donmoyer, R. (2000). *Generalization and the Single-Case Study*. In: R. Gomm, M. Hammersley, & R. Foster (Eds.), *Case Study Method*. London: Sage.

Bromley, D. B. (1986). *The Case Study Method in Psychology and Related Disciplines*. Chichester: Wiley.

Hamel, J. (1993). *Case Study Methods*. London: Sage.

Hammersley, M., & Gomm, R. (2000). *Introduction*. Cited in R. Gomm, M. Hammersley, & R. Foster (Eds.), *Case Study Method*. London: Sage.

Kazdin, A. (1982). *Single-Case Research Designs—Methods for Clinical and Applied Settings*. Oxford: Oxford University Press.

Merriam, S. (1998). *Qualitative Research and Case Study Applications in Education*. San Francisco: Jossey-Bass.

Meyer, C. B. (2001). A case in case study methodology. *Field Methods*, 13(4): 329–352.

Platt, P. (1988). What can case studies do? *Studies in Qualitative Methodology*, 1: (1–23).

Stake, R. (1995). *The Art of Case Study Research*. London: Sage.

Stake, R., (2000). *The Case Study Method in Social Inquiry*. Cited in R. Gomm, M. Hammersley, & R. Foster (Eds.), *Case Study Method*. London: Sage.

Yin, R. (1984). *Case Study Research—Design and Method*. London: Sage.

CHAPTER TEN

Exploring the unknown in psychotherapy through phenomenological research

Julia Cayne and Del Loewenthal

Introduction

This chapter examines how a particular phenomenological method was developed and utilized in: "describing individuals' lived experience of feeling ready to call themselves psychotherapists." The study began with a rather vague idea about how psychotherapists find their own place as a psychotherapist and was concerned more with how people speak of their own sense of feeling ready compared with validation through professional bodies. The researcher's own experience suggested that there is a gradual awareness, an evolutionary process, rather than a sudden arrival at a predestined place. It seemed likely that many factors would contribute to this awareness, not least the therapist's personal development. For example, Strupp (1989) emphasizes the importance of personal process alongside "skilful execution of professional craft" and Gilbert, Hughes, & Dryden (1989) point to the dangers of relying on technique, which they argue occurs as a result of insecurities in the therapist, rather than "being in a psychotherapy relationship".

Heaton (1990) also questions the way technique and certification can be used to validate practice rather than "judgement of a way of life", which is based upon a philosophical approach. While he acknowledges the place of theory, he also argues that such an approach is not about imposing rules but engaging with the other and states:

> It is a practice of thoughtfulness which reveals points of tension and conflicts and shows the consequences of commitment. It is more like a game, an art, a drama, a conversation than the application of a technique based on a theory. [Heaton, 1990, p. 6]

The idea of the internal supervisor where the psychotherapist is able to function with more immediate insight (or, indeed, able to wait patiently too) as opposed to the hindsight or foresight that are useful in supervision (Casement, 1985) would seem to require an ability to make such judgements about one's own practice. Casement also suggests that the movement towards such an internal supervisor and away from dependence on the external supervisor requires a shift in autonomy (*ibid*.). Thus, it seemed that being able to make judgements about one's own readiness to call oneself a psychotherapist would be useful and, indeed, it seemed likely that individuals already do so.

This paper highlights the phenomenological approach utilized in "describing individuals' lived experience of feeling ready to call themselves psychotherapists" and presents some aspects of the findings in order to illustrate the actual data analysis process. The final discussion offers a critique illustrating how the methodology was helpful as well as suggesting that the particular phenomenological method could not do what the researcher set out to do. This was, in part, because the question being asked: "What helps you feel able or not able to call yourself a psychotherapist?", stemmed from a naïve idea that conversation would be initiated in such a way that it would lead to a series of responses that could be seen to have a direct bearing on the research question or phenomenon under study. What went unrealized was the inherent difficulty of the question, which opens up uncertainty because it is not seeking a technical, quantifiable reply and because the responses were inferential rather than coming only from a place of knowing.

The phenomenological research method

Phenomenology is concerned with "the appearance of things, as contrasted with the things themselves" (Spinelli, 1989, p. 2). This means that we understand the world from the point of view of our individual perception so that rather than being able to "know" an objective reality we can only know such things as they appear to us. The phenomenological approach of Husserl thus requires us to notice both phenomena that are given to us and their modes of emerging (Husserl, 1929). Essentially, phenomenology is concerned with thought and in attending to thoughts that may at first seem strange or out of place. We need to attend to such thoughts, but also to the ways in which they come to us. So, while the main thesis in phenomenology is concerned with conscious thought, unconscious effects are not discounted.

Thus, trusting our experience of the world is crucial, although we need to be able to question it too because of the effects created by unconscious processes, which in research are recognized by Hollway and Jefferson (2000). In order to attempt this different way of thinking, we need to engage in several disciplines that then become the cornerstone of phenomenological research. These are: first, bracketing, which is the setting aside of judgements, presuppositions, and theories including personal theories, which incidentally can be the most difficult to notice, in order to remain open to our experience as it is given; second, description, which is related to bracketing in that the phenomenon is described rather than, for example, analysed from the position of any particular theoretical leanings; and third, horizontalization, which requires each piece of information to be treated with equal regard rather than ascribing too quickly significance of one thing over another (see Husserl, 1960).

Thus, the concern in phenomenological research is an attempt to reconsider a phenomenon such as "feeling ready to call oneself a psychotherapist" from the point of view of not believing you already know what this entails. Of course, in order to take this viewpoint it is also necessary to explore what assumptions one already holds about the phenomenon. Thus, bracketing does not mean ignoring one's assumptions but, as with brackets in mathematics, what is within the brackets needs attending to first.

Crotty makes an additional point about bracketing, suggesting that it is not just the researcher who must set aside their presuppositions but also the interviewees, and it is the researcher's role to engage with them in such a way that phenomena are discerned as given by the participants and not as constructed by the researcher (Crotty, 1996). The researcher's approach is then to facilitate description rather than "analytical reflection" or "scientific explanation", in order to restrict judgements in terms of both personal knowledge and theoretical knowledge (see, for example, Merleau Ponty, 1962). The researcher then becomes interested not just in what sense or meaning people make of certain phenomena but also in which phenomena people attach meaning to.

Qualitative research generally involves a number of processes before actually undertaking the data collection and analysis, although the order of the processes may change and the way they are managed may vary depending on the methodology underpinning the research. The major processes include: selecting a research topic; conducting a review of the literature, including identifying a theoretical underpinning or methodology for guiding the research; refining the research question; addressing ethical issues; selecting participants; methods of data collection and analysis; and presentation of findings (see, for example, McLeod, 1993; Moustakas, 1994; Silverman, 2000). The main emphasis in this chapter is on the data collection and analysis using Giorgi's empirical phenomenological research method (Giorgi, 1975, 1985) combined with some ideas from Becker (1992).

The stages of the research method are outlined by Giorgi (1985) as follows: first, reading of the transcripts; second, discriminating naturally occurring units of meaning within each transcript; third, defining the major element of meaning within each meaning unit; and fourth, the researcher questions how the meaning units and their elements relate to the research question for each participant. Becker (1992) suggests turning these units and elements into descriptive portraits of each participant before moving away from "individual life worlds" in order to present the structure of the phenomenon under study. Thus, stage four involved the constructing of individual descriptive portraits and stage five a construction of a general descriptive statement about the phenomenon.

In fact, Giorgi's empirical research method can be seen to focus mainly on how to analyse data collected through interviews (Giorgi, 1985). The method seemed to have a logical flow and it claimed a relationship with Merleau Ponty's phenomenological philosophy (Giorgi, 1985). A number of key factors, according to Kvale (1996) link Giorgi's method with phenomenological philosophy. These are: "fidelity to the phenomena, the primacy of the life world, a descriptive approach, expressing the situation from the viewpoint of the subject, the situation as the unit of the research and the search for meaning" (Kvale, 1996, p. 196). These principles seemed to convey the essential elements of phenomenology already outlined above.

Kvale (1983) proposes that interviews used in qualitative studies have the purpose of gathering "descriptions of the life-world of the interviewee with respect to interpretation of the meaning of the described phenomena" (p. 174). The phenomenological emphasis in this study was on each individual's description, meaning, and personal experience of "feeling ready to call oneself a psychotherapist", which seemed apposite with Kvale's ideas about how understanding emerges in qualitative interviews (see Table 1).

In qualitative research the participants are purposely selected on the basis of the needs of the study, the findings from which are not intended to be generalizable (Morse, 1991). Morse further argues that random sampling violates the main principle of qualitative

Table 1.   Modes of understanding of qualitative research interviews.

– Centred on the interviewer's life-world

     – Focuses on certain themes

– Seeks to understand the meanings of

     – Open to ambiguities and phenomena in the life-world

     – Changes

– Qualitative

     – Involves interperson ineraction

– Descriptive

     – May in itself be a positive experience

– Specific

– Presuppositionless

(see Kvale, 1983, pp. 174–179)

research, which acknowledges that participants do not have the same knowledge or experience and ignores the fact that some respondents are more willing to be interviewed than others. In this study, it was decided to interview between six and eight people who had undertaken an MSc in counselling and psychotherapy, although only two men and two women agreed to be interviewed within the time scale available. They had completed training between one and three years previously and all had a background in health care. It was felt that these participants would provide a range of experiences within a very specific sub-group. This addresses the issue of balancing uniqueness of experience with shared patterns as indicated by Patton (1990).

Once people had agreed to take part in the study, a letter was sent out clarifying the purpose of the research, seeking written consent, and pointing out that the participant could withdraw at any time. Interviews were then arranged at mutually convenient times and venues. As part of the interview process the researcher again reminded participants that they could withdraw at any time. Real names and places were changed during transcription of the interviews in order to aid confidentiality.

The researcher had only one prepared question, which was "What helps you feel able or not able to call yourself a psychotherapist?" As the interviewees considered this question and spoke about the phenomena, other questions were brought to mind, whereupon reflections were used to seek elaboration, further description, and clarification. Generally the idea of letting people's experiences unfold through listening without interruption (Kvale, 1996) seemed the most helpful suggestion. Sometimes, repeating the initial question would set off a new train of thought until either the interviewee felt they had nothing else to say or until the one hour allocated to the interview ran out.

The research methods/findings

Stages 1 & 2—transcription of interview tapes and discrimination of naturally occurring meaning units

Following the interviews the tape recordings were transcribed and read, and the process of data analysis began, using the method outlined earlier. The second stage of "discriminating the naturally occurring units of meaning" within each transcript led to questions about what comprises a unit of meaning and how you discriminate between one meaning and another, especially when a single sentence can convey several meanings at once. Continually going back to the original tape recordings also helped to get a feel for the context of what was being said, although it was difficult, using this particular phenomenological method, to convey the slip and slide between the meaning of the interviewee and that of the interviewer. There did, however, seem to be slippages from one line of thought to another that were identified as transitions in meaning and that enabled the researcher to identify chunks of dialogue that seemed to be addressing a particular issue or group of issues. Therefore, this stage involved discovery and description rather than theoretical verification (Giorgi, 1985) and enough material had to be presented (see Table 2) to provide the context for then identifying the major elements of meaning in phase three.

Stage 3—defining the major elements of meaning

The major element of meaning within each natural meaning unit was defined. This step involved the researcher trying to grasp the meaning of the text (in the transcribed interviews) with assumptions bracketed. Giorgi (1985) advised transforming the meaning into psychological language rather than the words of the participants. This transformation was, however, seen as problematic, because it meant moving towards theory and away from description, not sustaining the phenomenological reduction through bracketing, and leaving individual life-worlds too quickly. In fact, Becker's (1992) approach stays with the original words of the participants at this stage and into the writing up of individual descriptive portraits. It did seem useful, however to present the naturally occurring meaning units and the major elements of meaning alongside each other as Giorgi (1989) suggests. A section of the analysis of the data for stages two and three, from one interview (a participant named Bill), is presented in Table 2. Numbering the meaning units provided a way of locating particular data.

Table 2.   Meaning units and main element of meaning.

Bill	
Constituents of the natural unit	The main element of meaning
(14) For my supervisor there was the certainty of having had years of experience and therapy three times a week, which gave her certainty and a position to work from. I found it difficult talking about the certainties that came from that position rather than about the relationship with the client and the uncertainties that brings. Others need to bring out a theory like centredness because it is safe or say that something comes from free association, from the client. Something about finishing the course helps you know who you are and helps you to ask how you can be so sure.	(14a) A question of whether amount of experience and therapy are seen as contributing to one's ability to interpret what the client says through free association. (14b) Theories being about a place of certainty but what of the place of the relationship that brings uncertainty. (14c) Completing the course helps one to question certainty.
(15) I find it difficult to open dialogue in supervision because I am always questioning the problem with knowing. This is what doing a number is also about, that psychoanalysis and psychology enable one to have a place of security and certainty and therapy can be like that, providing a place for someone to be certain from. My personal work, therapy and study, has been about having the confidence to question that. At first, when asked to defend and explain this position, I would be more inarticulate than usual, but I am getting more at ease with unease. This can make me more helpful for clients who want me to sort out their problems.	(15a) Personal therapy and study help one to have the confidence to question certainty both for oneself and in practice where clients might desire certainty too. (15b) The difficulty of dialogue between positions of certainty and uncertainty.

Stage 4—individual descriptive portraits

As suggested above the individual descriptive portraits still attempted to stay with the language and meanings of the participants. Certainly Hollway argues that descriptive data needs to be allowed to speak for itself (Hollway, 1989), and Wertz (1984) challenges the researcher to maintain a presence to the data by slowing down and patiently dwelling with details and meanings. Each interview transcript was analysed and then individual descriptive portraits were constructed by placing together all the main elements of meaning, as far as possible in the order in which they arose, but also attempting to link what seemed to be related issues. The descriptive portraits are intended to illuminate the structure of the phenomenon under study specific to each individual participant, which is: "the lived experience of feeling ready to call oneself a psychotherapist". The descriptive portrait for Bill is presented here (Table 3) because it highlights a number of aspects or units of meaning relating to the phenomenon as they emerged from the interviews.

Stage 5—general descriptive statement

The final descriptive statement is a summary of the general nature of the phenomenon as suggested by Giorgi (1985). Generally, phenomenological research seems to move away from individual life-worlds at this stage and involves presenting a general structure of the phenomenon while also using examples from the verbatim description of the participants to demonstrate how this structure actually arose.

Four main meaning clusters were generated from the meaning units:

1.   Psychotherapy and counselling
2.   The influence of others
3.   Validation
4.   Speaking about being a psychotherapist and doing psychotherapy.

One meaning cluster will be outlined here to demonstrate some constituents that made up the cluster, illustrated with examples from the verbatim descriptions by participants.

Table 3.   Descriptive portrait: Bill.

Bill felt he could call himself a psychotherapist until he was caught off guard the other day and without thinking found himself saying that he was training to be a psychotherapist. Until the researcher had asked the question, when arranging the interview, he had not really thought about whether he could call himself a psychotherapist.

At first during supervision, Bill found it difficult to say what his method was, and he struggled with his supervisor's need for certainty, but gradually he found confidence in saying he could not define what his method was. Bill felt that his supervisor saw an amount of experience and personal therapy as contributing to being able to interpet what the client said through free association. He felt that others needed the safety of a theory like centredness. He valued a position of uncertainty that came from the relationship with the client and saw his supervisor's position as one of certainty. Completing his own training course had helped him to stay with his uncertainty. Bill also saw his personal therapy and study as enabling him to question a position of certainty both for himself and for his practice, where clients might also desire that. Part of feeling more confident is about being helpful in a way that does not try to direct people but rather allows something to emerge between them.

Bill felt that it would be easier if someone else told him that he is a psychotherapist, such as his supervisor, or those involved with accreditation. He thought that his past experience in nursing led him to think about the need to be registered or accredited before he could call himself a psychotherapist. It seemed that just because he calls himself a psychotherapist and someone else perceives that as so does not make it valid. For Bill, validity was to do with accreditation, which helps him with his insecurity because then no one can question his calling himself a psychotherapist. He felt that he could seek accreditation because of the way he is working, but he didn't have enough hours in order to demonstrate that he is practising. While accreditation seems to give protection to himself and his clients, he was not so sure that it does. It seems that having the hours validates one as a psychotherapist but the diversity in theoretical orientation and practice leads to difficulty in setting a standard. This is illustrated by the way his supervisor could talk about finances but not about clients; the very language was different in the way one spoke about defining what a client meant while the other questioned how that was possible.

(*continued*)

Table 3. (continued)

Bill was also unclear about the differences between counselling and psychotherapy. He was unsure whether counselling can be termed as problem-solving and psychotherapy as being deep, but he called himself a psychotherapist and does not see himself as a counsellor any more. There was a dilemma, though, in calling himself a psychotherapist, in that once you call yourself this it seems as though you are not training any more, but Bill was. In some ways he was, and in some ways he was not. While he felt that finishing his research for an MSc helped his confidence and justified his saying that he is a psychotherapist, he was also continuing with training and research and therefore he felt that he was continuing to become a psychotherapist. He did not know when that would stop.

Speaking about being a psychotherapist and doing psychotherapy

The participants spoke about the language of psychotherapy and the problems of how we speak to others about what we do and the effect of how they speak to us. The issue of confidence was raised in connection with others, with Dave saying, "The core of the difficulty is to do with kind of being confident about knowing what I am doing when I am talking to someone, when I am being a psychotherapist."

There was also an issue about having confidence in what one actually does as a psychotherapist, which is about having a relationship rather than a theory. This could be undermined by those who were seen as having confidence, as the ones who did more complicated and different sorts of psychotherapy, or as those who do have the language. Another way of viewing confidence could be linked to being able to question the need for such certainty, for example with a supervisor. Bill said:

> She was a psychotherapist really. There was something about her that needed some certainty. And when I was unable to provide certainty, the interpretation of the client's thoughts, there was difficulty there. And when I would challenge her she would say, "Well, obviously it is this". I would find that difficult, for someone to say that is supervision without having seen the client.

For Bill, something about this struggle had changed: "I bring this back to my research and my reflections and my therapy as well . . . I found confidence in saying that I couldn't define what I was doing."

There was also the struggle with one's own need for certainty, and finding a way of working that is helpful but in a way that doesn't try to direct people even if that is what they want. As Dave said:

> On one level I do feel as though I know what I am doing and I think that I am actually quite good at it. But on another level I think, I really, you know, I mean what I do I do well. All I do is sit and talk to people, you know, and I don't particularly sort things out for them. Quite often they go away more muddled than when they came in. You know, how is that helpful to them? And um, and on the other level I think it is helpful to them in the long run.

While Sue talked about psychotherapy being synonymous with branching out on one's own, she was not sure what it would take for you to feel you are a psychotherapist. Even when individuals can call themselves psychotherapists there is still something ongoing, like being able to go out and find business by saying "I'm a psychotherapist" or acknowledging that completing a course justifies one in saying "I'm a psychotherapist but I'm also continuing with it".

This short extract attempts to highlight how each cluster is made up of various constituents, such as confidence, being able to speak to others about one's approach, the need for certainty, uncertainty, and what being a psychotherapist means in terms of a continuing dynamic process of becoming. It is also intended to illustrate how the previous stages of data analysis are used to build the picture of the phenomenon "feeling ready to call oneself a psychotherapist".

Some of the difficulties encountered included how the relationship between clusters could be shown, how the clusters/constituents could be shown to be related to the original research question, and how to show the unspoken and inferential nature of the data. In fact, the difficulty of the struggle to speak directly of feeling ready to call oneself a psychotherapist was really recognized only after the research was written up. Perhaps the researchers' own process made it difficult to hear, and perhaps some research questions led to inferential data that need a different kind of attention.

Discussion

The fundamental ideas of phenomenology have been developed by a number of researchers into a series of stages or phases in light of the times or, as Crotty puts it, "grafted on to the local stock" (Crotty, 1996). There is a danger with this in that such stages change the essential nature of phenomenology because there is an expectation that certain things should be done at certain times rather than staying with what appears when it appears. Such approaches may, however, help one to find a way of conducting phenomenological research by providing a structure for the study of phenomena, while at the same time phenomenology requires a critique and, thus, also recognition of the limitations of such an approach.

By exploring one way of undertaking phenomenological research this chapter shows how a phenomenological research method helped to reveal the phenomenon under study while simultaneously concealing it. It provided a way into phenomenological enquiry by beginning a conversation about what it means to feel ready to call oneself a psychotherapist. The method was less helpful in addressing the discourse between researcher and researched because it seemed more like a kind of content analysis as opposed to exploring the interpersonal and intrapsychic processes of discourse, whether conscious or unconscious.

Thus, a serendipitous finding that was either missed by the researcher's inexperience or was difficult to recognize through the method (or both) was related to the sense of inference in what people spoke of. Unknown forces were at play. It is also argued that there is an essential paradox in the idea of empirical phenomenological research, because phenomenology is concerned less with the provable, disprovable, or explainable and more with the paradoxical, the unknown, and the mysterious, as Merleau Ponty states:

> The world and reason are not problematical. We may say if we wish that they are mysterious, but their mystery defines them: there can be no question of dispelling it by some "solution" it is on the hither side of all solutions. [Merleau Ponty, 1962, p. xx]

These ideas have led to a new direction for future research because an essential way of knowing that is often mentioned in the psychotherapeutic literature, but rarely empirically developed, is unknowing, perhaps because the idea of unknowing is paradoxical itself; in other words, how can you know the unknown, how can you speak the unspeakable?

A number of questions arose with regard to the three main processes of phenomenology and that concerned the extent to which the researcher is engaged in an interpretive as opposed to a purely descriptive activity, how and why the researcher includes or rejects aspects of the data such that horizontalization is difficult to stay with, and the problem of understanding bracketing as being simply about setting aside one's own presuppositions, which seem continually to arise and metamorphose in unexpected ways. There is only space here to consider the latter further.

Should bracketing be seen as an either/or option rather than as a process of considering when it is appropriate and when it is not? Simply deciding to bracket one's assumptions rather than continually examining them and their impact on the study does not seem to be enough. Kvale (1996) illustrates this as a difference between the hermeneutic and empirical phenomenological perspectives in research interviews. He highlights the way hermeneutics focuses on interpretation of meaning, with the interviewer attending to their prior knowledge of the phenomenon as they engage in conversation with the interviewee, while the empirical phenomenological interviewer is open to the frame of reference of the interviewee with prior knowledge bracketed (Kvale, 1996).

Some of the difficulties associated with separating out the way these perspectives view bracketing arose during the research; for example, in connection with the researcher's own struggle with becoming a psychotherapist. Initially, however, the researcher felt that the ethical imperative of putting the other first (Levinas, 1969) meant staying with the empirical phenomenological approach and the experience of the other. On reflection, however, it seems that Merleau Ponty does not see these perspectives as mutually exclusive. As we are in time continually forming and reforming the story (Merleau Ponty, 1964), it seems there needs to be a continual process of checking out presuppositions and their impact. Lipson puts this rather succinctly, stating the need "to both keep yourself in there and out at the same time" (Bergum, 1991).

If as Merleau Ponty (1962) suggests, phenomenology has a concern with what lies outside (on the hither side) that is the context as well as the text, it will be interesting to consider how a phenomenological approach to research could allow the unspoken to be spoken and to enable the researcher to engage with their own experience as well as the participants'. Can we see the other while being subject too?

References

Becker, C. (1992). *Living and Relating*. London: Sage.

Bergum, V. (1991). Being a phenomenological researcher. In: J. M. Morse (Ed.), *Qualitative Nursing Research. A Contemporary Dialogue* (pp. 55–71). London: Sage.

Casement, P. (1985). *On Learning from the Patient*. London: Routledge.

Crotty, M. (1996). *Phenomenology and Nursing Research*. Melbourne: Churchill Livingstone.

Gilbert, P., Hughes, W., & Dryden, W. (1989). The therapist as a crucial variable in psychotherapy. In: W. Dryden & L. Spurling (Eds.), *On Becoming a Psychotherapist*. London: Tavistock Routledge.

Giorgi, A. (1975). An application of the phenomenological method in psychology. In: A. Giorgi, C. Fischer, & E. L. Murray (Eds.), *Dusquesne Studies in Phenomenological Psychology: Vol. 2* (pp.82–103). Pittsburgh: Dusquesne University Press.

Giorgi, A. (Ed.) (1985). *Phenomenology and Psychological Research*. Pittsburgh: Dusquesne University Press

Heaton, J. (1990). What is existential analysis? *Journal for the Society of Existential Analysis*, 1(1): 2–6.

Hollway, W. (1989). *Subjectivity and Method*. London: Sage.

Hollway, W., & Jefferson, T. (2000). *Doing Qualitative Research Differently*. London: Sage.

Husserl, E. (1929). Phenomenology. In: R. Kearney & M. Rainwater (Eds.) (1996) *The Continental Philosophy Reader*. London; Routledge.

Husserl, E. (1960). Cartesian meditations. An introduction to phenomenology. In: M. Freidman (Ed.) (1991) *The Worlds of Existentialism. A Critical Reader*. New Jersey: Humanities Press International.

Kvale, S. (1983). The qualitative research interview. *Journal of Phenomenological Psychology*, 14(2): 171–195.

Kvale, S. (1996). *Interviews. An Introduction to Qualitative Research Interviews*. London: Sage.

Levinas, E. (1969). *Totality and Infinity: An Essay on Exteriority*. Pittsburgh: Duquesne University Press.

McLeod, J. (1993). *Doing Counselling Research*. London: Sage.

Merleau Ponty, M. (1962). *The Phenomenology of Perception*. London: Routledge.

Merleau Ponty, M. (1964). *The Primacy of Perception*. Evanston: Northwestern Universities Press.

Morse, J. (1991). Strategies for sampling. In: J. Morse (Ed.), *Qualitative Nursing Research. A Contemporary Dialogue*. London: Sage.

Moustakas, C. (1994). *Phenomenological Research Methods*. London: Sage.

Patton, M. (1990). *Qualitative Evaluation and Research Methods*. CA: Sage.

Silverman, D. (2000). *Doing Qualitative Research*. London: Sage.

Spinelli, E. (1989). *The Interpreted World*. London: Sage.

Strupp, H. (1989). My career as a researcher and psychotherapist. In: W. Dryden & L. Spurling (Eds.), *On Becoming a Psychotherapist*. London: Tavistock/Routledge.

Wertz, F. (1984). Procedures in phenomenological research and the question of validity. In: C. Anastoos (Ed.), *Exploring the Lived World. Readings in Phenomenological Psychology. West Georgia College Studies in the Social Sciences*, 23: 29–48.

CHAPTER ELEVEN

Heuristic research

Theresa Rose and Del Loewenthal

Introduction

The aim of this chapter is to explore heuristic research as a method for researching psychotherapy. Initially, the heuristic approach to research is discussed, followed by the process of conducting a heuristic inquiry; an eight-step approach is described. A discussion is provided on the application of heuristics for psychotherapeutic research, followed by a discussion on the potential merits and limitations of heuristic research. An overview of what is required in the research report concludes the chapter. Heuristics is considered here to be a relational research method that facilitates exploration of the lived experience of psychotherapy.

Definition

Heuristic research is a method located within phenomenological research and is premised on how an individual interprets their experiences (Moustakas, 1994; Patton, 1990). Heuristic "comes from the Greek word *heuristkein*, meaning to discover or to find" [original italics] (Moustakas, 1990, p. 9). He goes on to state: "A heuristic inquiry is a process that begins with a question or problem that the researcher seeks to illuminate" (Moustakas, 1990, p. 15), whereas Patton (1990, p. 71) states that this method "brings to the fore the personal experience and insights of the researcher". Thus, a distinction of heuristics from other research methods is the explicit nature of the researchers' involvement with the phenomenon that is being investigated. The research question emanates from the researchers' lived experience; the subject is of interest to them in their own lives and they wish to know more about the subject, and to elicit "what is other people's experience of this phenomenon?" The process of elicitation is underpinned by the concept of tacit knowing; Moustakas (1990, p. 22) states "the tacit dimension underlies and precedes intuition and guides the researcher into untapped directions and sources of meaning".

Another distinction with heuristics is the emphasis on the word "illuminate", for it is more about an exploration to discover/uncover the many facets/nuances that coalesce to form the phenomena of the inquiry/investigation/research activity. The researcher is seeking to find out about people's lived experience of the phenomena/subject, and through the research process to come to a new/increased understanding of the phenomena/subject; to see the phenomena from a more informed viewpoint.

Process of conducting a heuristic research inquiry

Moustakas (1990) suggests that there are six phases in a heuristic inquiry:

(i)   initial engagement—formulating the research question;
(ii)   immersion into the topic in question—the topic permeates every aspect of day to day living;
(iii) incubation—the topic is put on hold, this process facilitates tacit knowing and intuition;
(iv)   illumination—the topic is seen in a different light;
(v)   explication—making known to others this new light;
(vi)   culmination of the research in a creative synthesis—the researcher, through being familiar with the topic, the generation

and analysis of data from others with lived experience of the phenomena studied, is able through the processes of tacit knowing and intuition to share their new understanding of the research question.

These phases informed Moustakas's framework for conducting the research process. The framework has been modified here in light of the author's experiences of undertaking heuristic research, and is presented in eight steps, and includes Moustakas's guidelines for data analysis from which the creative synthesis emerges.

1. *The research focus.* This step requires the researcher to define the subject area of "lived experience" for the investigation. The researcher should consider the following questions: from your experience what is it that you wish to know more about?; why do you want to know more about this phenomenon?; why does it interest you?; has this topic been researched before?; how would your investigation add to the body of knowledge in the field? Answers to these questions assist with the development of the research question.

2. *Researcher's "lived experience".* The researcher is required to record in a research journal their "lived experience" of the phenomenon. Moustakas advocates that the researcher should keep a reflexive journal to record thoughts and feelings during the research investigation. Thus, the self of the researcher is actively involved in the study; the researcher makes transparent their personal experience.

3. *Identifying potential participants.* This is an important aspect of the investigation, as this research method requires that at interview participants are asked only one question, "What is your experience of *x*?", where *x* is the phenomena being investigated. To ask more questions has the potential to take away from the participant's "lived experience"; their experience is filtered through what the researcher wishes to know. Thus, the researcher needs to consider who is most likely to have had experience of the phenomena. Participant numbers are usually small, in the region of 10–15; it is the quality of the information rather than the quantity that is particularly pertinent with this research method. Prior to contacting potential participants, the researcher should adhere to ethical

[handwritten margin notes: "Ethical issues does this not conflict with what the point is? Previous paragraph?" and "Allows the participant to change something?"]

guidelines for conducting research within their organization. Potential participants need to be provided with sufficient information to enable them to make an informed choice about being involved with the proposed investigation (see McLeod, 2003). Information should include (i) the purpose of the study; (ii) what they are required to do; (iii) confidentiality; (iv) right to withdraw from the study at any time; (v) how they may be affected by participating, e.g. support required if in speaking of their "lived experience" unresolved issues are raised. The foregoing information should be included on a consent form that participants sign prior to their involvement with the study.

4. *Recruiting participants.* Informing potential participants of the study/investigation (e.g., advertisement in journals, word of mouth, names from databases—people who have accessed a service, or members of an organization with experience of the phenomena). Once contact has been made, the researcher provides information on the study as identified in point three. Those who wish to proceed sign the consent form.

5. *Data generation.* As previously mentioned, only one question is asked during the interview (either face-to-face, one-to-one or in a group, or via the telephone). Other questions may be asked for clarification. Experience of conducting this type of interview highlighted that, on the whole, participants were initially reluctant to respond to one question, stating "Is this what you want?" The researcher's role is to acknowledge the concern, but to reassure that it is their experience that is important. Interviews may vary in time (from fifteen minutes to two hours), depending on the participant's ability to articulate their experience. Participants are then sent transcripts of the interviews to check for accuracy. They are required to sign a declaration stating that they are willing for all/or some/or none of the material to be included in the study. Alternatively, participants may choose to write of their experience.

6. *Immersion.* The researcher immerses themselves in the phenomena of the investigation; examples of the phenomena are noticed in the media, in conversations, etc. This recognition is similar to that which occurs when you decide to buy a car of a particular make or colour; suddenly you become aware that there are many cars like

that on the road, a fact that previously you had not registered. Thoughts and feelings arising from this process are recorded in the research journal, thus adding to the pool of data for analysis. The researcher also immerses themselves in the data. Re-reading transcripts, looking for commonalities in experience, these are grouped together and form the first phase of presentation of findings, themes emanating from the "individual depictions" of people's experience of the phenomena. The second phase is a "composite depiction", a group presentation of the lived experience. The third phase is the presentation of exemplary portrait(s): these are individual stories of the phenomena. At each of these stages, participants (some or all) may be involved in checking that the findings capture the "lived experience". Because of this involvement, Moustakas referred to participants as co-researchers.

7. *Incubation.* This requires the researcher to do the reverse of the immersion phase, in essence, to switch off from the subject, to take a break, to do something different. An analogy of this process is when trying to remember the name of someone and you just cannot remember it, but by not focusing on the activity of trying to remember, the name suddenly comes to you. This process is thought to enable new meaning to become apparent, and fosters intuitive knowing.

8. *Creative synthesis.* This final step of data analysis requires the researcher to draw upon the knowledge gained during the investigation and elucidates for others their understanding of the research question posed; the lived experience of the phenomena. Moustakas (1990, p. 52) suggests that this may be in the form of "a narrative, story, poem, work of art, metaphor, analogy, or tale".

Application of heuristics for psychotherapeutic research

Researching psychotherapy is both challenging and complex (Garfield 1992; Roth & Fonagy, 1996). Conventional methods of research do not capture practice, for practice concerns a specific relationship, one that is difficult to quantify. Perhaps there is a need for the research method to be located within the field of relational research. Where the relationship developed between the researcher and the research participant is the primary relationship, the relational aspect is further demonstrated through the process of data analysis that culminates in the research report (Rose, 2002). Relational research is research that is mindful of re-presenting the other. It could be said that therapists are involved in a form of relational research through the supervisory relationship. Here they recount to another what went on behind the closed door of the consulting room, with the intention of gaining a new perspective; gaining new knowledge on the relationship, knowledge that has the potential for informing future practice.

This knowledge emanates from practice, with practitioners involved in the therapeutic process. Rustin (2001) makes reference to how the consulting room can be seen to be a laboratory. Relational research places the consulting room as the research field. This has the potential of opening up the possibility of demystifying the research process, for research is positioned as something practitioners can be actively involved in, in their day to day practice. Research is thus one component of practice, rather than seen as something "others" (those who are not involved in its practice) do. There is thus a shift from evidence-based practice (theory informing practice) to practice-based evidence (practice informing theory). The researcher as practitioner opens up potential conversations on how practice may provide "a series of opportunities to erect hypotheses concerning the patient which are then tested out in the course of treatment (and its supervision)" (Mace & Moorey, 2001).

Heuristics can be seen to be a feasible research method for researching psychotherapy, particularly as its central tenet is for the researcher to have experience of the phenomenon of the study. The researcher is involved in the study, not as an objectified observer, but subject to the process. This places the practitioner who (through the process of their personal therapy) has experience of both client and therapist perspectives of practice (i.e. to have been a user and provider of a psychotherapeutic service) as a potential researcher of heuristic inquiries.

Discussion of the potential merits and limitations of heuristic research

A potential merit of heuristic research is that it offers a methodical way of exploring the lived experience of therapy, either from the client and/or therapist perspective. It provides a method for researching personal experience. Through this process there is potential for making known some of the many facets of the therapeutic relationship; to gain an insight into what makes therapy effective or ineffective. It could be said that there is a similarity with other relational research methods presented in this book. What is it that makes heuristics distinctive?

The main issue is that the researcher has had direct experience of the phenomena being studied, and that this interest is named, is made transparent in the research report; this is said to increase the legitimacy of findings (Sword, 1999). It could be said that all research stems from the interest of the researcher in the subject, as this interest provides the impetus for a study. But not all methods require the researcher to declare this interest; it can be lost under the name of scientific rigour, or under the guise of validity, reliability, and generalizability. This was considered particularly so within the objectified stance of positivistic research, i.e., quantitative methods. However, with the shift to post-positivism (and qualitative methods), the view of the researcher changed from an objectified observer to a subjective participant (Denzin & Lincoln, 1994), and there was an increasing focus on the relationship between the researcher and research participant and how this impacted on the knowledge generated (Lather 1991; Rose, 2002; Scheurich, 1997).

However, this distinction can also present a potential limitation premised on the ability of the researcher to communicate their understanding of the phenomenon to both self and others. For what of their blind spots? What is it that they unconsciously bring to the study that may manifest in countertransferential issues, issues that have implications for how they hear and interpret the story of the other? Do they hear only if it resonates with theirs? This factor is alluded to by Reason and Rowan (1981) when commenting on "New Paradigm Research" that the researcher may only hear what they want to hear. They make the case for the researcher to have support during the analysis of data, a fact that Moustakas does not acknowledge. Rose and Loewenthal (1998) make the case for the researcher to have support to enable the working through of potential blind spots, blind spots that may emerge particularly during the immersion stage of a heuristic inquiry. This support is aimed at minimizing the potential for consensus collusion, and it could be said that it is akin to the psychotherapeutic supervisory relationship.

Justification

Another distinct aspect of a heuristic inquiry is that the data generation stage requires a leap of faith by the researcher. For only one question is asked at interview, "What is your experience of ...?", and the research participant responds from their frame of reference. The researcher does not know beforehand what data will be generated. In other approaches (e.g., grounded theory, case study, phenomenology) the researcher asks more specific questions, questions that emanate from their frame of reference, and as such can anticipate the data that will be generated. Heuristics requires the researcher to be open to what may emerge in the meeting with the research participant.

There is similarity here between the therapeutic relationship, where the parameters or boundaries are known in advance (e.g., time and place, confidentiality), and the heuristic interview, the boundaries imposed by the informed consent of the research participant, but what may be told in both meetings (therapy session, research interview) is unknown. This can present a dilemma to the researcher: what if I do not get the answers I expect?; how can I complete the project? In essence, these statements are about providing closure to the "lived experience" of the other, rather than being open to the new. It is about the researcher being open to what may emerge in the research interview, similar to the therapist being open to what may emerge in a therapy session. There is a distinction in that the researcher needs to be mindful that it is a research interview and that any questions asked are aimed at clarification, not exploration, of why the person thinks this way (Hart & Crawford-Wright, 1999).

Moustakas suggests that a heuristic investigation continues until the whole story is told. There is a similarity here with grounded theory, where the researcher continues checking out the emerging theory until no new material arises (Strauss & Corbin, 1990). But how realistic is this? A more realistic view is posited by Stake (1994) when he advises caution when employing a case study method, that the whole story can never be captured or told. It is suggested here that all relational research methods can do is to present a "snapshot", an in-the-moment experience of a phenomenon. A heuristic approach is distinct from grounded theory in that generalizations are not made from the findings; rather, the researcher presents a creative synthesis that represents his or her understanding of the phenomenon. Any attempt at generalization occurs when others who have experience of the phenomenon read the text and it resonates with their experience; the generalization does not emanate from the researcher.

A potential limitation of heuristics is that the researcher is at the centre of the meaning-making process, which is acceptable if viewed from the modernist perspective, but is open to question from the postmodern perspective; and the "de-centred self" where the "I" is subject to (Sarup, 1993, p. 15). Can heuristics be an acceptable research method from a postmodern perspective? The authors suggest that heuristics would need to be expanded to included further analysis that would then reconceptualize the method as post-heuristic. The key element in post-heuristic research is that there are two cycles of interpretation, the first cycle culminates in the creative synthesis, the second involves a deconstruction of the text (creative synthesis); the deconstruction represents the questioning of the privileged voice (Derrida, 1996). Thus, the self of the researcher is not at the centre of the meaning-making process; they are subject to it. Additionally a critique of the research process is an integral component of post-heuristics as this provides the opportunity for exploring and questioning the research process: to make known the tensions inherent in the process of attempting to represent the other (see Rose, 2002).

Conclusion

Heuristics is a research method focusing on the exploration of the lived experience of a phenomenon. The researcher needs to have direct experience of the phenomenon being investigated. The process of conducting a heuristic inquiry involves eight steps (research focus, researcher's lived experience, identifying potential participants, recruiting participants, data generation, immersion, incubation, creative synthesis). The research process culminates in the research report. Initially the researcher is required to define and locate the research focus in the literature, and identify what brings them to the study, i.e., their experience of the phenomenon. This is followed by a discussion of the literature. As heuristics is located within a phenomenological approach, it is recommended that a detailed review of the literature is conducted after the data analysis so as not to skew the findings. The next section is a discussion of the research design and method, followed by a presentation of findings; this includes the themes that emerged from the individual depictions; composite depiction (a representation of the group's experience of the phenomenon); exemplary portrait(s) (individual stories that reflect the lived experience of the phenomenon); and a key issue is to include verbatim data generated during participant interviews. The presentation of the creative synthesis concludes the findings section. The next section is a discussion of the findings located in the relevant literature, followed by a conclusion that includes discussion on the research process, limitations of the inquiry, and suggestions for further study.

Heuristics is a relational research method that is applicable for researching the lived experience of psychotherapy, where therapists are research practitioners with direct experience of the phenomenon they choose to study and have the potential to generate knowledge that is practice-led.

References

Denzin, N. K., & Lincoln, Y. S. (1994). Entering the field of qualitative research. In: N. K. Denzin & Y. S. Lincoln (Eds.), *Handbook of Qualitative Research* (pp.1–17). Thousand Oaks, CA: Sage.

Derrida, J. (1996.) The play of substitution In: W. T. Anderson (Ed.), *The Fontana Postmodern Reader* (pp. 82–87). London: Fontana Press.

Garfield, S. L. (1992). Major issues in psychotherapy research. In: D. K. Freedheim (Ed.), *History of Psychotherapy: A Century of Change* (pp. 335–359).USA: American Psychological Association..

Hart, N., & Crawford-Wright, A. (1999). Research as therapy, therapy as research: ethical dilemmas in new paradigm research. *British Journal of Guidance and Counselling, 27*(2): 205–214.

Lather, P. (1991). *Getting Smart: Feminist Research and Pedagogy with/in the Postmodern*. USA: Routledge.

Mace, C., & Moorey, S. (2001). Evidence in psychotherapy: a delicate balance. In: C. Mace, S. Moorey, & B. Roberts (Eds.), *Evidence in the*

Psychological Therapies: A Critical Guide for Practitioners (pp. 1–11). Hove: Brunner-Routledge.

McLeod, J. (2003). *Doing Counselling Research* (2nd edn). London: Sage.

Moustakas, C. (1990). *Heuristic Research: Design, Methodology and Applications.* London: Sage.

Patton, M. Q. (1990). *Qualitative Evaluation and Research Methods* (2nd edn). London: Sage.

Reason, P., & Rowan, J. (1981). Issues of validity in new paradigms research. In: P. Reason & J. Rowan (Eds.), *Human Inquiry: A Sourcebook of New Paradigm Research* (pp. 227–238). Chichester: John Wiley and Sons.

Rose, T. (2002). An exploration of counselling and psychotherapy as a form of learning, with particular reference to people with a facial difference. Unpublished PhD Thesis: University of Surrey.

Rose, T. M., & Loewenthal, D. (1998). An heuristic investigation: is there a need for a counselling/psychotherapy service for people with cleft lips? *The European Journal of Psychotherapy Counselling and Health*, 1(1): 105–120.

Roth, A., & Fonagy, P. (1996). *What Works for Whom? A Critical Review of Psychotherapy Research*. New York: Guilford Press.

Rustin, M. (2001). Research evidence and psychotherapy. In: C. Mace, S. Moorey, & B. Roberts (Eds.), *Evidence in the Psychological Therapies: A Critical Guide for Practitioners* (pp. 27–45). Hove: Brunner-Routledge.

Sarup, M. (1993). *An Introductory Guide to Post-Structuralism and Postmodernism.* Hemel Hempstead: Harvester Wheatsheaf.

Scheurich, J. J. (1997). *Research Method in the Postmodern.* Bristol, USA: The Falmer Press.

Stake, R. E. (1994). *The Art of Case Study Research.* Thousand Oaks, CA: Sage.

Strauss, A., & Corbin, C. (1990). *Basics of Qualitative Research.* Thousand Oaks, CA: Sage.

Sword, W. (1999). Accounting for presence of self: reflections on doing qualitative research. *Qualitative Health Research*, 9(2): 270–278.

CHAPTER TWELVE

The use of postmodern feminist methodology to examine the influences of therapists' sexuality*

Julie Ryden and Del Loewenthal

T he purpose of this chapter is to describe experiential analysis and briefly outline what happened when this discourse analytic perspective was used as part of a method involving triangulation of interview, literature analysis, and reflective diary methods. The actual study explored the influence of therapists' sexuality upon lesbian experiences of therapy and particularly the influence of marginal and dominant discourses within the process.

This research, arising from an MSc in Psychotherapy by one of the authors (Ryden, 1999), employed this postmodern feminist methodology, specifically the approach termed "experiential analysis". Experiential analysis was originated by the feminist researcher Shulamit Reinharz in 1983, and later developed by Bungay and Keddy in 1996 to reflect a more postmodern influence.

Experiential analysis seeks to explain the relationship between the knowledge produced or accepted in a particular society at any

---

* This chapter is drawn from Ryden, J., & Loewenthal, D. (2001), Psychotherapy for lesbians: the influence of therapist sexuality. *Counselling Research, 1*(1).

time, and the other dimensions of that society (Bungay & Keddy, 1996). Its focus is upon:

> ... the social construction of knowledge, power, language, meaning, and subjectivity. More specifically, it explores how and what knowledge gets created, disseminated, and perpetuated, and how this can contribute to the definition of our own subjectivity; the differences between this discourse and our experiences; and how our experiences have been influenced by this discourse. [Bungay & Keddy, 1996, p. 446]

A focus for this study was the discursive influences upon the narratives of a group of lesbians when exploring how perceptions of therapist sexuality affected their therapy experience. How were the narratives of these lesbians shaped by the world in which they live?

Essentially, experiential analysis employs three methods: an analysis of the discourses available within the literature; interviews; and a reflective diary written by the researcher. It is within the analysis of the data emerging from these three methods that Bungay and Keddy have particularly developed Reinharz's methodology. Their perspective upon the analysis is that the discourses available within the texts are reviewed to reveal the power relations governing the language used, and the areas of resistance contained within the texts (Bungay & Keddy, 1996). While their account provides pointers to the method of analysis, this was limited in its depth, and therefore this research drew additional guidance from the method of discourse analysis. This method moves the focus from a correspondence model, where texts refer to external objects in an unproblematic and consistent manner, to a "relational model", where: ". . . new meanings and 'objects' are presumed to be formed within the text, and the textual discourse is enmeshed with power systems" (Parker, 1992, p. 47).

Texts become ". . . a repository and a reflection of other processes . . .", and interest is focused not upon the experiences of the speakers, but rather their value in clarifying the wider processes of power, and the accompanying discursive practices (Grbich, 1999, p. 152).

The literature was analysed to identify the discourses available within the psychotherapeutic literature. The aim of the review is to explore the language and assumptions present within the literature, and to reveal the dominant and marginal standpoints (Bungay & Keddy, 1996).

Interview transcripts were scrutinized for a number of elements: the similarities and differences between texts (*ibid.*); the predominant and consistent themes or categories (*ibid.*; Potter & Wetherell, 1987); the functional purpose of language (*ibid.*) including evidence of dominant and marginalized discourses (Bungay & Keddy, 1996; Parker, 1992); the metaphorical constructions within the text (Sampson, 1989); the rules and codes employed within the text (Potter & Wetherell, 1987); evidence of absences (Parker, 1992); challenges or resistances to discourses (Grbich, 1999); the internal contradictions (Bungay & Keddy, 1996; Kitzinger & Wilkinson, 1997; Potter & Wetherell, 1987); and finally, the possibility of undermining the obvious, or making the familiar unfamiliar (Slaughter, 1989, cited Kincheloe & McLaren, 1998).

Excerpts from the reflective diary were used throughout the project to locate the reader within the researcher's subjectivity, but were also analysed for evidence of discourses apparent within the text.

The literature review showed some discursive influences upon a lesbian within a therapeutic context, and these will be considered in relation to the lesbian texts within the interview analysis.

Interview sample

Word of mouth and a newsletter were used as methods to access a convenience sample from two lesbian networks. Criteria for inclusion within the study included self-definition as a lesbian, a minimum of two therapy sessions, and being within two years of completing their episode of therapy. A minimum of two sessions was employed to avoid exclusion of clients with negative experiences, but who h,ad gained sufficient evidence for *their* perception to be confirmed.

The sample consisted of six women, whose experience of therapy ranged from six weeks to several years. Personal characteristics, such as occupation, social class, and age, were not obtained for reasons of confidentiality; however, all respondents were white and able-bodied, as is the case with many lesbian studies (Lemon & Patton 1997).

Interviews

A semi-structured interview was employed, containing three broad question areas. First, the interview enquired about the process by which interviewees had chosen their therapist, and factors influencing this choice. Second, whether the sexuality of the therapist had any influence upon their experiences, necessitating them to disclose their perception of the therapist's sexuality and the factors influencing this judgement. Finally interviewees were asked to speculate on how they thought a lesbian therapist might have influenced their experience.

The approach taken within the interviews followed the feminist exhortation to reciprocity, indicating personal involvement of the researcher (Maynard, 1994; Reinharz, 1992). Such an approach aims to reduce the power differential between interviewee and interviewer, although the issue of oppression within the interview process became an uncomfortable experience for the researcher. The use of a reflective diary raised awareness of a sense of conducting a "smash and grab" raid on interviewees' stories. Using their words to earn an educational qualification, inviting them to re-experience their past for the researcher's benefit, and rewriting their stories according to the researcher's priorities. The issue of the researcher's power and violence, ironically within an emancipatory methodology, is pursued elsewhere is more detail (Ryden. 1999).

Written consent was obtained and the interviews lasted between one and two hours. Interviews were taped, subject to interviewee consent, and then transcribed by the researcher. The transcriptions were not returned to interviewees to amend or develop as recommended by Reinharz (1983), since this presents the illusion of attaining a complete and whole picture, which is fixed and static. The postmodern beliefs underpinning this research would reject such a possibility, preferring to believe that social worlds and identities are themselves being constructed through the interview process, and continue to evolve and develop without reaching a fixed and defined end-point (Shotter & Gergen, 1989). However, the written consent allowed participants to withdraw their consent up to one month after the interview date.

Interview analysis

The analysis focused upon two sites of contradiction within the interviews: the "employment/rejection of lesbian stereotypes", and the "danger/safety inferred through the sexuality of the therapist". Contradictions within texts are said to arise from competing discourses (Kitzinger & Wilkinson, 1997; Potter & Wetherell, 1987), and therefore become a focus for locating the dominant and marginal discourses and possible resistances as required by experiential analysis (Bungay & Keddy, 1996).

Implications for psychotherapy

The discursive nature of a lesbian's experience revealed within therapy should be open to question and examination. Of particular note might be her construction of the therapist's sexuality, which, according to O'Connor and Ryan (1993), has to be available for analysis with regard to its implications within the transference and the therapeutic relationship. Constructions of therapist sexuality may reveal the homophobic stereotype, whose constraints upon self-image and impression management might be usefully explored. Client endeavours to "educate" the therapist can be a site of enquiry, since they may reflect the client's discursive image of both herself and the therapist.

Discourses of sexuality should be a necessary feature of a psychotherapist's knowledge and self-awareness; without such examination the possibility for a collusion of discourses is likely, regardless of the sexuality of the client or therapist. Indeed, this study would perpetuate the heterosexual normality discourse if it only recommended implications for practice with lesbian clients. Surely, the assumptions and sexuality discourses of heterosexual clients should be open to equal deconstruction, in order to challenge the definitive binary and open the "normal" to question.

Concluding note

The selected methodology of experiential analysis proves suitable in the philosophical sense, yet unsuitable in terms of the word and time constraint. The use of three methods, and particularly their analysis, could not be adequately covered within the word and time limits. The analysis presented in al three areas is limited and curtailed, which does not do justice to the methodology itself. The analysis of discourse within the literature and reflective diary proved an insightful conjunction to the interview analysis.

References

Bungay, V., & Keddy, B. C. (1996). Experiential analysis as a feminist methodology for health professionals. *Qualitative Health Research*, 6(3): 442–452.

Grbich, C. (1999). *Qualitative Research in Health: An Introduction.* London: Sage.

Kincheloe, J. L., & McLaren, P. L. (1998). Rethinking critical theory and qualitative research. In: N. K. Denzin & Y. S. Lincoln (Eds.),*The Landscape of Qualitative Research: Theories and Issues* (pp. 260–299). London: Sage.

Kitzinger, C., & Wilkinson, S. (1997). Validating women's experience? Dilemmas in feminist research. *Feminism and Psychology*, 7(4): 566–574.

Lemon, G., & Patton, W. (1997). Lavender blue: issues in lesbian identity development with a focus on an Australian lesbian community. *Women's Studies International Forum*, 20(1): 113–127.

Maynard, M. (1994). Methods, practice and epistemology: the debate about feminism and research. In: M. Maynard & J. Purvis (Eds.), *Researching Women's Lives from a Feminist Perspective* (pp. 10–26). London: Taylor & Francis.

O'Connor, N., & Ryan, J. (1993). *Wild Desires and Mistaken Identities: Lesbianism and Psychoanalysis.* London: Virago.

Parker, I. (1992). *Discourse Dynamics: Critical Analysis for Social and Individual Psychology.* London: Routledge.

Potter, J., & Wetherell, M. (1987). *Discourse and Social Psychology: Beyond Attitudes and Behaviour.* London: Sage.

Reinharz, S. (1983). Experiential analysis: a contribution to feminist research. In: G. Bowles & R. Duelli Klein (Eds.),*Theories of Women's Studies* (pp. 162–191). London: Routledge and Kegan Paul.

Reinharz, S. (1992). *Feminist Methods in Social Research.* Oxford: Oxford University Press.

Ryden, J. (1999). Psychotherapy for lesbians: the influence of therapist sexuality. MSc Dissertation, Psychotherapy and Counselling as a Means to Health, University of Surrey.

Sampson, E. E. (1989). The deconstruction of self. In: J. Shotter & K. J. Gergen (Eds.), *Texts of Identity* (pp. 1–19). London: Sage.

Shotter, J., & Gergen, K. J. (1989). Preface and introduction. In: J. Shotter & K. J. Gergen (Eds.), *Texts of Identity* (pp. ix–xi). London: Sage.

CHAPTER THIRTEEN

Researching sensitive and distressing topics

Thaddeus Birchard

A s part of a doctoral research programme jointly sponsored by the Metanoia Institute and Middlesex University, I am developing a modular training unit to teach psychotherapists and counsellors to assess and work with the problems of sexual addiction and compulsivity. This module could stand alone or within a programme of continuing professional education, or it could be integrated into an existing counselling curriculum. It is constructed in such a way as to recognize the growing role of Internet pornography in addictive compulsive patterning. This is a professional studies academic programme with an expectation of a product-orientated outcome rather than the preparation of a traditional dissertation destined for the library and not the workplace.

I had intended, before the current project, to research the relationship between religious behaviour, sexual behaviour, and sexual offending. After four months of indecision and distress, I set this to one side to develop this other work, the teaching and training programme on sexual and romantic addiction. This is of more interest to me and, I believe, of wider benefit to the community. The other research was leading professionally away from my main areas of clinical interest. I also made that decision because I found the other research distressing and disturbing.

The data for the earlier project was to come from interviews with paedophile Roman Catholic priests and those who specialize in working with offenders. What had seemed feasible in the environment of the classroom became depressing and distressing in the field. This paper is an examination of some of the implications and consequences of handling painful, sensitive, distressing, and potentially explosive, subjects in the pursuit of the twin goals of academic and clinical research.

The distress began at the end of 2001, and early in 2002, as I began to interview offenders and those who work with them. These are the relevant extracts from my research journal:

Monday 7th January 2002

In typing up the interview with RW I am very aware of his anxiety and a sense of contagious shame that extends from him to me and I feel that I am bordering on nothing less than despair.

The entry is followed by reflective notes under the following headings, "heuristic and reflexive", "hermeneutics and phenomenology", and "social construction".

Tuesday 8th January 2002

I am experiencing feelings of paranoia and a sense of contamination. I have been exposed to a culture of fear.

Wednesday 9th January 2002

I keep having dreams of being victimised and at the mercy of predators which I connect to the nature of the research. I woke up feeling angry and trapped.

Sunday 13th January 2002

I had two bad dreams last night, one about breaking china and another about a woman falling to her death on a roller coaster. This feels like it is about an encounter with evil. This is about a confrontation with evil, the ordinariness and all pervasiveness of evil in the human condition.

Similar entries follow throughout the timetable of the interview process. During this period I began to drink too much and became vulnerable to old, and long abandoned, addictive compulsive patterns. Over four months I discussed this "toxic leakage" into the rest of my life with my academic adviser, clinical supervisor, and personal therapist. Eventually, the way forward crystallized at conference, where I was giving a paper on sexual addiction and the Internet. The transition became complete when I discussed the future of the work I was doing then with the head of the London Marriage Guidance Council. I quote him, ". . . such a change represents the creative movement of the heuristic process". This paper grows out of that "creative movement" and is, thus, an exploration into some of the particular characteristics and requirements that can accompany heuristic qualitative research when the research, and particularly the data gathering, is associated with sensitive issues, distressing behaviours, and/or high levels of fear, opprobrium, and social anxiety.

The experience of "distress" is subjective and cannot be made by others or necessarily predicted in advance. Sexual abuse is not the only distressing or sensational topic likely to come into the researcher's remit. For some researchers it might be work with drug addicts, abortion, terminal illness, domestic violence, or crime. A staff member at the Medical Foundation for the Treatment of Victims of Torture reported a similar experience to me in the preparation of his own doctoral dissertation. His research, "Mind and body: the treatment of the sequelae of torture using a combined somatic and psychological approach" (Korzinski, 1997), was a qualitative case study analysis of important but disturbing material. What may seem manageable in the classroom can feel much less clinical and much more personal in the field or in the consulting room.

In my experience, research with sensitive and distressing topics has a possible impact at six interconnected levels:

- academic;
- administrative;

- ethical;
- political;
- professional;
- personal.

Sieber and Stanley (1988, p. 49) define "socially sensitive" research as research "in which there are potential social consequences or implications, either directly for the participants or for the class of individuals represented in the research". In this case, the consequences and implications were mostly for the researcher and grew out of the research journey and the heuristic and reflexive nature of the qualitative process.

Academic

Working with sensitive and stigmatizing topics has a number of potential effects upon reception and location within an academic environment and within the academic community. This is particularly true at entrance level and for the novice researcher and when the research constitutes a debut into an academic community.

Having begun to establish a reputation as a psychotherapist with an interest in addiction, I began to notice that the new research was subtlely altering my reputation to someone who is interested and experienced in the field of paedophilia. Even at an early stage, I had been booked for a workshop on "Men, religion and offending" and asked to join a national working party on sexual abuse in the church. Next came an invitation to a conference in the United States on working with paedophile offenders. While this "establishment of reputation" would be true of any directional development in research, it seems to me that this is more pronounced in the case of research that explores the extreme. The extreme, stigmatizing, and sensational make it more memorable and invite speculation and comment. This is especially true of a "product orientated" dissertation that requires, for example, the preparation and publication of books or journal articles as part of the academic outcome. In degree programmes that require a traditional dissertation, the actual subject matter of the dissertation may not so extensively determine academic repute, because the dissertation often sits, unpublished and unread, in the recesses of a university library.

Research that is proposed and seems reasonable in an academic environment can become unexpectedly and unforeseeably problematic once in the field. As my diaries show, discomfort set in only at the beginning of the interviews when I was exposed to the horrific content of the material and working on the deeply depressing interface with the tragedy of my informants. The distress was multi-factored and involved not only the nature and history of the people interviewed, the character of the stories told, but included repeated winter visits to the dismal physical setting of secure accommodation. All this was set in the wider context of a media outcry and moral panic that spilled over into my interviews, both here and in Ireland. While interviewing participants in one establishment, the security of the setting was invaded by vigilantes with cameras. I had to remain locked in the building until it was judged that I might not be mistaken for an offender and that it might be safe for me to leave unharassed, unfollowed, and unphotographed.

Fear and shame have been primary feelings experienced in the process of research. I felt shame that I would be perceived by the Academic Committee to have chosen badly, to be lacking in resolve, to be a person without academic substance. I became aware that when I read the e-mails of my tutor, before choosing to change the direction and character of the research, I experienced them as cheerful and helpful. Once I made the decision to change, I projected unfriendly feelings on to these e-mails. As far as I can see, they do not, in words, vary from the ones before.

The levels of fear and shame that accompanied the academic character of this research extended more widely into my professional and personal life. The important thing for a researcher to bear in mind is that the affect of the participants, in this case the toxic fear and shame of the interviewees and those who work with them, had the power to leak into the academic, as well as the professional and personal, life of this researcher.

Administrative

Research with sensitive and distressing topics and research into areas of social opprobrium can bring with it extra, onerous, and time-consuming administrative requirements. These include, among others, a need for more long-term planning, unexpected administrative difficulties, and special issues of confidentiality.

In the first place, I found it difficult to access my participants. The institutions that work with sexual offenders are discrete, cautious, and have high levels of security. Phone numbers were unlisted, calls screened, and access to decision-makers slow and difficult. I had to plan carefully, deliberately target and cultivate contacts, and build credibility over a two-year period. It was a case of strategically targeting people of influence and courting the gate-keepers. Because of the difficulty of access, longer lead-in times are required and exceptionally careful preparation is necessary. It is also important for the researcher to "snowball" contacts, to use one gatekeeper to set up connections and appointments with other gate-keepers.

Given the highly confidential and even sensational nature of the taped material, I soon realized that there needed to be exceptional commitments to confidentiality. For example, I could never leave my computer, notes, or briefcase in my car, or the window open in my ground-floor study. For extra security, tapes and notes were transferred to specially designed double-lock filing cabinets. In working with sensitive material any security breach, however unlikely, will bring with it risk and fear to the participants and heavy criticism to the researcher.

The long-term timetable had been built upon the expectation that my secretary would type up the interviews. Once I had begun to do the interviews, it became clear to me that the recorded data would have been too distressing and disturbing for her to hear. I would have to do the transcription and typing myself. This would add four or five unplanned extra weeks to the research timetable.

Ethical

All research projects raise "ethical, moral, and political questions" (Renzetti & Lee, 1993, p. 14). In addition to the special administrative considerations of doing research with sensitive and distressing topics, there are also special ethical considerations. The topic of sexuality raises, in its own right, a set of ethical issues, and has to be dealt with in a sensitive way.

Renzetti and Lee (1993) emphasize the importance of the following: privacy, confidentiality, safety, respect, consent, and the avoidance of deception. The Council for International Organisations of Medical Sciences had the following guideline for maintaining ethical standards in sensitive research, especially around sexual issues: respect for persons, beneficence, non-malficence, and justice (Ringheim, 1995). I found four major areas that required attention: confidentiality, the issue of free and informed consent, the problem of psychological harm/benefit, and the problem of "unacceptable truth".

The principal of confidentiality is one of only three principles that appear "without exception" (Kimmel, 1988, p. 88) in American and European codes for psychological research. I have already delineated the extra administrative security provisions to double-insure the confidentiality that needs to be put in place while working with sensitive material. It is also important to clearly state, to your participants, the context and the limitations of confidentiality, especially working with paedophile offenders where there is a possibility that the content of the interview might disclose previously unknown offences. Knowledge of some behaviour might be required for disclosure by law or by a code of professional conduct. The confidentiality contract between the researcher and the research participant requires good clarity and appropriate wording.

Most of my research was done with men living in secure residential accommodation. Some were there either in advance of trial and sentencing or as an alternative prison. Davison and Stuart argue (1975) that it is not possible to do ethical research in an involuntary and coercive setting. Ethical questions can be very complex and sometimes there are no clear and obvious answers. In this case, although the accommodation was secure, the men in residence were there on an optional basis. The voluntary nature of the research participation was made abundantly clear. Even so, it was obvious to me that non-participation would have been common knowledge throughout the institution. This could not help but affect judgements and perceptions. While these interviews took place in an inherently coercive setting, it seems to me, that this was within an acceptable context, and I was grateful that participation was experienced and reported by my informants as positive and beneficial.

While recognizing that it is important not to harm my participants, the purpose of the project was to gain information to prevent my participants from harming other people. This is recognized in *Research Methods in Clinical and Counselling Psychology* (Barker, Pistrang, & Elliott, 1994),

> In general, research should not harm the participants. However, some people may freely consent to suffer harm for the greater good of humanity . . . there is a trade-off between any harm caused to the participants and the potential gain to humanity from the knowledge acquired.

In the preparation for my schedule of interviews I was able to call a meeting of all my prospective clergy participants and address them as a group, answer questions, and invite them to participate. At the end of the questions one man in the group agreed to participate. He said, "I can't change the harm I have done but this is the least I can do to put something back." All the other men agreed and all of them volunteered to participate. Given the sensitive and disturbing nature of the material that could emerge with each interview, plenty of time was left over at the end of each interview for a full debriefing. In every case I had reports from my participants that they had found the interview therapeutically helpful and that it had been, for them, an act of repair, restitution, and reparation. The ethical implications of this process, and it may well be the same in working with other types of participants, is that the actual research creates a sense of benefit, especially where participants have been stigmatized or have experienced isolation and opprobrium.

Another ethical dilemma that emerged from the project came not from the format or the participants but from the outcomes of the study and the general public. I call this the problem of "unacceptable truth". It became clear to me that the high level of public outrage around the issue of sexual abuse in the Roman Catholic Church had created an environment where some views were acceptable and other views were not acceptable. Seiber and Stanley (1988) make this point in this way, "society will enthusiastically embrace ideas that suits it and that will be done irrespective of the validity of the application or the validity of the research".

There are transient orthodoxies in the charged world of strong feelings, abuse, allegation, counter-allegation, vigilantes, and public protest. According to Jenkins (1996, p. 152) concern over child abuse has followed a cyclical pattern, alternating between extravagant claims with far-reaching legislation until the public grows sceptical and the "crusade" itself becomes seen to be the problem. He cites this as the pattern with the sex-offender panics of the 1930s and 1940s. In the 1970s it was widely held that single incidents of sexual abuse did little lasting harm and at least one authoritative text is quoted saying that "Early sexual contacts do not appear to have harmful effects on many children *unless the family, legal authorities or society reacts negatively*" (Jenkins, 1996, p. 88, original italics). This view would not be acceptable now. It could not be promoted even if it were established as an incontrovertible fact. There is, thus, an additional heightened ethical difficulty—the problem of "unacceptable truths"—in the conduct and publication of sensitive and distressing research in the coercive context of a time of moral panic.

Political

There are other important political issues to consider in the process of researching sensitive or controversial subjects, particularly in climates of social concern or in times of moral panic. These may include having to handle, harness, or avoid media interest, respond to personal criticism and unfriendly scrutiny, recognize problems of prejudice and exercise vigilance and dexterity in fielding potential legal and political issues.

Whatever the preferences of the researcher, sensational subjects are attractive to the media and invite press interest. This may have advantages for the researcher. It may create an advantageous public perception around the career of the researcher or clinician. To be seen as an adviser to the stars or a confidante of royalty might well have a generous impact on career development and clinical or academic reputation and therefore client demand. However, if the subject is unpopular, the opposite is likely with the consequences in reverse. When the residential treatment centre was under siege by vigilantes and press photographers, I became very aware that my concern to understand causation could be presented to the public not as explanation but as justification. This would not have had a welcome effect on public standing, academic reputation, or my clinical referral system. It was this kind of interpretative controversy that enveloped Cherie Blair in the media response to her comments on suicide bombings—explanation was taken, probably deliberately, by the press and her political enemies—as justification.

It also has seemed to me that hostile methodological scrutiny and even deliberate misrepresentation of the work are more likely when doing research on sensitive and distressing topics. The competition for funding or reputation creates an environment where it can be economically advantageous for those with one view to criticize and attack those with another competing view. Similarly, with subjects that generate strong feelings, either positive or negative, research findings and statistical information will be taken up or ignored to suit different political agendas. This is potentially true of all research, but I believe that this is especially problematic for researchers investigating sensitive, controversial, or distressing topics.

Those who research extreme subjects and socially marginal groups need to remember that research outcomes have the capacity to generate prejudice as well as reveal truth. I became aware that the publication of my research into Roman Catholic paedophile offending would have the power to contribute to the generation of additional prejudice against the clergy and the church. Just to write about this subject tarnishes reputations and inflames the potentials of prejudice. Most of the men I interviewed were Irish and from a culture and time quite different from our own. I have wondered to myself how much prejudice came into play in the assessment, treatment, and evaluation of such men. In writing a paper on sexual misconduct in the Church of England, I was aware of my own prejudice operating, in that instance to protect the church from insinuation and attack. Issues of prejudice come into play with all research, but when researching areas of controversy and sensational subjects, the ethical and political implications of prejudice are more far-reaching and of greater consequence.

Sensational and sensitive topics, by their nature, may be circled by special legal requirements that require the attention of the researcher. In the case of my own research, I was concerned about the requirements of disclosure in relationship to the material given to me in the interview. What if I were made aware of an offence that had not come to light to others? What exactly were the legal requirements? What would be required under the Code of Ethics and Practice of my professional body? Attention to the law and to codes of practice will need to be heightened in researching issues of controversy. In cases of sexual abuse in the Republic of Ireland there is a tariff of compensation paid depending upon the nature and level of the abuse. It becomes in the financial interest of the victim to have been badly abused and to have suffered greatly. This point highlights the complex and consequential legal nature of some kinds of behaviours that the researcher may research. This is particularly true where documents, statistics, and outcomes might be cited in a court of law or in other circumstances involving custody, settlement, or compensation.

Professional

In counselling and psychotherapy research it is not absolutely possible, right, or desirable to separate out the academic, the professional, and the personal. However, I have done so in this paper for conceptual clarity and ease of organization. The professional problems that emerged for me were connected with the requirements of immersion, conflicts of empathy, and the heuristic character of psychotherapy research.

There were a number of lesser problems attached to my status as a novice researcher that should be noted by other novice researchers investigating sensitive or sensational subjects. The first is to recognize that those working with such topics can experience a kind of "professional contamination". One can become "the odd one" and can suffer an alteration or imputation of reputation. I found myself characterized as "the one interested in paedophilia" rather than "the one interested in prevention". Doctoral studies can create the professional identity of the researcher. I found that my professional identity had begun to conform to the topic. I am not especially interested in paedophilia or sexual offending as an end product. I am primarily interested in the generic process that, I believe, lies behind the majority of these behaviours. I found this shift of professional reputation undesirable and unwelcome.

I have come to the view that research with sensitive subjects, or subjects with the capacity to contaminate the researcher, should be "department anchored". By "department anchored" I mean commissioned and held by an organization rather than by the individual and/or lone researcher. This takes the speculation and media attention off the researcher. It allows the researcher to be supported and grounded, and to hand over public interface to an impersonal organization. I noticed that when the residential treatment centre was attacked, all responsibility was directed away from the sponsoring organization and individual staff members and handed over to the Home Office. This anchored the work outside the work itself.

Qualitative research uses empathy as a major heuristic tool and many qualitative researchers regard participant empowerment as a legitimate, even central, purpose of the research (Sieber & Stanley, 1988). Client empathy is central to the psychotherapist's task and essential for the creation and development of the therapeutic alliance. Our academic and clinical tradition has grown out of medicine, and this places the primary duty of care to be towards the client rather than to a third party. I found myself in "empathy competition", a contest between the capacity to feel empathy for the perpetrator, who is seen, and the requirement to feel empathy for the victim, who is unseen. Worst of all, I found that my empathy for the offender (necessary to the qualitative process) was being characterized by others as an absence of empathy for the victim.

This was made worse because much of the offender treatment world, at least that based in the prison system and the probation service, takes the view that psychotherapy is not helpful in the treatment of offenders. It might even make it worse. This, it was suggested, inclines to make a psychotherapeutic approach "well meaning" but, in effect, complicit in offender behaviour. I understand that this view of psychotherapy is the prevailing view and that this has determined some aspects of the Home Office funding policy for intervention and treatment. During this research I observed in myself many disturbances of empathy and empathy competition, and I found this to be exacerbated by the political and professional agenda of others.

Stiles (1993, p. 604), writing in *Clinical Psychology Review*, made the point that "in contrast to the idealised detachment sometimes advocated in received-view research, qualitative research seems facilitated by immersion in the material". McLeod (2001, p. 6) prescribes the necessary foundation for the qualitative researcher as "becoming a knower". The single most difficult aspect for me of this research was the expectation and requirement of immersion in the qualitative process. I had to hear distressing material, not once, not twice, but over and over again. I would hear it at the time of the interview. I would hear it again on the tape, sometimes two or three times more, because of the way a transcription machine works, and then read it over and over again in the analysis process. I found it distressing to hear once, but I was unprepared for its cumulative impact. Other researchers working on sensitive and distressing topics would do well to make provision to minimize this effect. The research is important, but for me, it is not my first priority and it is not right at this stage of my own development. I will say more about immersion in the next section.

Personal

The literature on qualitative research emphasizes the importance of protecting the well being of the research participants. There is not much on protecting the researcher. There is an emphasis on the use of the self as the principal tool of the researcher; however, I did not come across mainstream material for prospective researchers warning them that research material has the capacity to enter, in a disturbing way, into the personal process of the researcher. The requirement for immersion exacerbated my sense of personal contamination. This was made worse by what I call "the incongruity of the lyrical requirement" and the way in which the research activated some of my own inner psychological scripting.

The principal issue is that the primary components of heuristic qualitative psychotherapy research, immersion, ethnography, hermeneutics, and reflexivity, are the same components that allow leakage from the professional back into the personal, the psychological equivalent of stomach acid reflux. In the same way as the heuristic process affects the nature of the research, so too, does the research affect the nature of the researcher. It is the heuristic nature of qualitative psychotherapy research that brings the leakage as well as the insights to bear.

Strauss and Corbin (1998) in *Basics of Qualitative Research* describe the process of qualitative research as "like a piece of music", and Moustakas (1990), in particular, waxes lyrical, and becomes poetic in his descriptions of the heuristic contribution required of the qualitative researcher. I found this lyricism incongruous and inimical to my own research. Delightful and inspiring as it might be in many research projects, it sets an inappropriate and discouraging tone for those doing qualitative research into the sensitive, distressing, and disturbing.

I am clear that shame and the shame of public opprobrium are the most powerful scripts that operate in my inner world of feeling and thinking. Shame, in particular, I experience as involuntary and excruciating and, when activated, it seems to have a life of its own. In my family of origin and in the community of my adolescent formation, sexuality was both sought after and experienced shamefully. Although the issues are different, I experienced this research as an activator of my own shame, as shame by association.

Shame has a contagious nature. People can feel shame when they see someone else acting in a shameful way, especially if others think that they are somehow associated with the shameful person. This is what I think happened to me. Whenever anyone would ask my research topic they would grimace and look away in disgust. I suspect that this registered in me, in an involuntary place, that I was shameful and disgusting. It is not logical but I think that somehow this research project, dealing with maximum sexual shame and maximum social opprobrium, activated powerful inner scripts that now account for my distress and disturbance. Other researchers working in different but equally distressing and disturbing areas or interest ought to be mindful of the capacity of the subject matter to engage their own archaic memories and deeply imbedded scripts.

Recommendations

In addition to that the recommendations and "good advice" that are implicit in the text I would like to highlight the following points.

- Perhaps, as a novice researcher, avoid sensitive and distressing research topics.
- Do not choose sensitive and distressing topics unless you are willing to undergo media scrutiny and public identification.

- The willingness to quit and the willingness to continue are choices of equal value.
- Create a peer support team that can meet with you as a group on a regular basis to interpret, support, challenge, and create perspective.
- If you are indecisive about the continuation of your work, take advice from the experts and set a time-limited reflection period and a decision-making timetable.

Most important of all, if you decide to quit, the next day you will have wished you had decided to stay, and, if you decide to stay, the next day you will have wished you had decided to quit.

Conclusion

People have assumed when I talk about the sensitive and distressing nature of the subject matter that I mean I have met wicked monsters and heard horrendous tales of the unimaginably vile. This has not been true. Two quite different and unexpected things have upset me in this study. The first has been the reality of the goodness of these men, and, these acts excepted, their commitment to service, the reality of their faith, and the confusion, deep suffering, profound despair and hopeless nature of their circumstances. The second has been a recognition of the similarities between the psychology of the offender and the psychology of the crusader (Firman & Gila, 1997). The yearning that creates and drives the offender seems, to me, to be the same yearning that drives the crusader—both are driven by the need to matter and the dread of non-being. The child abuser and the "abuser abuser" share a common psychological profile, only the end product is different. To understand this is to understand something of the nature of evil.

References

Barker, C., Pistrang, N., & Elliott, R. (1994). Research methods in clinical and counselling psychology. Chichester: John Wiley and Sons.

Bell, J. (1993). *Doing Your Research Project*. Buckingham: Open University Press.

Davison, G., & Stuart, R. (1975). Behaviour therapy and civil liberties. *American Psychologist, 30*: 755–763.

Firman, J., & Gila, A. (1997). *The Primal Wound*. Albany, NY: State University of New York Press.

Jenkins, E. (1996). *Paedophiles and Priests*. New York: Oxford University Press.

Kimmel, A. (1988). *Ethics and Values in Applied Social Science*. Applied Social Science Methods Series, Vol. 12, Sage Publications.

Korzinski, M. (1997). Mind and body: the treatment of the sequelae of torture using a combined somatic and psychological approach. Unpublished PhD Thesis: University of Chicago.

McLeod, J. (2001). *Qualitative Research in Counselling and Psychotherapy*. London: Sage.

Moustakas, C. (1990). *Heuristic Research: Design, Methodology and Application*. Newbury Park, CA: Sage.

Renzetti, C., & Lee, R. (1993). *Researching Sensitive Topics*. London: Sage.

Ringheim, K. (1995). Ethical issues in social science research with special reference to sexual behaviour research. *Social Science and Medicine, 40*(12): 1691–1697.

Sieber, J., & Stanley, B. (1988). Ethical and professional dimensions of socially sensitive research. *American Psychologist, 43*: 49–55.

Stiles, W. (1993). Quality control in qualitative research. *Clinical Psychology Review, 13*: 593–618.

Strauss, A., & Corbin, J. (1998). *Basics of Qualitative Research*. Thousand Oaks, CA: Sage.

PART III

RESEARCHING THE
THERAPEUTIC PROCESS

CHAPTER FOURTEEN

A heuristic–dialogical model for reflective psychotherapy practice

Christine Stevens

This is an account of how I went about developing a research method that was compatible with my day-to-day practice of Gestalt psychotherapy, how I applied it in a small scale study of my work, and the impact it has had on my professional development.

My aim in writing this account is to elicit critical responses to the methodology as a contribution to the debate about ways of doing psychotherapy research. In the space available I have chosen therefore to focus on the research process rather than simply report on my research findings.

During the research period, my work was based in a GP surgery, and was funded by the local Health Authority. I was working with brief client contracts of 6–8 weekly sessions of fifty minutes of therapy. Through my training I had come to appreciate the involvement of the therapist's active, authentic self as an intrinsic part of Gestalt therapy, rather than the sophisticated application of appropriate techniques. My training, however, presented a model of psychotherapy that was normatively long term and open-ended. Furthermore, my exploration of the literature showed Gestalt therapy was barely represented at all in studies of brief work in primary care.

What I wanted to look at was how I used my self as a therapist in the work I was doing—was it possible to work dialogically within a brief therapy contract?

There is a danger in talking about the therapist's use of self that this becomes reified as a technique, a clinical "tool" in the hands of a skilled practitioner. What I am concerned with here is self as neither an entity nor the core of existence, but an inherently and profoundly relational process—self as the contact-boundary at work, actively engaged in figure-formation as initially defined by Perls, Hefferline, and Goodman (1951, p. 235).

The challenge was to find a way of researching my work that was congruent with the demands of Gestalt therapy for therapist authenticity and presence, and that was not merely of academic interest, but was useful for me as a practitioner. Most studies of therapy in primary care have been outcome research. Although beloved of managers and commissioners, my frustration with these is that to date they offer little benefit in terms of informing my practice. A basic flaw in outcome studies is the reductionist assumption that there is a linear logical correlation between process variables and outcomes. Psychotherapeutic interaction is responsive to this client in this particular moment by this therapist with their own therapeutic perspective. Anticipated outcome feeds back into the therapy process. Some minor event can cause the field to reconfigure in unexpected patterns and have a significant effect on outcome. We simply do not know enough about how this occurs. As Fonagy has pointed out, the problem is that "the outcome of psychotherapy is what outcome measures happen to measure" (1995, p. 174).

With some important qualifications, the research method which I felt most facilitated my exploration was the heuristic approach developed by Moustakas (Douglas & Moustakas, 1985; Moustakas, 1990), which shares some common ground with existentialism and phenomenology. Ethical considerations in co-opting current therapy clients as co-researchers prevented me from using co-operative inquiry. Other qualitative methods include case study research, which provides rich narrative description of a bounded system over time. A grounded theory approach enables substantive theory to emerge from the systematic collection of data about a phenomenon. I incorporated aspects of both these approaches into my data handling and analysis. However, neither of these approaches incorporates active self-awareness as an intrinsic part of the research process in the way that heuristics does. Phenomenology encourages the researcher's detachment from the phenomenon being investigated, whereas heuristics retains the essence of the person in experience. The heuristic researcher derives the raw material of knowledge and experience from the empirical world, typically through dialogue with one's self and with participants—a process very akin to that of therapy. Clarkson, in fact, has suggested that the Gestalt approach is intrinsically "qualitative research in action" (Clarkson, 1997, p. 35). A condition of heuristic research is that the investigator must have had a direct, personal involvement with the phenomena being investigated. This certainly applies to reflective practice in psychotherapy. Intrinsic to the heuristic research process is self-awareness and a valuing of one's own experience in the recognition that this is deeply connected to what is being perceived and investigated "out there" in relation to others. This parallels the therapist's use of self through awareness of transference and countertransference processes.

What makes heuristic methodology so useful for therapy process research is that it explicitly operates at third-order awareness—awareness of awareness—creating a cognitive discourse that makes the subjective experience of doing therapy accessible for research through self-reflection. Moustakas has identified a number of non-linear processes by which meaning is heuristically constructed. I briefly summarize these and show how I applied them in my research.

Identifying with the focus of the inquiry

Aligning oneself with what one is seeking to know. My research was a subjective inquiry into my use of self in the therapeutic relationship with my clients.

Self-dialogue

Allowing the phenomenon to speak directly to one's own experience, and being receptive to all aspects of it. Through the personal exploration of the meanings, to be able to depict the experience in its many aspects into core themes or essences. This is very congruent with reflective psychotherapy practice, in which I understand self as a relational process and dialogue as an intersubjective dynamic.

Tacit knowing

The basis for heuristic discovery is knowledge that we do not know that we know, but that forms the ground of our perceptions. In looking at the use of self in therapy, this touches on existential issues of what it is to be human. If, as Lynne Jacobs asserts, we are "wired to be dialogical" (Hycner & Jacobs, 1995 p. 94), then this forms the tacit dimension for much of what takes place in the therapeutic encounter.

Intuition

The bridge between the tacit and the explicit which makes possible the perceiving of things as wholes. In my research, I understood this process of knowing as facilitating my choice of questions and methods as well as the therapy process itself.

In-dwelling

Turning inward to seek a deeper or more extended comprehension of a quality or theme of human experience. This was my experience as I focused intently on my practice during the research period. I felt that "up-welling" was a more accurate description, however, as much of my search for deeper meaning was expressed in the context of relationships between my self and others.

Focusing

The sustained process of systematically contacting the more central meanings of the phenomenon in order to see the thing as it is. In terms of my clinical practice, this was the experience of sustained reflective inquiry that both informed and was informed by my way of being with my clients.

Internal frame of reference

The understanding of the meaning and essences of any human experience depends on the internal frame of reference of the person doing the experiencing: "Our most significant awarenesses are developed from our own internal searches and from our attunement and empathic understandings of others" (Moustakas, 1990, p. 26).

In my research, I explore the meaning for therapy in bringing my awareness of my own internal frame of reference into the meeting with my client. I see this as an element of the "between" in the dialogical encounter.

This heuristic model is a way of attending rigorously to the process of knowing so that subjective experience becomes qualitatively accessible to scientific investigation. If Gestalt therapy is qualitative research in action, heuristics provides a conceptual framework for the observing ego. However, it is not the whole story. If the heuristic processes are plotted in relation to the Gestalt cycle of experience (Figure 1), the reflective process of awareness

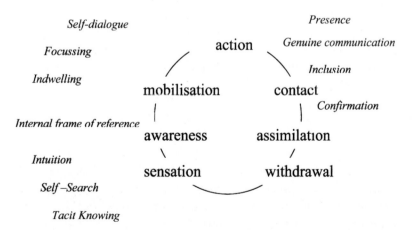

Figure 1. Heuristic–dialogical processes in relation to the Gestalt model of experience.

becomes clear. What the heuristic process does not illuminate so well is self-in-relation-to-other, the contacting process itself. However, here the cognitive tools are available through the dialogical processes of presence, inclusion, confirmation, and genuine communication. When the heuristic process is enriched by a dialogical perspective, we have an qualitative methodology for psychotherapy process research that is both accessible and relevant to the reflective practitioner.

Moustakas sub-divides the process of a heuristic study into six phases; initial engagement, immersion, incubation, illumination, explication and creative synthesis. I will give a brief account of each phase, relating it to the process of my research.

Initial engagement

In this phase the researcher is involved in an inner search to discover a topic that has compelling personal meaning, often with autobiographical and relational involvement within a social context. The question about which I feel passionate concern emerges from the inner processes of self-dialogue, tacit awareness, and intuition.

I think there is also a dialogical dimension to this phase, with meaning derived from self-in-relationship. The personal context from which my research interest emerged was a journey from sociological research (self as "detached observer") through social casework and counselling to experiential psychotherapy training and practice. Behind my research questions was an intense personal interest in the quality and nature of the process of meeting and being met.

Immersion

Once the question has been discovered and the terms defined, immersion is the process of living the question, awake, asleep, in dreams, in dialogue with others, alert to all the possibilities for meaning and growing in understanding of it.

I identified this phase of my research as a period of intense excitement as I seemed to make daily discoveries through the books

I read, the clients I worked with, meetings I attended, discussions with colleagues, and my work in personal therapy. My dreams were infused with themes of presence and connectedness, and I wrote creatively in my journal.

Incubation

During this phase the researcher's intensive focus fades and other tasks become figural. The research questions move out of awareness into ground. Moustakas argues that growth occurs none the less. The tacit dimension of knowing operates outside immediate awareness, giving rise to new understanding or perspectives.

Having gathered the clinical data for my research report, I spent the following four months engaged in fulfilling other demands of my training course and in clinical work. Re-engaging with the material in an intensive writing-up phase, however, I discovered that I had been working on the issues continuously without fully recognizing this. In particular, my practice as a therapist had evolved over the six months of the study, significantly influenced by the discoveries I had been making during that time.

Illumination

These phases are not necessarily sequential. Illumination is the breakthrough into awareness of qualities or themes inherent in the question through the processes of tacit or intuitive knowing. This can happen at any part of the research process. In this way discoveries take place of hidden meaning, new knowledge is gained, or distortions corrected. One morning, for example, I woke up early with the realization that dialogic understanding contributed what was missing to the heuristic model as a tool for Gestalt therapy process research, which I then represented in Figure 1.

Explication

In this phase the researcher attends to the levels of meaning, apprehended through the processes of awareness such as in dwelling, focusing, and self-searching. Added to this are the experiences and understandings derived from interpersonal dialogue. Eventually, through the processes of focusing and in-dwelling, the major components of the phenomenon are clarified and explicated in detail. The discoveries of meaning are organized into a "comprehensive depiction of the essences of the experience" (Moustakas, 1990, p. 31). This is then written up as the presentation and analysis of data in the research report.

Creative synthesis

This is the final phase of heuristic research, the bringing together of all the major constituents of the data, core themes, qualities, explications, into a connected whole. This may be in the form of a narrative depiction using verbatim material and examples, or some other creative form. In my study, this took the form of a statement and illustration (Figure 2).

I shall now give a brief summary of how I applied this approach.

During the research period I was funded by the Health Authority and employed by a GP for six hours a week to work in a one-doctor inner city practice with a list size of around 2000 patients. All new NHS referrals during a three-month period were

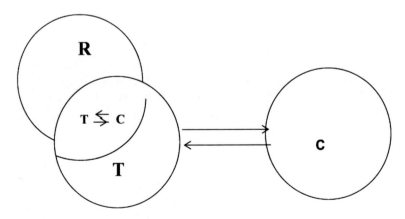

Figure 2.   Reflective-self-in-relation-to client and therapist (**R** = researcher; **T** = therapist; **C** = client).

sent a letter with their first appointment, asking if they would be willing to participate in a research project. In the first session, their consent was sought, further explanation given, and a written contract signed. None of the clients opted out of inclusion in the study.

The study comprised seven clients. Each was offered an eight-session contract, including initial assessment and final review. Four clients attended all eight sessions. The study continued over a four-month period, comprising a total of forty-three therapy sessions of approximately fifty minutes each, which were tape-recorded. In addition, process notes of each session, supervision notes, and letters were kept in the usual way. The process notes and tapes were shown to my programme leader and formed the basis for tutorial discussions.

With such a rich database, a range of methodologies would have been possible, including detailed textural analysis. However, using the approach I have described, I was able to stay with what was figural for me as therapist in the work with each client, thus using a research technique that closely parallels the process of Gestalt therapy itself.

Instead of transcribing each session, I used my process notes and recollections, augmented by listening to taped material and transcribing extracts when needed, to produce an individual depiction of each of the seven clients. Each depiction was a constructed, sequential narrative, from my perspective as a therapist, of the process of the interaction between the client and myself over the course of the sessions attended. These detailed depictions were presented in the appendix to my research report.

From these depictions, from my engagement in the heuristic process previously discussed, and from additional listening to taped material, I developed a thematic structure depicting my use of self as therapist, which I illustrated with examples from the clinical data. In the body of the report, therefore, I presented for each client a list of themes that for me characterized the work. For example, for one client I wrote, "shyness, difficulty making friends, longing for contact, feeling unwanted, worried about what other people think, afraid to upset others". This was followed by a depiction of my use of self as therapist, using the dialogic concepts of presence, inclusion, confirmation, and unreserved genuine communication (or self-disclosure) as a framework and a category for other aspects not included in this list. For example, for this client under "presence", I noted that sometimes I felt tired and heavy or bored and distant. Sometimes I realized I was working very hard to reach her. Through inclusion I came to appreciate her feelings of being ineffectual, her low expectation of other people being interested in her. I attended carefully to my phenomenological experience of our meeting and gave her accurate feedback. She felt confirmed by this degree of attention and made a connection between this and her enhanced self-esteem. I frequently disclosed my experience of her in the moment in order for her to have accurate information to challenge the projections and fantasies that were her habitual way of interrupting contact.

Having done this for each client, distilling the major themes, I was then able to present a composite depiction and discussion of my use of self as therapist, which I presented under the themes previously identified. This was a reflective process informed by the heuristic elements of self-awareness and illustrated by specific examples from the research data. I became more aware, in the course of my study, about the personal challenges of being able to sustain sufficient vulnerability to be authentically present with my clients. My capacity for this varied between clients and at different times. Sometimes it felt safer to "seem" than to risk being fully present as "I", but the nature of the encounter was poorer as a result.

The synthesis of this work was the discovery of a process by which I can engage as reflective-self-in-relation-to client and therapist both as clinician and researcher, which is illustrated in Figure 2. This uses the relational qualities of I–It in the service of I–Thou. The I–It reflective activity helps me as therapist–researcher to disengage from confluence, and the I–Thou process helps me to move out of isolation. From my perspective as therapist, meaning is made available through the heuristic processing of third level awareness, or the reflective-self-in-relationship.

From my research, I found that a dialogical approach to Gestalt therapy can be used in brief psychotherapy, in a primary care context. This does not require sophistication on the part of the client. Most of the clients in my study had not been in therapy before. The attention to the quality of contact rather than on problems and solutions helps clients to become more aware of who they are and therefore be more able themselves to take the decisions and actions that will make a difference to their lives.

This was a research study that I was able to conduct in the context of my normal clinical work, using a method congruent with the practice of Gestalt therapy. Using heuristic processes of knowing informed by dialogic encounter in this way helped me to develop a reflective practice directly relevant to my personal and professional development as a psychotherapist.

References

Clarkson, P. (1997). Gestalt therapy is changing: part II—which future? *British Gestalt Journal*, 6(1): 29–40.

Douglas, D., & Moustakas, C. (1985). Heuristic inquiry: the internal search to know. *Journal of Humanistic Psychology*, 2(3): 39–55.

Fonagy, P. (1995). Is there an answer to the outcome research question?—"waiting for Godot". *Changes*, 13(3): 168–177.

Hycner, R., & Jacobs, L. (1995). *The Healing Process in Gestalt Therapy*. Highland, NY: Gestalt Journal Press.

Moustakas, C. (1990). *Heuristic Research: Design Methodology and Application*. London: Sage.

Perls, F.S., Hefferline, R., & Goodman, P. (1951). *Gestalt Therapy— Excitement and Growth in the Human Personality*. Highland, NY: The Gestalt Journal Press.

CHAPTER FIFTEEN

Psychotherapy research in a postmodern world: discourse analysis and psychoanalysis

Colleen Heenan

Introduction

I n this paper I broaden out the focus of psychotherapy and psychotherapy research in order to contextualize it within postmodern debates. I take two ideas from postmodern and poststructuralist thinking—the idea of the self as socially constructed and the idea of knowledge as discursive—and use Foucault's concept of "discourse analysis" to deconstruct a piece of therapeutic text in order to demonstrate how psychotherapy constructs meaning. My aim is to make clear that discourse analysis is not simply a positivistic research tool but a perspective that challenges taken-for-granted ways of understanding psychotherapy. However, this challenge can be beneficial to practitioners, patients and researchers.

First, I outline some key ideas that inform discourse analysis. Next, I give a discourse analytic reading of clinical material and outline the usefulness of a discourse analytic perspective in relation to psychotherapy theory, research, and practice. However, I also indicate some of the tensions that arise in attempting to amalgamate ideas from discourse analysis and psychoanalytic theory, particularly in relation to issues of agency. My intention is to encourage both psychotherapists and psychotherapy researchers to think more critically about their practices.

Discourse analysis

My interest in discourse analysis came from trying to think about some of the tensions between feminism and psychotherapy, especially in relation to eating disorders therapy (Heenan, 1996a,b, 1998a,b). For instance, if, as a feminist, I regard eating disorders as arising out of gendered notions of normal and abnormal eating, how do I reconcile this political focus with the individual problem-solving approach of psychotherapy, especially psychoanalytic psychotherapy? Further, how do I reconcile the desire of some female clients to ignore the impact of the social world on their dissatisfaction with body image or struggles with food? I was unable to find a paradigm within psychotherapy research that would allow me to explore these tensions in a creative way.

In a postmodern framework, discourse is "a system of statements, practices, and institutional structures that share common values" (Hare-Mustin, 1994, p. 19). Discourse analysis is a way of approaching "all forms of spoken interaction, formal and informal, and written texts of all kinds" (Burman & Parker, 1993, p. 2) as performing a function rather than revealing content. There are different emphases within discourse analysis; for instance, Potter & Wetherell's "interpretative repertoire" approach focuses on the linguistic tools speakers use "to justify particular versions of events, to excuse or validate their own behaviour, to fend off criticism or otherwise allow them to maintain a credible stance in an interaction" (Burr, 1995, p. 117). However, I am going to focus on explicating the "ideological dilemmas" at work on text rather than the speakers' linguistic tools.

Discourse analysis has three aims: to "facilitate a historical account of psychological knowledge, [to] mount a critique of psychological practice by challenging its truth claims, and . . . [to] transform . . . our notions of what a good methodology should be like" (Burman & Parker, 1993, p. 9). Although discourse analysts are interested in individual subjectivity and self-awareness, their interest is in how subjects are discursively positioned by language within wider social discourses. This deconstructive stance is not only concerned with how language is used to construct notions of selves, but also how the very notion of a "self" has come to be constructed. Discourse analysts replace the term "self" with that of "subject", in order to make clear "the way in which [they believe] the social domain constitutes subjects rather than the other way round" (Henriques, Hollway, Urwin, Venn, & Walkerdine, 1984, p. 2).

Discourse analysis draws on ideas from postmodernism and post-structuralism: first, they reject the idea that the self is "organised, stable . . . that selfhood comprises a core element of each individual's personality and subjective existence" (Frosh, 1991, p. 2). Second, they believe that meaning is not fixed by language but is contextual and temporary. So, for instance, personality becomes a concept, not a concrete thing (Burr, 1995). Third, they draw on Derrida's notion of deconstruction; that is, clarifying the way in which identity implicitly defines what it is not (e.g., if an eating disorder, then not normal eating), and how language is based on binary oppositions (either individual or social) that not only hide what is not being spoken about but also privilege what is (objectivity in research).

Central to analysing ideological dilemmas are the ideas of Michel Foucault (1961, 1972, 1978a,b), who was interested in how certain "domains of knowledge" come to be regarded as truth—for instance, scientific knowledge or positivism. He argued that power is exercised "by drawing on discourses that allow our actions to be represented in an acceptable light" (Burr, 1995, p. 64). Further, power only emerges when there is resistance. Foucault suggested that the population of modern societies is managed not by forceful oppression but by means of "bio-power" or "power over life" (1978)—for instance, ideas about the self are constituted through the generation of knowledge about humans (for instance, from the theory and practice of psychotherapy). Individuals participate in the process of subjection through partaking in self-disciplined practices. From a Foucauldian perspective, then, psychotherapy is simply one more technology of subjectivity, constituting therapeutic selves, wherein everyday experiences are regarded as "exemplary and exceptional" (Rose, 1990, p. 244). For the "therapeutic" self, work is not an exchange of labour for cash rewards but a matter of fulfilment and identity; mundane experiences become "life events" that are regarded as psychologically meaningful; experiences of life and death become "part of the work of life itself" (*ibid.*, p. 245) and interactions become potentially meaningful "relationships" of varying degrees.

Constructing eating disordered subjectivities

I now offer a discourse analytic reading of clinical material. This is a brief extract from a short-term psychodynamic eating disorders therapy group for women in which I was both the therapist and researcher. By using a reflexive discourse analytic paradigm for my research, I was able to run the group as I usually would, with only the tape recorder as a disruption. I later transcribed the tapes along with tapes of my clinical supervision and analysed excerpts from both. For the purposes of this paper my analyses of the extract are clearly selective and strategic.

In this extract (from the first group session), Maureen and Laura (names changed) discuss their "compulsive eating":

Maureen: How do you feel when you're actually, when it's actually in your mouth?

Laura: I just want to get rid of it as soon as possible, swallow it so I can have more. I don't know. I just eat everything so fast and I just, 'cause normally there's no, there's no—I don't—there's no thought process/

Maureen:/No/

Laura:/It just happens and that's it/

Maureen:/There's no feeling then before it happens, then?/
Colleen: I think the difficulty is, is that there is a process, which is why I'm asking you to try and pay attention to that because it isn't, you know, someone doesn't come along and inhabit your body and go and do this. There, there is a process and there are thoughts and feelings that go on but that, as you're describing, the food blocks out the thoughts and the feelings so that it just becomes, you know, as if the action took place before you know, you even thought about it.

Within a discourse analytic framework this clinical material can be "read" as performing the function of constructing eating disordered subjectivities. As discourse analysts, we would be asking questions such as, "What discourses about eating, about eating disorders or about therapy, are drawn upon by the group participants?"

Let's look more closely at the words in the text: Maureen's question to Laura as to how she feels about having food in her mouth presupposes that she could, or indeed, should, have feelings about "having food in her mouth". Given that this is a psychodynamic therapy group, this assumption is not surprising. However, since it is the first group, it also indicates the way in which psychoanalytic discourses ("eating as a meaningful activity") have permeated into everyday talk (Parker, 1997). Further, this talk could only occur within a specific historical, cultural and economic context that makes the issue of eating and hunger distressing in a very particular way—because there is too much food, not too little.

We might also want to ask, "How are women positioned by discourses about food, body size, and shape?" In contemporary western society, there are particular moral, medical, and consumerist discourses about the amount or type of food it is appropriate for women (or men) to eat, or the appropriateness, healthiness, and appeal of particular body sizes and shapes or lifestyles. By drawing on, as well as competing with, each other, these discourses make available certain subject positions for women—in this case, problematic positions that warrant the intervention of experts: psychotherapists and, indeed, feminists.

In the context of an eating disorders group in which eating is regarded as "meaningful" and worthy of study, therapeutic discourse becomes more powerful through Laura's resistance: she presents her eating as simply functional, saying "I just want to get rid of it as soon as possible, swallow it so I can have more". Laura requires education and as the therapist I take an overtly pedagogic position ("there is a process, which is why I'm asking you to try and pay attention to that"). This also promotes a particular theory ("the food blocks out the thoughts and the feelings") as well as warding off potentially competing discourses, such as madness or badness. At the same time, there is a hidden moral discourse at work that involves Laura and Maureen taking responsibility not just for "getting to know" themselves but also changing themselves.

Finally, I am aware that this particular extract doesn't indicate any feminist discourses at work—instead, it perhaps makes clear that feminist psychodynamic therapy (like other therapies) is permeated by different discourses—in this instance, cognitive–behavioural, pedagogic, and moral discourses. However, I am going to leave this text here and turn to the relevance of discourse analysis for us as practitioners, as researchers, perhaps as patients or clients.

Discourse analysis, psychotherapy and psychotherapy research

I now want to comment briefly on three issues—the self, agency, and defence mechanisms—before I conclude by focusing on psychotherapy research. Although psychoanalytic theory does not draw upon postmodern and post-structuralist thinking, its notion of the therapeutic subject is similar. The focus is on the irrational—unconscious processes—that in itself is not directly accessible. Language is the medium for constructing the subject and meanings become temporary constructions. It is perhaps Melanie Klein's notion of "positioning" that offers the clearest non-linear framework for viewing the fragmented, shifting, multiple ways in which the psychoanalytic self can be experienced (Ogden, 1994).

However, given that the broad intention of psychotherapy, is to facilitate clients' self-understanding and bring about change in the self, indeed sometimes to enable clients to find a self, how do we deal with the idea of a non-agentic subject? Despite the post-structuralist "death of the author", there clearly is a self—a corporeal self, alive and breathing but also capable of thought. However, as Harré put it, "[t]o be a self is not to be a certain kind of being, but to be in possession of a certain kind of theory" (in Burr, 1995, p. 125). The difficulty is in confusing the function of reflexivity with a belief in the self as an object. There is no true self waiting to be excavated by therapy, but a core self with the capacity to experience itself as agentic, or non-agentic (Flax, 1990, 1993). It is the historical and cultural value placed by contemporary western thinking on agency that compounds the confusion.

Given that we live in contemporary western society, it is crucial to one's sense of identity to be able to offer a coherent and meaningful account of one's self. This is contradicted by the employment of defence mechanisms like eating disorders, which, while initially experienced as "liberating", act upon the person, not just constituting them but also tying them to identities. The women in the group seemed to experience their subjectivities only through being positioned by their eating disorders. Foucault's notion of "subjection" may help us understand the non-linear nature of defence mechanisms—if power is an effect of resistance, then the "forbidden" only becomes powerful through the psychic resistance of defence. Defences are not linear—cause and effect—but dynamic and self-sustaining.

Offering a therapeutic discourse that posits eating disorders as functional, or a feminist discourse that posits eating disorders as socially constructed, offers not only competing narratives but enables participants to construct more coherent and meaningful accounts of themselves. From a combined therapeutic and discursive perspective, what is problematic—and crucial—is to enable patients to develop a "sense of selves", through explicating the constitution of subjectivities—"the point of contact between identity and society" (Parker, 1992, p. 117), and to promote the management of the myriad emotions that arise out of the inevitable tensions that result from being positioned through particular discourses about selves, gender, and bodies. An understanding of the constructive function of language and the ways in which meaning is discursive does not liberate patients, but enables them to know more. However, therapists need to acknowledge which notion of self they are offering.

Finally, I want to say something more specifically about psychotherapy research. Most of what I have said about the discursive nature of psychotherapy can be applied to research. It is crucial that we think about research not as the revelation of truth but as the construction of certain types of knowledge that privilege some accounts and render others invisible. I am not suggesting this is some sort of conspiracy, but I do want to advocate taking a more critical and reflexive approach to the work in hand. This means not being tied to a belief in positivism as truth, or objectivity as neutral, but as a particular discourse that clearly holds a great deal of power—perhaps made more evident by the growing resistance to it.

References

Burman, E., & Parker, I. (Eds.) (1993). *Discourse Analytic Research: Repertoires and Readings of Texts in Action.* London: Routledge.

Burr, V. (1995). *An Introduction to Social Constructionism.* London: Routledge.

Flax, J. (1990). *Thinking Fragments: Psychoanalysis, Feminism, and Postmodernism in the Contemporary West.* Berkeley, CA: University of California Press.

Flax, J. (1993). *Disputed Subjects: Essays on Psychoanalysis, Politics and Philosophy.* New York: Routledge.

Foucault, M. (1961). *Madness and Civilisation—A History of Insanity in the Age of Reason.* R. Howard (Trans.). London: Routledge.

Foucault, M. (1972). *The Archaelogy of Knowledge.* A. M. Sheridan Smith (Trans.). London: Routledge.

Foucault, M. (1978a). *Discipline and Punish: The Birth of the Prison.* Alan Sheridan (Trans.). New York: Vintage.

Foucault, M. (1978b). *The History of Sexuality. Volume 1.* R. Hurley (Trans.). London: Penguin.

Frosh, S. (1991). *Identity Crisis: Modernity, Psychoanalysis and the Self.* London: Macmillan.

Hare-Mustin, R. (1994). Discourses in the mirrored room: a postmodern analysis of therapy. *Family Process, 33*:19–35.

Heenan, C. (1996a). Feminist psychotherapy and its discontents. In: E. Burman, P. Alldred, C. Bewley, B. Goldberg, C. Heenan, D. Marks, J. Marshall, K. Taylor, R. Ullah, & S. Warner, *Psychology, Discourse & Social Practice,* London: Taylor & Francis.

Heenan, C. (1996b). Women, food & fat—too many cooks in the kitchen? In: E. Burman, G. Aitken, P. Alldred, R. Allwood, T. Billington, B. Goldberg, A. J. Gordo Lopez, C. Heenan, D. Marks, & S. Warner, *Challenging Women: Psychology's Exclusions, Feminist Possibilities.* Milton Keynes: Open University Press.

Heenan, M. C. (1998a). Discourse analysis and clinical supervision. Paper presented at Clinical Psychology Forum 114, Division of Clinical Psychology, British Psychological Society, April.

Heenan, M. C. (1998b). Feminist object relations theory and therapy. In: I. B. Seu & M. C. Heenan (Eds.), *Feminism & Psychotherapy: Reflections on Contemporary Theories and Practices.* London: Sage.

Henriques, J., Hollway, W., Urwin, C., Venn, C., & Walkerdine, V. (1984). *Changing the Subject.* London: Methuen.

Ogden, T. (1994). *Subjects of Analysis*. London: Karnac.

Parker, I. (1992). *Discourse Dynamics: Critical Analysis for Social and Individual Psychology*. London: Routledge.

Parker, I. (1997). *Psychoanalytic Culture: Psychoanalytic Discourse in Western Society*. London: Routledge.

Potter, J., & Wetherell, M. (1987). *Discourse and Social Psychology: Beyond Attitudes and Behaviour*. London: Sage.

Rose, N. (1990). *Governing the Soul*. London: Routledge.

CHAPTER SIXTEEN

Identifying cohesion in group psychotherapy process

Georgia Lepper

Introduction

One of the problems in researching the psychotherapy process is how to identify clinically significant events and link them to theory. Many of our clinical concepts were derived from experience in the consulting room and then used to develop theory. Where clinical concepts are drawn from other kinds of theory—systems theory, or cognitive theory, for example—the same problem arises: how can we link clinical events in the practice of psychotherapy reliably to the clinical concepts that shape our understanding of the process and our interventions? First, the researcher must seek ways to identify clinically significant elements or moments in the process; and then, if the research is to be of use to clinical practice, seek to understand what it was about those moments that was significant.

One such clinical concept that informs practice, but is little understood, is the concept of "group cohesion". It was Yalom (1975), in his original study of patient responses to the group process, who first studied the clinical concept of "cohesion". In doing so, he employed the subjective report. He compared his concept to that of the "therapeutic alliance". Like the concept of "therapeutic alliance", "group cohesion" is a heuristic concept, a combination of some research findings and the experience of clinicians and group members. In their 1994 review of the research literature on cohesion, however, Bednar and Kaul conclude that "there is no consensus about the definition or composition of the cohesion construct" (p. 651). Some of the research into cohesion which has been undertaken to date (Kivlighan , Multon, & Brossart, 1996; Marcus & Kashy, 1995; Silbergeld, Koening, Manderscheid, Meeder, & Hornung, 1975) has attempted to bring empirical methods of study to bear on these clinical concepts. They use subjective reports of the therapist and patients and the ratings of observers to measure the phenomenon. This strategy has, however, left us with an unanswered question: is there any way to identify what is happening in the interaction when, as participant observers, we have the experience of cohesion? Do therapists' clinical interventions promote it? Or do they hinder it?

The study presented in this chapter takes as a starting point the need for further research in order to specify the phenomenon of cohesion. Is there any other recourse than to "subjective" reports? This single case analysis seeks to explore the possibility of building an empirical strategy that combines two methods in order to identify and analyse critical moments in psychotherapy interaction that could be contributing to the experience of "cohesion". The two methods used are the Therapeutic Cycles Model (Mergenthaler, 1996)—a computerized approach to text analysis that identifies patterns over large quantities of text; and Conversation Analysis (CA) (Sacks, 1992), an observational method developed originally to study social process, which enables a micro-analysis of interactional events in the actual talk of the session. First, I describe the two methods, and then I show how they were applied to the analysis of a group therapy session. Finally, some of the interaction will be analysed in detail, in order to open to investigation how a therapist intervention affects the overall process of the session.

The Therapeutic Cycles Model (TCM)

Developed by Erhard Mergenthaler (1996), this computerized text analysis software identifies the frequency of occurrence of emotion and abstraction words in a text. Emotion and abstraction words were chosen as relevant linguistic markers of psychotherapy process. The model is based on a standardized dictionary of words denoting emotion and abstraction that were derived empirically from the analysis of a wide variety of texts. A separate dictionary for German, English, Spanish, and Italian has been developed using the same process for each language. The software identifies the frequency of emotion and abstraction words in preset blocks of x number of words (which may be altered for the purpose at hand), and represents them graphically as deviations from a mean. One hundred and fifty-word blocks have been found empirically to represent features of the text most reliably. This analysis reveals characteristic patterns in the occurrence of these words in the many psychotherapy sessions which have been analysed. Beginning with psychoanalytic psychotherapy texts, a frequently occurring cycle was identified. Later work on the text of other kinds of psychotherapies—CBT, for example—revealed the existence of the same cycles, although in these the high and low occurrence of abstract and emotion words came in a somewhat different shape. An example of a TCM graph looks like this:

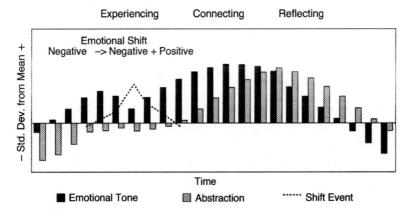

Figure 1.

This is session 9 of a group therapy session, which will be the subject of the following analysis. The graph represents the deviation above and below the mean occurrence of the emotion and abstraction words identified in the text. Two cycles occur in word blocks 24 to 38, and in word blocks 47 to 56, where the number of emotion and and abstraction words rises above the mean (0) axis, to a level of more than +1 standard deviation (SD) above the mean, from the period of "relaxing", before each cycle begins, where the incidence of emotion and abstraction words is below the mean.

More recently, Fontao and Mergenthaler (2000) analysed the cycles occurring in a series of group therapy sessions. This analysis revealed that while the cycles did not occur in the speech of the individual speakers (as they normally appear in dyadic exchanges), nevertheless the cycles appeared when the speech of all the speakers taken together was analysed. This finding suggests that the TCM analysis captures a process that is supra-ordinate to the contribution of individual members in the group interaction. This study is based on an interpretation of this finding—that it may provide evidence for a basic concept of group theory, which holds that it is qualities of group process, such as "cohesion", that provide the therapeutic vector in individual outcomes.

The TCM is a method that analyses context-free patterns of linguistic markers. It does not concern itself with content, or with interaction. It provides a surface map of some of the events occurring in process of the therapy session. It could be compared to the way a geological map might locate the surface features of the earth's geological processes. Interpreting what the observed cycles might represent in terms of processes (in and over time) is the next step in the course of empirical enquiry. Mergenthaler suggests that the cycles can be understood as representing different kinds of activity within the session: "relaxing", where levels of both emotion and abstraction are low; "experiencing", where levels of emotion are high, and levels of abstraction are low; "reflecting", where levels of abstraction are high but emotion is low; and "connecting", where

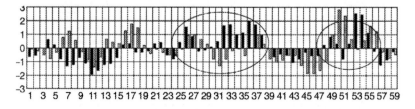

Figure 2.   Therapeutic Cycle Model (source: Mergenthaler 2004).

levels of both emotion and abstraction are high (above +1 SD). In the course of a therapeutic interaction, all of these phases will typically appear. Mergenthaler also hypothesizes that the occurrence of "connecting" represents moments of heightened connection between thought and feeling, marking the presence of therapeutic work, and the potential for change.

The TCM provides a map of the psychotherapy session that plots the location of linguistic markers of affect, abstraction, and narrative, but it does not tell us about the actual events at the level of the talk between therapist and patient(s). The cycles, none the less, can be thought of as indicating where phenomena of interest might lie, and directing analytic attention to specific features of the therapeutic discourse. To analyse those features at a different level of enquiry—at the level of the actual talk in the session—we turn to Conversation Analysis (CA).

Conversation analysis

Conversation analysis was conceived by the social science researcher Harvey Sacks in the 1960s, and developed by his co-workers after his death in 1974. In a lecture, Sacks proposed that "the aims of researchers . . . are to try to get at sets of properties that something has, see how they work" (1992, Vol. I, p. 476). Sacks aimed to demonstrate that it was at the level of interaction that social processes are shaped and sustained, and that, therefore, the analysis of turn-by-turn conversation itself could form the basis of an empirical approach to the study of social order, grounded in systematic observational data. Following his death, a number of different lines of development of the methods emerged, and today CA provides an important corpus of findings in sociology, ethnography, linguistics, and more recently in psychology. One line of development, of interest to this study, is the study of "topic coherence", defined by Sacks in a lecture:

> Talking topically constitutes ways of talking which involve attention to "topical coherence". But one could perfectly have a sequence of talk in which each person talked with an orientation to talking topically, in a topically coherent way with the last, in which

> nonetheless one would find—if one were engaged in seeing what the topics were, that each person "talked on a different topic" . . . and when you open a topic you may be assured that others will try to talk topically with what you've talked about, but you can't be assured that the topic you intended was the topic they will talk to. [Sacks, 1992, Vol I, p. 762).

What he suggests here is that topic coherence is sustained not by content, but in the structure of the conversation: the means by which co-participants in a conversation hear, respond to, and sustain turn-by-turn coherence through "tying" each utterance to the preceding utterance. Joint topic production may include narratives, interactional agreements and disagreements, contributions of experience relating to an agreed topic. Often topical conversation will incorporate rhythms—or "prosody"—when speakers acknowledge each other's utterances with small sounds, with tone of voice, and through a choice of words that link as much through sound affinity as through meaning. Most importantly, topic coherence relies on contextual resources, "the phenomenal environment that provides for the ongoing intelligibility of talk, action and situation" (Goodwin, 1995, pp. 131–132).

The study of conversation as an achievement of people in relation to each other embeds an implicit epistemology: it

> regard[s] a conversation as a rather wonderful device available to human beings by means of which separate minds are able to influence and be influenced by each other, managing to some extent, but always imperfectly, to bridge the gap that inevitably exists between separate selves. [Chafe, 1997, p. 52]

From this perspective, the study of conversation provides an important potential method for the study of the therapeutic process. However, it generates a highly detailed map of the phenomena of talk: how do we know which events are therapeutically significant? How do we place them in the larger context of our theories?

This study proposes to link two "maps" of the interactional process of one session, in order to identify interactionally significant moments, and to test the hypothesis that the process of "topic coherence" can be rendered "visible". It is based on these assumptions:

- Topic coherence is what we, as participants, experience subjectively as "group cohesion'
- There will be evidence of increased topic coherence within the cycles.

To test these assumptions, three important features of topic coherence will be identified in the text: topic content, sequential structure, and participation structure (Linell & Korolija, 1997), and linked to the TCM cycles which appear in the session.

Method

Development of Sacks's original proposal about topic coherence—that topic in conversation is sustained on a turn-by-turn basis by the activity of speakers and hearers—has subsequently been undertaken by researchers in the field of CA. Three elements of topic that together contribute to the maintenance of topical coherence have now been identified (Linell & Korolija, 1997):

- Topic content: what is being talked about?
- Sequential structure: how do speakers link each turn to a previous turn in a way that hearers will follow, and which will enable the next speaker to link in turn?
- Participation structure: who is talking?

In the field of CA, answering these *how* questions has generated a large body of general evidence for the orderliness of talk and the (learned) rules for generating coherent talk. However, some problems in applying CA to the analysis of psychotherapy texts need to be addressed:

1. given that CA analysis is so detailed, analysing every feature of even one session is a very lengthy task;
2. CA does not have anything to say about clinical relevance;
3. How, then, does the researcher select which elements in a text to analyse?

The analysis builds on the findings of Linell and Korolija, and applies them to the text of a psychotherapy session in three stages. In order to analyse the topic content, the method of "Grounded Theory" originally developed by Glaser and Strauss (1967) is used to identify the main categories in use by simple counting, identifying the categories-in-use (Lepper, 2000), and aggregating them into conceptual groups, which can then be identified as topics. By using this procedure, the discovery of topics is grounded in the categories used by the participants themselves, rather than imposed on the talk by the researcher's interpretation of the text. Next, the participation structure is analysed by linking the text to the word blocks created by the TCM analysis, and identifying the speakers in each segment of text. Finally, the sequential structure is analysed using segments of text identified as "connecting" moments by the TCM analysis: what are the significant features of the turn-by-turn interaction at these points in the session?

Basic to CA is the assumption that coherent talk is constructed on a turn-by-turn basis by the participants in a conversation. Sacks (1992) proposed that conversational interaction is characterized by what he called "order at all points": no part of a conversation is accidental. All talk is built on procedural rules that are attended to by all participants. Breaks in conversational order are subject to repair through the mutual efforts of speakers and hearers. These basic characteristics of conversation are termed "sequential order". However, in practice, examination of every turn in even one entire conversational event, such as a therapy session, would be a daunting task. In order to examine some of the features of the sequential structure within this session, the decision was made to restrict detailed analysis of the text to the ten-word blocks in the session that were identified as "connecting moments" by the TCM: moments in which both abstraction and emotion are high. Mergenthaler hypothesizes that it is at these times that clinically significant interactions, leading to insight, may occur. The aim of this analysis is to address in detail the question: what is happening in the turn-by-turn interactions of the participants in the group at these key moments?

Each feature of topic cohesion is analysed in relation to the text within cycles in the session, identified by the TCM, and compared to the text outside the cycles. Finally, a segment of text identified through this process is analysed in detail, in order to examine how a specific interactional event shapes the overall topical coherence of the session.

The data

The session to be analysed is the ninth of the fifty-three sessions of an psychodynamic psychotherapy group for seven women diagnosed with an eating disorder, as part of a treatment and research programme within the Health and Social Action Department of the University of Buenos Aires. The treatments typically consisted of forty-eight sessions, conducted in either a CBT or a psychodynamic model. The study group was conducted by a psychodynamically qualified therapist in Spanish. All the sessions were tape-recorded and transcribed, and then analysed by the TCM programme.

Session number 9 was selected to be analysed for a pilot study because it demonstrated the presence of a very clear cycle in a session with six patients and the therapist (in many sessions there were only two or three patients in attendance). In the first analysis, Fontao analysed some of the linguistic features—identifying topics and analysing speech proportions and the timing of the therapist's interventions. The present analysis takes that work forward by formalizing the analysis of topic and applying the detailed analysis of CA to some of the text.

For the purposes of the present analysis, the session was translated into English, although the TCM analysis is of the original Spanish text.

Analysis

Topic content

The most commonly occurring categories overall in the text were "mother" and "father", followed far less frequently by "sister", "brother", and one instance of "uncle". These, with a few references to medical staff, constituted the "person" categories-in-use. In accordance with the original grounded theory method, the higher order concept of family, or "family ties" (using the category chosen by the therapist herself) was created to identify these categories as a topic. An additional incumbent of the person categories in the text was the category "a normal person". The category "eating disorder" with its varieties of "vomiting", "bingeing" occurred with some frequency, particularly in the first third of the session. These were aggregated into the category "an ill person", noting that throughout the session, these higher order categories constitute a topic—the difference between an "ill person" and a "normal person". Proceeding in this way, the major categories-in-use were identified and aggregated into higher order categories, or topics. Table 1 shows the results of that analysis of the topics.

The main topics were identified as family ties; illness (eating disorder)/normal person; "put in a box" (trapped)/change; give/get help; be perfect/fail; make an effort/rebel; feel good/feel bad (angry, sad, confused, upset) Additionally, there was a significant topic introduced by the therapist—"your feelings". This was not the same as the topic "feel good/bad" as developed by the patients, which was characterized by concrete terms. The therapist's "your feelings" was introduced in its higher order conceptual form, as was the form "family ties", in contradiction to the patients' more concrete use of categories ("my mother", "Dad", etc). Generally, the categories offered by the therapist as candidate topics were higher order concepts.

Finding

The number of categories identified as significant to the topics is higher in the cycles word blocks than it is in the non-cycles word blocks. The average density of topic words in the cycles word blocks is 3.7 categories per block, compared to 2.7 categories in the word blocks outside the cycles. Applying a standard statistical analysis, this difference was found to be significant at the level $p < 0.01$ This result suggests that topic content is significantly richer within the cycles and is consistent with the hypothesis that the cycles indicate higher levels of coherence. Turning to the content, the dominant topic is "family ties". Although the therapist seeks to change the topic to "your feelings" at key points in the session, the group participants continuously return to "family ties" until the last cycle.

Table 1. Labels and frequency for topics found in session 9.

Label	Frequency
Father	17
Mother	36
Family ties	4
Normal person	5
Illness	11
Change	5
Get/give help	10
Make mistakes	2
Be perfect	9
Eating	15
In/out of control	6
Attack/fight	10
Talk/keep things in	15
Fail	5
Make an effort/try	5
Rebel	4
Categorized/put in a box	4
Barrier/prison	5
Your feelings	5
Angry/annoyed	12
Love	5
Hate	1
Feel bad	9
Feel good	2
Confused	1
Alone/lonely	2
Happy	3
Sad	5
Upset	2
TOTAL	215

Participation structure

The second element of topic coherence to be looked at is "participation structure": who is speaking? In group discourse, complex speaker patterns become possible, from monologues and dialogues to multi-party talk. The task of topic coherence becomes increasingly complex as the number of speakers increases. Sacks noted that question and answer sequences frequently provide the "floor" for a topic. A question requires an answer, and the response should address the topic introduced. Where there are several parties actively contributing to developing topics, however, the task of coherence becomes more demanding and abrupt topic changes may occur. Three kinds of talk were identified in the session: question and answer sequences—two-party talk that is structured by the therapist's questions; narrative talk—extended sequences in which patient narratives predominate (these tend to be characterized by a higher incidence of emotion words); and reflective talk—sequences in which reflection, or intellectualization, predominate (characterized by a higher incidence of abstraction words). Table 2 expresses the occurrence of the three kinds of talk—question and answer sequences, narrative sequences, and reflection sequences—for each of the fifty-nine segments of text. It also indicates whether these basic kinds of talk occur as two-party talk, or as multi-party talk. In each cell is an indication of who the speakers are—therapist and/or patient.

Looking at the tables, some patterns in the interaction emerge. The first third of the session is dominated by two-person talk, mostly prompted by therapist questions. The patients tell their stories. Only eight of the twenty word blocks are multi-party talk. A period of reflection in a two-party exchange (word blocks 15 to 19) is followed by multi-party narrative episodes which occupy ten of the twenty word blocks. A long cycle (*in italics*) occurs in word blocks 24–38, with two connecting events at word blocks 26–27 and 37–38. The cycle ends with a question asked by the therapist: "Isn't your father an alcoholic?" and a question and answer sequence between Patient 3 and the therapist follows. The question and answer sequence between Patient 3 and the therapist continues (with low emotion and abstraction levels) from word block 39 until word block 46, when the therapist introduces a new topic. It is an interpretation: "because if she goes out with your dad, you must be angry". This heralds a second long cycle (*italics*) that begins with the therapist inviting Patient 4 to speak, and the topic "anger" is taken up. This leads to a connecting moment (WB 49–50) and then to an extended episode of multi-party reflection on the topic of change (WB 53, 54, 55) and a further connecting moment (WB54–55).

Table 2. Participation structure.

Word block	Q&A	Two-party talk Narrative	Two-party talk Reflection	Multi-party talk Narrative	Multi-party talk Reflection
1	T/P				
2		T/P			
3					T/P
4					T/P
5				T/ P	
6				T/ P	
7	T/P				
8	T/P				
9	T/P				
10				P	
11				T/P	
12	T/P				
13		P			
14				T/P	
15			*T/P*		
16			*T/P*		
17			*T/P*		
18			*T/P*		
19			*T/P*		
20					*T/P*
21			T/P		
22				T/P	
23		T/P			
24					T/P
25				*T/P*	
26				*T/P*	
27				*P*	
28	*T/P*				
29	*T/P*				
30		*T/P*			
31		*T/P*			
32		P		T/P	
33		P			
34				P	
35				*P*	
36	*T/P*				
37	*T/P*				
38	*T/P*				
39		T/P			
40		T/P			

(continued)

Table 2.   Participation structure (*continued*).

		Two-party talk		Multi-party talk	
Word block	Q&A	Narrative	Reflection	Narrative	Reflection
41			T/P		
42				T/P	
43				T/P	
44			T/P		
45		T/P			
46			T/P		
47			T/P		
48				T/P	
49			T/P		
50					T/P
51			T/P		
52			T/P		
53					T/P
54					P
55					T/P
56					T/P
57					T/P
58		T/P			
59			T/P		

T = Therapist
P = Patients
italics= cycles word blocks

Findings

- As anticipated, the participation structure moved away from two-party and question and answer sequences towards multi-party talk as the session progressed.
- Participation structure in the cycles is characterized by a higher level of multi-party talk: 13/25 of the word blocks within the cycles (52%), compared to 12/34 of those outside the cycles (35%). Statistical analysis established that these differences were significant.
- Connecting word blocks occur in predominantly multi-party talk: six of the eight connecting word blocks (75%) are characterized by multi-party talk, except for the question and answer sequence in word blocks 37–38.

This finding suggests that the participants move from the simpler, and more predictable, format of question and answer exchanges to the more complex task of maintaining multi-party talk as the session progresses, and that the connecting word blocks in particular show evidence of a high degree of participation among the group members. It provides further evidence of a higher degree of topic cohesion within the cycles. However, the return to a Q&A sequence in word blocks 37–38 does not follow the expected pattern, and will be the subject of further analysis.

Sequential structure

In order to represent and analyse the sequential structure, Table 3 was assembled to examine some of these properties of the text. The columns show which of the topics, identified through the analysis of the categories-in-use in the first stage of the analysis, are in play in each of the connecting blocks, which are represented by the rows. Column 2 indicates who the speakers were. To further represent the participation of the group members, the unshaded box indicates that the topic was first introduced by a patient, and the black box that it was introduced by the therapist.

Findings

- The "connecting" word blocks are topic rich: every key topic identified in the initial analysis of the text is represented.
- In word blocks 16–17 (weak connecting), seven of the eleven key categories that were introduced by patients at some point in the session are included in the speech of Patient 7; the therapist introduces her preferred topic, "your feelings".
- In word blocks 26–27, Patients 1 and 5 take up the topics "normal person", and "bad feelings" of sadness, anger and failure
- In word blocks 37–38, talk between Patient 3 and the therapist revolves around the topic "Family ties", despite the therapist's introduction of her preferred topic, "your feelings" in WB 37. It is already known from the analysis of the participation structure that this is a question and answer sequence which follows

Table 3. Properties of the text

Word block	Speaker	Illness (eating)	Normal person	Family ties	Get/give help	Change	Make an effort/rebel	Attack/ fight	Love/ hate	Failure	Feel (bad, sad, angry)	Feelings
26	P1		*□							*□		
	P5											
27	P1		*							*	*□	
	P5		*									
37	P3			*□			*□					
	T			*							*	■
38	P3			*			*					
	T			*			*					
49	P4			*							*	
	T			*							*	
50	P6			*					*□		*	
	P1										*	
	T						*				*	
54	P5	*□		*				*□	*			
	P6				*				*			
	T		*	*	*□							
55	P5					*			*	*		
	P6					*			*			

an extended period of multi-party talk. How does the topic return to "family ties"? Again, as observed in the analysis of the participation structure, word blocks 37 and 38 seem to deviate from the expected patterns. These observations suggest that this episode needs detailed analysis.

- In WBs 49–50, the topic "family ties" co-occurs with topic "bad feelings'; therapist response ties to the topic "family ties" in WB 49, then to "bad feelings" in WB 50. This episode then leads quickly to a second connecting sequence in WB 54–55. Taken together these final connecting episodes are topic rich (10/12 key categories in use) multi-party talk, leading to the topic "change".

Deviant case analysis

An important task for systematic research is the demonstration of its validity. The validity—i.e., the significance—of the quantitative components of this research was tested using accepted statistical tests. One of the principles of validity governing textual, qualitative research is the principle of "deviant case analysis", according to which every instance in the corpus of a data analysis must be accounted for in theory building. Deviant cases—those observations which do not support the exploratory hypotheses—are in need of further analysis. Either the hypothesis needs to be revised to accommodate them, or, in some cases, further analysis of the deviant case may support the hypothesis. In this analysis, it was expected that the three components of topic coherence—content, participation and sequential structure—would be at their richest in the "connecting" WBs. That is, that they would be topic rich, that participation would be high, and that tying between WBs would be high. Analysis of the connecting WBs has supported this expectation in every case except in WB 37–38, where the participation structure returned from a higher level of multi-party talk to the question and answer format found in the earlier phase of the session. At the same time, despite the therapist's tying to the topic "your feelings" in WB 37, the patient returns to the topic "family ties" in WB 38. What is happening in the conversation in this episode that might explain this deviant case? Looking at the text in

WB 36, just before the question and answer sequence begins, we find this exchange:

1. P1: Do they know about your eating habits?
2. P7: They know . . . my mum does. I told them, well I started to let them know
3. what was happening to me—I told my mum and dad—I went especially to
4. Tucumán to tell them (laughter) yes . . . because I needed them to help me more
5. than anything (noise of cars) I think my dad more than my mum—because my
6. mum is in no condition to help me whereas my dad is.
7. T: isn't your dad an alcoholic?
8. P7: no.
9. (pause: 11secs)
10. T: And who would like to say anything about how they see their mother?
11. P 1: I see her as very sad . . . with her life—ruined (dogs barking)
12. T: ruined?
13. P1: out of tune—with everything. she is a good person, her heart is in the right
14. place, but I don't want to be dragged down with her, that's (36) why I don't feel
15. right at home, I'm not comfortable, I'm not at home. her marriage is a failure, her
16. personal life . . . I don't know, but it upsets me.
17. T: you are upset?

P1 and P7 are engaged in an ongoing discussion on the topic "family ties", when the therapist enters the conversation with a question (Line 10): "Isn't your father an alcoholic?" Following this is a pause of eleven seconds (Line 9), which, in the context of an ongoing multi-party conversation, is very long, and creates a problem for the speakers. Evidence that something has gone wrong can be observed when the therapist (Line 10) begins a repair sequence, asking a question in order to restart the conversation: "And who would like to say anything about how they see their mother?" In doing so, she links back to the topic "family ties", and P1 collaborates in this repair with a reply about her own mother. The question and answer sequence continues, with the therapist asking direct questions about "your feelings" (her preferred topic) first of P1, and then of P3, who enters into the extended Q&A sequence of WBs 37 and 38.

With her question, the therapist brings a period of multi-party talk to a temporary end, and creates an interactional problem for the group. How did this happen? First, although the question was partially on-topic (family ties), the high level of emotion words (+2 SD) in this word block suggests that the primary topic was the "bad feelings" being expressed. The therapist's question fails to tie to the topic and generates breakdown in the talk, which is in need of repair. This episode brings this cycle to an end, and an extended period of "relaxing"—low abstraction and low emotion—follows.

What does the analysis of this deviant case add to the working hypothesis proposed by this study? The initial expectation was that the cycles, and in particular the "connecting" episodes, would be characterized by high levels of topic coherence, and that this in turn would provide evidence of group cohesion. This cycle was characterized by increasing levels of multi-party talk and topic rich content. That it ends with a breakdown in the talk, at the point of the therapist's question, in fact supports the hypothesis that the cycles are markers for a high level of topic coherence at the level of sequential order.

To further explore the analysis of this deviant case, and its implications for understanding the nature of the cycles and their relationship to the actual talk, the end of the second cycle in the session was examined. Looking at the last three word blocks, there is a similar event. Here is the text:

1. P3: sure but my mum knows about it—hers doesn't.
2. P5: to have a problem + if you have a problem or—if you fail like she said—
3. and you stay there—that's not right but if you have a problem and you try to
4. find a solution like you did by coming here searching for help—why would

5. your mum feel that that everything goes wrong? on the contrary ok, she looks
6. for help.
7. T:—well—very + well.
8. P9: I must go to see the doctor at ten.

In this episode, the therapist again fails to provide a connection to a previous turn (Line 7). Here she is facing the familiar problem of a therapist who must find a way to bring the session to an end, especially when the participants are into the kind of vigorous multi-party talk that we see in this cycle. In this case, she breaks the sequence deliberately, and again, she is aided by a group member— this time, by P9, who, hearing her, collaborates to start the topic "ending" (Line 8).

With this observation, the working hypothesis that the cycles may be good predictors of topic coherence therefore finds further support. This comparison supports the internal validity of the analysis and points the way to further analytic possibilities.

Conclusion

This pilot study was intended to explore whether it is possible to identify in the therapeutic discourse what it is that group participants experience as "cohesion". It has demonstrated that a specific feature of the therapeutic talk—"topic coherence"—can be reliably mapped on to the cycles identified by the TCM. This finding provides support for the claim of the TCM that it can reliably identify moments of the therapeutic process that are clinical interest. It also suggests that it is possible to identify and analyse communicative actions that make a difference to the therapeutic process without recourse to subjective impressions. For example, in this case, it could be tentatively stated that the therapist's question in WB 36 "caused" a breakdown in topic coherence and a rupture in the talk. Whether this was a therapist "error", or a therapist response to other dynamics—perhaps non-verbal dynamics—in the interaction is not possible to answer with this analysis. In either case, however, this observed interaction could inform clinical practice by noting that while asking open-ended questions may support the development of a coherent topic floor, asking a question that requires a yes or no answer in the context of an ongoing interaction is likely to impede the development of a cohesive group process.

Finally, what do these findings have to say about the concept of "group cohesion", and its function in the group process? The high level of correlation between topic coherence and the TCM cycles provides suggestive preliminary evidence for the hypothesis that what we, as participants, experience subjectively as "cohesion" may be related to the level of topic coherence in the talk, and that this can be rendered observable, through the combined empirical methods of CA and the TCM. This finding offers to the process researcher another strategy for building clinical theory through the identification of clinically significant data and the detailed study of the clinical process.

References

Bednar, R., & Kaul, T. (1994). Experiential group research. In: A Bergin & S. Garfield (Eds.), *Handbook of Psychotherapy and Behavior Change*. New York: John Wiley & Sons.

Chafe, W. (1997). Polyphonic topic development. In: T. Givon (Ed.), *Conversation: Cognitive, Communicative and Social Perspectives*. Amsterdam: John Benjamins.

Fontao, M. I., & Mergenthaler, E. (2002). Das Therapeutische Zyklusmodell: Eine Evaluation im gruppenpsychotherapeutischen Setting. *Gruppenpsychotherapie und Gruppendynamik, 38*(4): 349–371.

Glaser, B., & Strauss, A. (1967). *The Discovery of Grounded Theory*. London: Weidenfeld and Nicolson.

Goodwin, C. (1995). The negotiation of coherence within conversation. In: M. Gernsbacher & T. Givon (Eds.), *Coherence in Spontaneous Text*. Amsterdam: John Benjamins.

Kivlighan, D. M., Multon, K. D., & Brossart, D. F. (1996). Helpful impacts in group counseling: development of a multidimensional rating system. *Journal of Counseling Psychology, 43*(3): 347–355.

Lepper, G. (2000). *Categories in Text and Talk: A Practical Guide to Categorization Analysis*. London: Sage.

Linell, P., & Korolija, N. (1997). Coherence in muli-party conversation: episodes and contexts in interaction. In: T. Givon (Ed.), *Conversation: Cognitive, Communicative and Social Perspectives*. Amsterdam: John Benjamins.

Madill, A., Widdicombe, S., & Barkham, B. (2001). The potential of conversation analysis for psychotherapy research. *The Counselling Psychologist*, 29(3): 413–434.

Marcus, D. K., & Kashy, D. A. (1995). The social relations model: a tool for group psychotherapy research. *Journal of Counseling Psychology*, 42(3): 383–389.

Mergenthaler, E. (1996). Emotion–abstraction patterns in verbatim prorocols: a new way of describing psychotherapeutic processes. *Journal of Consulting and Clinical Psychology*, 64: 1306–1315.

Sacks, H. (1992). *Lectures in Conversation, Volumes 1 & II*. Oxford: Blackwell.

Silbergeld, S., Koening, G., Manderscheid, R., Meeder, B., & Hornung, C. (1975). Assessment of environmental systems: the group atmosphere scale. *Journal of Consulting and Clinical Psychology*, 43: 460–469.

Yalom, I. D. (1975). *The Theory and Practice of Group Psychotherapy*. New York: Basic Books.

CHAPTER SEVENTEEN

"The vehicle of success": theoretical and empirical perspectives on the therapeutic alliance in psychotherapy

Jocelyn Catty

"Transference of friendly or affectionate feelings ... which is admissible to consciousness and unobjectionable ... is the vehicle of success in psychoanalysis exactly as it is in other methods of treatment"

(Freud, 1912)

The importance of the "therapeutic alliance", "therapeutic relationship" or "working alliance" in psychotherapy has long been recognized, first in clinical practice and theory and latterly in a wealth of quantitative research. It has been shown in empirical studies to be one of the most powerful predictors of outcome in psychotherapy (Horvath & Symonds, 1991; Orlinsky, Grawe, & Parks, 1994), and is often seen as encompassing the common factors of the different schools of psychotherapy. This image of the alliance as common ground, however, may obscure crucial differences in definition and operation.

Despite the increasing interest in the alliance, I argue that two key questions remain unanswered. First, how successfully can a concept such as the alliance be transposed, either from one setting to another or from a clinical concept into a research instrument, and is its meaning irrevocably distorted in the process? Thus, what are the implications of using research measures based on the alliance in empirical studies and how do we interpret the findings of such studies? Second, how is it that the major proponents of the alliance have defined it as a means by which interventions are delivered and not curative in itself, while quantitative research increasingly links it to outcome?

Although the terms "therapeutic relationship", "therapeutic alliance" and "working alliance" are often used interchangeably, I shall use "therapeutic relationship" as a broad term covering all types of relationship and retain "therapeutic alliance" and "working alliance" for distinct aspects. This paper is about that "alliance", although inevitably it cannot be discussed without recourse to a range of conceptualizations of the relationship.

Psychoanalytic formulations of the therapeutic alliance: transference or reality?

The concept of the therapeutic alliance may be traced back to Freud, who referred to the patient being a "collaborator" with the doctor (Freud, 1895d), argued that we must "[ally] ourselves with the ego of the patient under treatment" (1937c), and defined the "analytic situation" as a "pact . . . to give [the patient's] ego back its mastery over lost provinces of his mental life" (1940a). This pact, however, he saw as a form of positive transference and he never clearly distinguished the alliance as an independent concept.

As the idea of the therapeutic alliance has been increasingly delineated, so both its distinction from the transference and its importance relative to transference interpretation have become increasingly contentious. The term "therapeutic alliance" was introduced by Zetzel (1956), who distinguished between classical analysts and the British Object Relations school in their formulations of the transference. The former attended to the alliance, seeing it, following Freud, as a form of positive transference; while seeing it as less important than the analysis of transference, they regarded it as the prerequisite for such analysis. The Object Relations school, by contrast, in emphasizing "the crucial role of transference as an object relationship", were less interested in the concept of alliance (Zetzel, 1956). The Kleinian emphasis on unconscious phantasy and the "total situation" of the transference (Joseph, 1985) ensures that every communication between patient and therapist be seen as a manifestation of transference and countertransference.

Greenson (1967) similarly emphasized the rational component of the relationship in delineating the "working alliance" as "the relatively non-neurotic, rational rapport which the patient has with his analyst" and "the patient's capacity to work purposefully in the treatment situation". He went further, however, in coining the term "working alliance" to emphasize its purposive function and in clearly distinguishing three separate concepts: the transference, the working alliance and the "real relationship".

Greenson (*ibid.*) argued that transference reactions are "unrealistic and inappropriate, but . . . genuinely, truly felt"; the "real relationship" is "the realistic *and* genuine relationship"; the working alliance, by contrast, is "realistic and appropriate, but it is an artifact of the treatment situation" in that it involves the patient's ability and commitment to work. He conceptualized the alliance as a "relatively rational, desexualised, and de-aggressified transference phenomenon", which might at any time "contain elements of the infantile neurosis which will eventually require analysis". As he argued, "not only can the transference neurosis invade the working alliance, but the working alliance itself can be misused defensively to ward off the more regressive transference phenomena". The working alliance, then, might draw on either transferential or realistic elements of the relationship, which it would put to the use of furthering the work of the analysis.

Whether or not the alliance exists as an independent phenomenon, however, is not the only controversy surrounding it. Even some of those who admit its validity as a separate entity have argued that it may prove a distraction: the danger being "the tendency to see the therapeutic alliance as an end in itself—to provide a new and corrective object relationship—rather than a means to the end of analysing resistance and transference" (Curtis, 1979). The mutative properties of the relationship continue to be debated. The role of non-verbal empathy and attunement is seen as curative in self-psychological and independent approaches (Bateman & Holmes, 1995), while in Kleinian psychotherapy, the relative importance of insight and "the corrective object relationship" (Segal, 1973) as mutative factors is still unresolved (Nuttall, 2000).

The way to seeing the working alliance as a corrective emotional experience may have been paved by early definitions of it as a "new-object relationship" (Bibring, 1937). It seems to have been compounded, however, by the conflation of arguments for its existence at all and those advocating an accompanying modification of technique. There seems to have been some confusion between the concept of the alliance as a phenomenon and the question of what technical implications it may have. This distinction is implied by Hanley (1994), who, in revisiting Zetzel and Greenson, attributes to them the claim of "an indisputable therapeutic agency on behalf of non-interpretative communications aimed at creating and sustaining a therapeutic alliance" (Hanley, 1994).

This may account for the tendency in psychoanalytic clinical theory to see non-transferential aspects of the relationship, such as the alliance, as "inferior, or even dangerous" (Wynn Parry & Birkett, 1996). Meissner (2001), indeed, suggests that negative reactions to Greenson's and Zetzel's work are based on such an "oppositional view" of the alliance and transference, whereby attention to the former is supposed to interfere with the latter. Hanley (1994), however, argues that "the therapeutic alliance is a necessary, but not a sufficient, condition of therapeutic change, whereas interpretation is a sufficient condition" and that the alliance is best strengthened by interpretation rather than non-interpretive interventions. He thus implicitly accepts that there is a conceptual difference between the alliance and transference, while rejecting the idea that enhancing it demands a different technique. The alliance, he implies, is necessary, but its role is as a facilitator of the truly mutative elements of the relationship.

Perhaps because of the pervading sense of the alliance's dangerous inferiority to the transference, it had received relatively little attention in the psychoanalytic clinical literature by the time Wynn Parry and Birkett published their "re-appraisal" (1996). They point out the contrast between theory and clinical practice, in which the idea of the alliance has gained a wide purchase (see also Sandler, Dare, & Holder, 1992); as we shall see, the contrast between theory and empirical research in this regard is equally striking.

Even within psychoanalytic theory, then, there are a range of different concepts and definitions of the alliance. Whether it exists at all as a phenomenon distinct from the transference remains contentious, as does the question of whether it requires a modification of technique. Finally, whether or not it is curative in itself has been debated. Curtis's (and, implicitly, Hanley's) alignment of the working alliance concept with "corrective emotional experience" may be a fundamental misreading of Greenson (Wynn Parry & Birkett, 1996), who clearly described it as "[making] it possible for the patient to . . . integrate and assimilate the material of the analysis" (Greenson & Wexler, 1969). Nevertheless, this controversy gains in power when the impact of the empirical literature is taken into consideration.

Development of the therapeutic alliance in other therapies

In referring to positive transference as "the vehicle of success in psychoanalysis exactly as it is in other methods of treatment" (1912), Freud clearly conceived it as not exclusive to psychoanalysis. Although the alliance as a delineated concept may have begun with psychoanalysis, it does not end there. In other models of therapy, however, it inevitably finds different incarnations.

The three "core conditions" which Rogers (1951) proposed as being both essential and sufficient for therapeutic change—empathy, unconditional positive regard and congruence—are conceptually different from the therapeutic alliance, but there is a clear overlap to which empirical research has testified (Horvath & Luborsky, 1993; Salvio, Beutler, Wood, & Engel, 1992). In transactional analysis, by contrast, the therapeutic alliance is conceptualized as "a contract or agreement between the Adult of the psychotherapist and the Adult of the client" (Clarkson, 1990): what in psychoanalytic terms might be seen as a collaboration between the egos or non-neurotic parts of the therapeutic couple. This would bring it close to Greenson's working alliance, although without his inclusion of transference elements. Alternatively, Buber (1970) proposed an "I–You" or "real relationship", more reminiscent of the "real relationship" in Greenson's formulation.

Although these concepts owe much to each other, there are clear differences between them both in how they are conceived and in the theoretical contexts in which they operate. In particular, Wynn Parry and Birkett (1996) emphasize the contrast between the concepts of the alliance implied by other psychotherapies and the psychoanalytic one; the "exclusive use of communication between one conscious ego to another" of these therapies gives the alliance concept an entirely rational function, contrasting with that of the psychoanalytic concept, the function of which is "ultimately to work with unconscious material". By delineating this difference in terms of function, they not only emphasize the importance of the unconscious in psychoanalytic work but also point again to the controversy over cure.

Measuring the alliance: the empirical paradigm

In their comprehensive review of process-outcome research in psychotherapy, Orlinsky and colleagues (1994) identify what they call the "therapeutic bond" as the element of psychotherapy that has been most investigated empirically, in more than a thousand studies, and that commands the strongest evidence. This is in striking contrast with the relative dearth of clinical psychoanalytic theory on the subject (Wynn Parry & Birkett, 1996). The strongest evidence, they suggest, links a global assessment of the therapeutic bond with outcome, but particular aspects of the relationship have also been studied (Orlinksy, Grawe, & Parks, 1994). While the clinical theorists, then, have given the alliance relatively little emphasis and its proponents have largely defined it as facilitative rather than transformational, the empirical researchers have given it far greater emphasis, perhaps more than any other element of therapy, and increasingly demonstrated its associations with outcome.

The origin of this wealth of research seems to have been less the status of the alliance in clinical theory than the increasing evidence from early empirical research of the importance of the so-called "non-specific factors". Such research failed to detect significant outcome differences between different therapies, leading to the inference that "non-specific factors"—usually taken to mean relationship factors—were driving outcome (Luborsky, Singer, & Luborsky, 1975). This led to an examination of relationship factors *per se*. As Martin and colleagues suggest, "several [researchers] have begun to conceptualize the alliance as a common factor across therapeutic disciplines", while some have argued that "the quality of the alliance is more important than the type of treatment" (Martin, Garske, & Davis, 2000).

This interest in common factors in turn gave rise to "pantheoretical" models of the therapeutic alliance, such as Bordin's (1979), which emphasizes the client's "positive collaboration with the therapist against the common foe of pain and self-defeating behavior" (Horvath & Luborsky, 1993). He defines it in terms of three areas: goals, bonds and tasks and, like Greenson, defines the alliance as the ingredient that "makes it possible for the patient to accept and follow treatment faithfully", rather than as curative (Bordin, 1994).

The wealth of research on the "therapeutic bond" is reflected in the existence of a great many empirical measures. Horvath and colleagues (1993) noted the existence of at least eleven measures, grouped into five clusters: the California Psychotherapy Alliance Scales (CALPAS) (Marmar, Weiss, & Gaston, 1989); the Penn Helping Alliance Scales (Luborksy, Crits-Christoph, Alexander, Margolis, & Cohen, 1983); the Therapeutic Alliance Scale (TAS) (Marziali, 1984); the Vanderbilt Therapeutic Alliance Scales (VPPS) (Hartley & Strupp, 1983); and the Working Alliance Inventory (WAI) (Horvath & Greenberg, 1989). Most can be used as self-report by either party or as observer-rated measures. Each assesses a "global level" of the alliance but also measures components in subscales (Horvath, Gaston, & Luborsky, 1993). They have been used to measure therapeutic alliance in a range of psychotherapies and, more recently, with different client groups (Plakun, 2001). The association of the alliance with outcome is the studies' usual area of enquiry, and a variety of outcomes has been used, from drug use to social functioning to global improvement (Martin, Garske, & Davis, 2000).

Horvath and Symonds (1991), in their meta-analysis of 23 studies, found a "moderate but reliable" association of 26% between the alliance and outcome overall, and this was replicated in the updated meta-analysis of 79 studies performed by Martin and colleagues (2000) (22%). Martin and colleagues' meta-analysis found the WAI to be most often used (22 studies). Associations were most often tested against measures of global outcome (38 studies), rather than symptom scales (24) or termination of therapy status (13).

Horvath and Symonds found some evidence that ratings of the alliance early on in therapy are more powerful predictors of outcome and that clients' and observers' ratings of the alliance were more predictive of outcome than therapists' ratings. Neither finding, however, was replicated in the later meta-analysis (Martin, Garske, & Davis, 2000), which found no evidence that the alliance is influenced by type of outcome measure, type of outcome or alliance rater, time of assessment or type of treatment.

The strong evidence of an association between global measures of the alliance and outcome may have the side-effect of masking the distinction between different elements within it or obscuring the differences between different conceptualizations, on which individual studies are based. Indeed, Horvath and Symonds see the alliance as "a pantheoretic construct". Given the variation of conceptualizations of the therapeutic relationship, alliance or bond both between and within different schools of therapy, however, one might wonder what chance there is of any two research instruments measuring the same phenomenon.

Horvath and colleagues (1993) consider whether all these instruments are based on the same underlying construct. They find that the theoretical perspectives of the groups of instruments differ. The Penn scales take a psychoanalytic perspective and the VPPS a "dynamic/eclectic framework", while the TAS and CALPAS are influenced by both "traditional psychodynamic concepts of the alliance" and Bordin's pantheoretical model; the WAI is based on the latter. The instruments share two elements of the alliance, which Horvath and colleagues call "personal attachments or bonds" and "collaboration or willingness to invest in the therapy process" (not further defined), while different instruments also investigate further aspects, such as goals, capacity to form a relationship and active participation. After examining the covariance among the measures, they conclude that the data are difficult to interpret, with greater agreement between the scales as global measures and lower correlations between the sub-scales. Only the Penn scales and the WAI are theoretically homogeneous, indicated by higher correlations between sub-scales.

The findings of the meta-analyses, then, are clearly being driven by two factors in particular, affective bonds and collaboration. Both of these concepts go back to Greenson and, indeed, to Freud. The idea of an affective bond could incorporate the positive transference and both Zetzel's and Greenson's conceptualizations of the alliance, while collaboration is the element particularly emphasized in Greenson's term "working". These findings can provide no answers about controversies over distinctions between the real relationship, the alliance and the transference, and indeed this is not their brief. For one thing, all the instruments used necessarily start from a preconception of the alliance, and necessarily presuppose that it exists. It is the level of alliance (however operationalized) in different samples of patients, as well as its relationship to further factors, that is their area of enquiry.

The question that *is* relevant, however, is how therapists of different persuasions should interpret such findings. They certainly demonstrate that the alliance, as each group of instruments conceptualizes it, has been shown to be associated with clinical outcome. The question remains, however, whether the ubiquity of this finding, which encourages the alliance to be seen as a common factor, threatens to obscure differences between distinct concepts. Once studies using different instruments are pooled, the resultant emphasis on the alliance as a global or generic factor may encourage us to see it as pantheoretical, or even atheoretical. We need to be aware, nevertheless, of significant differences between and within the theories that will impact on the way in which any alliance research will be interpreted by therapists using different theoretical models. This matters particularly when the clinical and theoretical implications of the studies and meta-analyses are considered. It also has methodological implications for the choice of instruments for research studies, which are considered below.

To date, the empirical researchers have naturally been most concerned with what the component parts of the broad spectrum of the therapeutic alliance may be and how they relate to outcome, while theorists have been more concerned with what kind of a phenomenon the alliance is and how it relates to other psychological processes. This may suggest that differences between conceptualizations of the alliance have more meaning in clinical theory and practice than in empirical research, perhaps because they are too subtle to detect quantitatively. These complementary activities, however, have implications for each other: even though empirical research seems not to be able to answer questions about the contribution of the transference to the alliance, or at least has not done so yet, it may have other things to contribute to clinical theory. According to these analyses, for example, bonds and collaboration seem to stand out as separate components, not necessarily highly correlated: components that are not distinguished conceptually by writers such as Greenson.

The associations demonstrated between alliance and clinical and other outcomes, however, have been seen as having the greatest implications. These links with outcome encourage us to think of the alliance as curative in itself, despite the widespread rejection of this model in theory. This may be due to a misunderstanding of the nature of the research, however. The alternative explanation, that the alliance may be a facilitator of other factors (perhaps harder to measure), has not yet been ruled out. After all, the identification of the alliance as a statistical "predictor" of outcome simply denotes an *association*, with no demonstrable direction of cause and effect; moreover, the proportion of the variation in outcome associated with the alliance overall has been found to be a modest 22% (Martin, Garske, & Davis, 2000). Martin and colleagues argue that their meta-analysis supports the view that it is therapeutic in itself, but acknowledge that alternative explanations are equally valid, such as the alliance interacting with other interventions or affecting outcome indirectly.

The empirical paradigm and the history of the empirical research into the alliance may actually encourage interpretation of the research as demonstrating the curative properties of the alliance. It is interesting that Orlinsky and colleagues (1994) identify the inspiration for the mass of empirical alliance research as Rogers' therapeutic model with its three core conditions: and ironic, given that these core conditions are far from synonymous with the alliance. This apparent disregard for the concept's origins in psychoanalysis may point to the connection between Rogerian therapy and empirical research. This connection—traditionally stronger than between psychoanalysis and research—seems to have ignited an interest in empirical alliance or relationship research. If this is correct, then we are presented with a curative paradigm for the alliance from the outset. A model of therapy that sees the core conditions as curative and that gives rise to empirical evidence associating them with outcome (Barratt-Lennard, 1985; Rogers,

Gendlin, Kiesler, & Truax, 1967) thus gives rise to further research increasingly linking the alliance with outcome.

If the empirical research, then, has been driven by an overtly curative theoretical model of the therapeutic relationship (the Rogerian one), or at least an implicitly curative model of research (the empirical model itself), then that may have influenced the interpretation of its findings. To enable interpretation of these findings in a meaningful way, however, empirical research would still need to tease out the mediating factors between alliance and outcome, which might include transference interpretation, transference *per se*, or the impact of the real relationship—phenomena whose distinction from the alliance is a vexed theoretical question.

Implications

We began this enquiry with two related questions. The first concerned the translation of concepts from one idiom into another, whether from clinical theory to quantitative research tools or from psychoanalysis to other therapies, raising the question: are we sure what we are measuring here, and are its ramifications the same in the new context? The evidence seems to suggest that the meaningful clinical and theoretical distinctions between different concepts are not fully reflected in the empirical literature, perhaps because quantitative research tools are too blunt to detect them, or because the global associations between tools based on different concepts blur the distinctions between them.

The methodological implications of this question are also far from straightforward. What might the implications be of using a particular instrument if its underlying construct is not congruent in nature and scope with those informing the studied model? While too close a degree of equivalence might lead to somewhat tautological research, there would seem to be a clear case for theory-congruent, or at last theory-compatible, research. While this might seem self-evident, the ubiquity of the association between alliance ratings and outcome and the high degree of association between the global scores of different alliance measures may encourage us to ignore this necessity, leaving the implications for the interpretation of findings difficult to establish.

The second question posed by the interplay of clinical theory and empirical research on the alliance concerns the implications of the empirical evidence linking it with outcome. While this evidence seems to be based on an at least implicitly curative paradigm, it has not yet answered the question of whether the alliance facilitates other factors or is curative in itself. The empirical research clearly has important clinical and theoretical implications, however: implications which we are in danger of avoiding or foreclosing if we either assume a curative model of the alliance or, conversely, ignore the empirical research and insist on a purely facilitative one.

Acknowledgements

This chapter is taken from a longer paper, " 'The vehicle of success': theoretical and empirical perspectives on the therapeutic alliance in psychotherapy and psychiatry", reproduced with kind permission from *Psychology and Psychotherapy: Theory, Research and Practice* (2004, 77, 255–272) © The British Psychological Society.

Thanks are also due to Tom Burns and Cathy Jacobs for helpful comments.

References

Barratt-Lennard, G. T. (1985). The helping relationship: crisis and advance in theory and research. *The Counselling Psychologist, 13*: 278–294.

Bateman, A., & Holmes, J. (1995). *Introduction to Psychoanalysis: Contemporary Theory and Practice*. London: Routledge.

Bibring, E. (1937). On the theory of the results of psychoanalysis. *International Journal of Psycho-Analysis, 18*: 170–189.

Bordin, E. S. (1979). The generalizability of the psychoanalytic concept of the working alliance. *Psychotherapy: Theory, Research, and Practice, 16*: 252–260.

Bordin, E. (1994). Theory and research on the therapeutic working alliance: new directions. In: A. Horvath & L. S. Greenberg (Eds.), *The Working Alliance: theory, research, and practice*. New York & Chichester: Wiley.

Buber, M. (1970). *I and Thou* (W. Kauffman, Trans.). Edinburgh: T. & T. Clark.

Clarkson, P. (1990). A multiplicity of therapeutic relationships. *British Journal of Psychotherapy, 7*(2): 148–163.

Curtis, H. C. (1979). The concept of therapeutic alliance: implications for the "widening scope". *Journal of the American Psychoanalytic Association, 27* (Suppl.): 159–192.

Freud, S. (1895d). Studies on hysteria. *S.E., 2*. London: Hogarth.

Freud, S. (1912b). The dynamics of transference. *S.E., 12*. London: Hogarth.

Freud, S. (1937c). Analysis terminable and interminable. *S.E., 23*. London: Hogarth.

Freud, S. (1940a). An outline of psycho-analysis. *S.E., 23*. London: Hogarth.

Greenson, R. (1967). *The Technique and Practice of Psychoanalysis*. London: Hogarth.

Greenson, R., & Wexler, M. (1969). The non-transference relationship in the psychoanalytic situation. *International Journal of Psycho-Analysis, 50*: 27–39.

Hanley, C. (1994). Reflections on the place of the therapeutic alliance in psychoanalysis. *International Journal of Psycho-Analysis, 75*: 457–467.

Hartley, D. E., & Strupp, H. H. (1983). The therapeutic alliance: its relationship to outcome in brief psychotherapy. In: J. Masling (Ed.), *Empirical Studies in Analytic Theories*. Hillsdale, N.J: Erlbaum.

Horvath, A., & Greenberg, L. S. (1989). Development and validation of the working alliance inventory. *Journal of Counseling Psychology, 36*(2): 223–233.

Horvath, A. O., & Luborsky, L. (1993). The role of the therapeutic alliance in psychotherapy. *Journal of Consulting and Clinical Psychology, 61*(4): 561–573.

Horvath, A. O., & Symonds, B. D. (1991). Relation between working alliance and outcome in psychotherapy: a meta-analysis. *Journal of Counseling Psychology, 38*(2): 139–149.

Horvath, A., Gaston, L., & Luborsky, L. (1993). The therapeutic alliance and its measures. In: N. E. Miller, L. Luborsky, J. P. Barber, & J. P. Docherty (Eds.), *Psychoanalytic Treatment Research: A Handbook for Clinical Practice* (pp. 247–73). New York: Basic Books.

Joseph, B. (1985). Transference: the total situation. *International Journal of Psycho-Analysis, 66*: 447–454.

Luborsky, L., Singer, B., & Luborksy, L. (1975). Comparative studies of psychotherapies: is it true that "everyone has won and all must have prizes"? *Archives of General Psychiatry, 32*: 995–1008.

Luborsky, L., Crits-Christoph, P., Alexander, L., Margolis, M., & Cohen, M. (1983). Two helping alliance methods for predicting outcomes of psychotherapy: a counting signs vs. a global rating method. *Journal of Nervous and Mental Disease*, 171: 480–491.

Marmar, C., Weiss, D. S., & Gaston, L. (1989). Toward the validation of the California Therapeutic Alliance Rating System. Psychological assessment: A. *Journal of Consulting and Clinical Psychology*, 1: 46–52.

Martin, D. J., Garske, J. P., & Davis, M. K. (2000). Relation of the therapeutic alliance with outcome and other variables: a meta-analytic review. *Journal of Consulting and Clinical Psychology*, 68(3): 438–450.

Marziali, E. (1984). Three viewpoints on the therapeutic alliance scales: similarities, differences and associations with psychotherapy outcome. *Journal of Nervous and Mental Disease*, 172: 417–423.

Meissner, W. W. (2001). A note on transference and alliance: II. Patterns of interaction. *Bulletin of the Menninger Clinic*, 65(2): 219–245.

Nuttall, J. (2000). Modes of therapeutic relationship in Kleinian psychotherapy. *British Journal of Psychotherapy*, 17(1): 17–36.

Orlinsky, D. E., Grawe, K., & Parks, B. K. (1994). Process and outcome in psychotherapy—noch einmal. In: A. E. Bergin & S. L. Garfield (Eds.), *Handbook of Psychotherapy and Behavior Change* (4th edn) (pp. 270–376). New York: Wiley.

Plakun, E. M. (2001). Making the alliance and taking the transference in work with suicidal patients. *Journal of Psychotherapy Practice and Research*, 10(4): 269–276.

Rogers, C. (1951). *Client-Centered Therapy: Its Current Practice, Implications and Theory*. London: Constable.

Rogers, C. R., Gendlin, G. T., Kiesler, D. V., & Truax, L. B. (1967). *The Therapeutic Relationship and its Impact: A Study of Psychotherapy with Schizophrenics*. Madison, WI: University of Wisconsin Press.

Salvio, M. A., Beutler, L. E., Wood, J. M., & Engle, D. (1992). The strength of the therapeutic alliance in three treatments for depression. *Psychotherapy Research*, 2, 31–36.

Sandler, J., Dare, C., & Holder, A. (1992). *The Patient and the Analyst* (2nd edn). London: Karnac.

Segal, H. (1973). *Introduction to the Work of Melanie Klein*. Reprinted London: Karnac, 1988.

Wynn Parry, C., & Birkett, D. (1996). The working alliance: a reappraisal. *British Journal of Psychotherapy*, 12(3): 291–299.

Zetzel, E. (1956). Current concepts of the transference. *International Journal of Psycho-Analysis*, 39, 369–376.

PART IV

RESEARCHING THERAPEUTIC OUTCOMES

CHAPTER EIGHTEEN

Outcome measurement

Richard Evans

The therapist as researcher

Most therapists in ordinary day-to-day clinical practice already routinely build up narrative case notes and supervision discussion notes about each client. And most therapists fairly frequently use those notes to ask themselves pertinent questions.

This process of reflecting on practice (sometimes referred to as "reflective research") was first recognized by Donald Schon (1983) as playing a crucial role in individual professional development (see also Argyris & Schon, 1992; Ghave & Ghave, 1998) in all professional fields. Therapists are possibly better versed in this process of reflective research than professionals in many other fields because of the nature of their training.

Unfortunately this form of reflective research is often overlooked in discussions concerning "research" in the psychological therapies field, which focus instead on formal psychological therapy research studies carried out by full-time, academic researchers. Reflective research is different in a number of important ways to the research carried out by academic researchers but it is complementary to it and of equal importance.

This chapter describes how the therapist engaged in reflective research can add quantitative outcome measurement data to the qualitative narrative notes that they already collect—and the ways in which this can enhance their reflective research.

Academic research on outcomes

In the academic world a high proportion of psychotherapy research studies carried out over the last few decades has involved the measurement of the outcome of therapy in quantitative terms.

Most of these studies (of which there have been some thousands) have taken the form of a randomized control trial (RCT) where the outcomes of treatment with a trial group of patients are compared with the outcomes for a matched, randomly assigned, control group of patients who have received no treatment. Many studies have been aimed at comparing two (or more) different kinds of treatment and so have involved setting up two or more trial groups of patients (alongside the control group) who receive different forms of treatment.

These studies have added a great deal to our understanding of the effectiveness of therapy and have underpinned the development of treatment guidelines such as those set out in DoH, 2001. The development of treatment guidelines is discussed in Cape & Parry, 2001; Parry, 2000; Parry, Cape, & Pilling, 2003; Roth & Fonagy, 1996 and elsewhere.

Bringing quantitative outcome measurement into clinical practice

A by-product of this academic research activity has been a great deal of development in the actual methods for measuring outcome. In the last few years these have matured to the point where they can now be used easily by therapists on a day-to-day basis. As a result, any therapist in clinical practice can now gather quantitative data on the outcomes of therapy with most of their patients on a routine basis.

Quantitative data gathered in this way, when added to the narrative notes already routinely collected by the therapist, makes it much easier for the individual therapist to obtain more definitive answers to questions about their own practice and thus better able to engage in reflective research. (For a wider discussion of outcome measurement in routine clinical practice see Cone, 2001.)

CORE

This chapter describes one system for measuring outcomes—the CORE system—and how it is currently used by therapists on a day-to-day basis. There are many other outcome measures that might be used, but CORE has become the most widely used in the UK with around 200 services and some thousands of therapists making routine use of it.

The design, development and results from the use of CORE are described at length in Barkham *et al.*, 1998, 2001; Evans, Mellor-Clark, & Margison, 2000; Evans *et al.*, 2002; Evans, Connell, Barkham, Marshall, & Mellor-Clark, 2003; Mellor-Clark, 2000a,b, 2002, 2003; Mellor-Clark, Barkham, & Connell, 1999; Mellor-Clark, Connell, & Barkham, 2001.

Measuring outcome

Prior to the first therapy session the client is asked to complete a questionnaire which asks them thirty-four questions about how they have been feeling and how their life has been going over the last week or so. Each question is then scored on a 0–4 scale and added to produce a total score. This can be compared with a "clinical cut-off" score to provide a measure of the client's level of distress. The clinical cut-off has been established by asking a large sample of people to complete the questionnaire. People in the ordinary population normally score below the clinical cut-off and those who are seeking help are usually above it.

Following the last session, the questionnaire is repeated. The comparison of the pre- and post-treatment scores provides a measure of "outcome"—that is, whether or not the client's level of distress has changed and by how much. Reassuringly, the data for some tens of thousands of clients shows that a high proportion of clients achieve clinical change (their level of distress moving from above clinical cut-off to below) and a substantial additional proportion achieve at least a statistically reliable level of improvement.

Contextual data

To increase the usefulness of the client outcome date most CORE users make use of a software programme (CORE-PC) to allow them to record a range of other contextual data about each client such as their age, gender, employment, and living status, number of sessions, how therapy was ended, the therapist's assessment of their problems, etc.

These data, along with the client's answers to the questionnaire, are stored in a database together with that for all clients. The software provides easy to use analysis, display and reporting facilities, which allows the therapist or service manager to explore a wide range of questions: how outcomes vary by age or type of problem; which kinds of patients are most likely to fail to attend sessions; what factors lead to unplanned ending of therapy; and so on. "Benchmark" data are published that allows the user to compare their own results with those obtained nationally.

Needless to say, one of the objectives in asking these sorts of questions is for the therapist to ascertain how much they themselves might be contributing to a particular outcome.

General acceptability

The CORE Outcome Measure questionnaire was designed and tested in conjunction with a wide cross-section of therapists drawn from different theoretical schools in order to ensure that it was acceptable to the majority of therapists. Thus, it can be best described as "pan-theoretical": to the extent that the questions reflect any theory of mental distress (or of therapy) they reflect an underlying theory common to virtually all schools that accept that the level of a patient's distress can be measured in terms of their well-being, symptoms, or problems, functioning and degree to which they are "at risk".

One consequence of the pan-theoretical design is that while the Outcome Measure provides an overall assessment of the patient's level of distress, it is not intended to provide any diagnosis of a specific disorder.

Risk assessment

Of particular importance when the therapist is working within the NHS, the patient's answers to a number of "risk" questions in the questionnaire provide an assessment of risk independent of the therapist's own assessment of risk. This can sometimes provide the therapist with an additional alarm signal alerting him or her to review risk for a particular patient.

The limits of CORE

The CORE Outcome Measure has been the subject of extensive research (e.g., Evans *et al.*, 2002) that has established that, for the majority of clients, it provides a useful and reliable indication of the level of distress, and that it is sensitive to change. But it is important to emphasize that, for a minority of clients, their CORE score may not always provide a fully inclusive indication of their level of distress. The complexities and variety of mental distress are too great to be captured by any single measure; therefore, this should be seen not just as something peculiar to CORE, but as a problem common to all outcome measures in the psychotherapy field.

Where the therapist's own assessment of the patient's level of distress differs markedly from that indicated by the CORE score the therapist will use their own clinical experience and judgement to decide what weight to give to the CORE score.

The future

A number of research studies over the past few years (Brown, Burlinghame, Lambert, Jones, & Vaccaro, 2001; Lambert *et al.*, 2001; Lueger *et al.*, 2001; Lutz, 2002) have asked the client to complete an

outcome measure at every session and then encouraged the therapist to use the score as a means of measuring progress over the
sessions. The results show encouraging improvements in outcome
amongst those 20% or so of clients for whom significant benefits
from therapy may not otherwise have been expected. It is anticipated that this way of using an outcome measure may well become
common in the future, and to this end shortened versions of the
CORE questionnaire have been designed, and CORE-PC software
upgraded.

Further information

Further information about CORE can be found at
www.coreims.co.uk or from CORE Information Management Systems Ltd, 47 Windsor Street, Rugby CV21 3NZ. Tel: 01788–546019.
E-mail: john@coreims.co.uk

References

Argyris, C., & Schon, D. (1992). *Theory in Practice: Increasing Professional
Effectiveness*. San Francisco, CA: Jossey Bass.
Barkham, M., Evans, C., Margison, F., McGrath, G., Mellor-Clark, J.,
Milne, D., & Connell, J. (1998). The rationale for developing and
implementing core outcome batteries for routine use in service
settings and psychotherapy outcome research. *Journal of Mental
Health, 7*: 35–47.
Barkham, M., Margison, F., Leach, C., Lucock, M., Mellor-Clark, J.,
Evans, C., Benson, L., Connell, J., Audin, K., & McGrath, G. (2001).
Service profiling and outcomes benchmarking using CORE-OM:
Toward practice-based evidence in psychological therapies. *Journal
of Consulting and Clinical Psychology, 69*: 184–196.
Brown, G. S., Burlinghame, G. M., Lambert, M. J., Jones, E., & Vaccaro,
J. (2001). Pushing the quality envelope: a new outcomes manage-
ment system. *Psychiatric Services, 52*: 924–934.
Cape, J., & Parry, G. D. (2001). Clinical practice guidelines development
in evidence-based psychotherapy. In: N. Rowland & S. Goss (Eds.),
Evidence-based Mental Health. London: Routledge.

Cone, J. (2001). *Evaluating Outcomes: Empirical Tools for Effective Practice.* Washington, DC: American Psychological Association.

Department of Health (2001). *Treatment Choice in Psychological Therapies and Counselling: Evidence Based Clinical Practice Guidelines.* London: DOH.

Evans, C., Mellor-Clark, J., & Margison, F. (2000) CORE: Clinical Outcomes in Routine Evaluation. *Journal of Mental Health, 9*: 247–255.

Evans, C., Connell, J., Barkham, M., Margison, F., McGrath, G., Mellor-Clark, J., & Audin, K. (2002). Towards a standardised brief outcome measure: Psychometric properties and utility of the CORE—OM. *British Journal of Psychiatry, 180*: 51–60.

Evans, C., Connell, J., Barkham, M., Marshall, C., & Mellor-Clark, J. (2003). Practice-based evidence: benchmarking NHS primary care counselling services at national and local levels. *Journal of Clinical Psychology and Psychotherapy, 10*: 374–388.

Ghave, A., & Ghave, K. (1998). *Teaching and Learning Through Critical Reflective Practice.* London: David Fulton Publishers.

Lambert, M. J., Whipple, J. L., Smart, D., Vermeersch, D. A., Nielsen, S. L., & Hawkins, E. (2001). The effects of providing therapists with feedback on patient progress during psychotherapy. Are outcomes enhanced? *Psychotherapy Research, 11*: 49–68.

Lueger, R. J., Howard, K. I., Martinovich, Z., Lutz, W., Anderson, E., & Grissom, G. (2001). Assessing treatment progress with individualized models of predicted response. *Joumal of Consulting and Clinical Psychology, 69*: 150–158.

Lutz, W. (2002). Patient-focused psychotherapy research and individual treatment progress as scientific groundwork for an empirically based practice. *Psychotherapy Research, 12*: 251–272.

Mellor-Clark, J. (2000a). Developing practice and evidence for counselling in primary care; the agenda. *British Journal of Guidance and Counselling, 28*(2): 253–266.

Mellor-Clark, J. (2000b). Evidence-based counselling in primary care. In: P. Tovey (Ed.), *Contemporary Primary Care & Change: Issues and Themes.* Buckingham: Open University Press.

Mellor-Clark, J. (2002). A CORE profile of counselling in primary care. *Psychiatry, 1*(4): 39–43.

Mellor-Clark, J. (2003). National innovations in the evaluation of psychological therapy service provision. *The Journal of Primary Care Mental Health and Education, 7*(3): 82–85.

Mellor-Clark, J., Barkham, M., & Connell, J. (1999). Practice-based evidence and a standardised evaluation system: informing the design of the CORE system. *European Journal of Psychotherapy, Counselling and Health*, 3: 357–374.

Mellor-Clark, J., Connell, J., & Barkham, M. (2001). Counselling outcomes in primary health care: a CORE system data profile. *European Journal of Psychotherapy, Counselling and Health*, 4: 65–86.

Parry, G. (2000). Developing treatment choice guidelines in psychotherapy. *Journal of Mental Health*, 9: 273–281.

Parry, G. D., Cape, J., & Pilling, S. (2003). Clinical practice guidelines in clinical psychology and psychotherapy. *Journal of Clinical Psychology and Psychotherapy*, 10: 337–351.

Roth, A., & Fonagy, P. (1996). *What Works for Whom: A Critical Review of Psychotherapy Research.* New York: Guilford.

Schon, D. A. (1983). *The Reflective Practitioner: How Professionals Think in Action*. New York: Basic Books.

CHAPTER NINETEEN

Psychotherapy research: the need for an aetiological framework

Tirril Harris

P sychotherapy research has often been crudely subdivided into the categories of *process* research and *outcome* research. The former focuses on what goes on in the therapy sessions, the latter on selected changes occurring since the start of the therapy. Such changes usually involve the mental state of the person attending the sessions (henceforth "client') using well-validated measures of symptoms such as the Beck Depression Inventory (Beck, Ward, & Mendelson, 1961) or the Spielberger State–Trait Anxiety Inventory (Spielberger, Goruch, Luchese, Vagg, & Jacobs, 1983) well-known in the world of psychiatry. A recent instrument, the CORE, has made such an approach more acceptable to non-psychiatric psychotherapists (Evans *et al.*, 2002). Others have chosen to target changes in the client's relationships, with the IIP instrument (Inventory of Interpersonal Problems—Horowitz, Rosenberg, Baer, Ureno, & Villesenor, 1988) the favourite among psychodynamic therapists, although some have developed their own instruments of interpersonal relating (Benjamin,1987; Birtchnell, 1999); while those with a perspective informed by Attachment Theory use measures of attachment style (Bifulco, Moran, Ball, & Bernazzani, 2002; George, Kaplan, & Main, 1985). Studies best approximating an assessment as to whether psychotherapy is really helping people to feel better investigate both process and outcome. However, a really thorough assessment must do more than look at process and outcome. It has to control for the role of other key factors; that is, the possibility that the outcome changes are not due to the therapy but to some other crucial determinants. For this it is necessary to have a theoretical model that can explain the client's initial mental state before entering therapy. The factors identified as explaining this need to be monitored during the course of the therapy in case it is they, rather than the experience of the sessions, that have improved the client's well-being; in case, for example, the depression that has been with a young man since he was made redundant has lifted because at last he has found work, not because he has had eight therapy sessions. In this chapter I use examples from studies of depression to expand this argument about the need for such a framework, wider than mere process and outcome, if the effectiveness of psychotherapy is ever to be properly assessed.

The aetiological framework: one example

Preliminary remarks

It may be helpful to set the scene by making two preliminary points to minimize misconceptions arising from academic "labels". First, the model of depression has evolved during a thirty-year period of data collection by George Brown's "medical sociology" research team, but it spans a wide range of social science disciplines. Brown himself, initially an anthropologist, later at the Institute of Psychiatry, would be better located in developmental psychology. Today the work is labelled "social psychiatry". Second, the methodology employed really bridges the gap between "quantitative" and "qualitative": Brown has sought to measure the meaning of people's experiences and, thus, he takes into account not just how they say they feel but also the context in which they say it, particularly their social roles, plans, and commitments; not just what they say about their attitudes but also what they tell us about their behaviour. Interviewers use semi-structured questionnaires with additional probing questions. The structured stem questions ensure all relevant scales are covered, but the flexible interviewing style allows respondents to answer at as much length as they choose, and the extra probes can encourage a narrative if a respondent is hesitant or monosyllabic. Interviews are not transcribed *as a whole* but rating schedules are designed so that there is space to record the subjects' detailed remarks beside the relevant rating scale. Thus, when deciding, say, how stressful a life event has been, the rater writes down a long description of that event and its consequences beside the digit he/she is allotting on the rating scale of "severity". Raters are encouraged to report new insights arising from the qualitative narratives. As new respondents report new aspects of stress, the research team may be instructed to rate a new scale (for example, not only the severity of stressfulness, but also its nature—humiliation, loss, danger, guilt-induction, to name a few). Thus, a project undertaken in the 1980s confirmed in a quantitative analysis the result of one from the 1970s that emotional support from an intimate confidante was protective against depressive onset. But it also opened the way for more refined *quantitative* work in the 1990s, because the 1980s respondents' detailed *qualitative* remarks about how people succeeded or failed to support them, led to the development of extra rating scales about the reasons for unsupportive behaviour, providing quantitative tests of differential impacts on depression (Harris, 1992). Thus, among unsupportive behaviours, criticism for being a "fusspot" was distinguished from criticism for having brought the stress upon themselves, contrasted with the lack of empathy by a thick-skinned but not *critical* Other, which was again different from someone failing to be totally on their side because of loyalty to a third party (the classic spouse vs mother-in-law situation).

The ability to move from qualitative to quantitative and back again is a true example of the value of grounded theory (Glaser & Strauss, 1967). It can occur not only between successive samples in the way described, but also within one project during the course of data collection, developing new scales for the last 85% on the basis of responses by the first 15%, subjecting these new scales to tests of inter-rater reliability and construct validity.

The aetiological model of depressive onset

Initial projects followed a stress–diathesis model: disorder results from a combination of provoking and vulnerability factors.

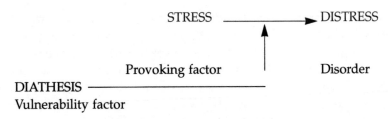

At first most attention was paid to the measurement of the *meaning* of stress, taking into account not only the contextual features of current roles, plans, and commitments, but also both evolutionarily-derived meaning (for example, special purpose appraisal systems responding to natural cues—see Bowlby 1988) and meaning arising from personal memory-linked schemata (for example, a parent facing a current crisis of school refusal by their child against a background of the bullying they themselves experienced aged eleven). Thus, some "discovering pregnancy" events could be experienced as positive (i.e., non-severe), for example, a planned third pregnancy to a comfortably-off solicitor's wife with a four-bedroom house and garden and a kind, supportive husband; some as mildly negative (i.e., still not severe)—an unplanned third pregnancy to a woman in similar circumstances who was hoping to go back to full-time work when the older two children were both in school but will now have to continue part-time for several more years, though freely choosing not to terminate the pregnancy; some as moderately negative (severe)—an unplanned third pregnancy to a separated woman on a low income living with her two other children under five in two rooms, whose religion forbids ending the pregnancy—and some markedly severe—a woman in similar circumstances to the last who, in addition, has suffered many hospital admissions during previous pregnancies.

Particular attention was paid to the dating both of events and of the onset of depressive symptoms in order to obtain a true picture of the time order, since anything postdating onset could not be of aetiological relevance. "Severe" events were identified as "provoking" depression through statistical comparison of depressed and non-depressed respondents (Brown & Harris, 1978). However, as mentioned above, qualitative work later pinpointed events involving actual loss as particularly depressogenic compared to other severe events involving future danger. Further qualitative distinction targeted humiliating/entrapping events as the most potent provoking experiences (Brown, Harris, & Hepworth, 1995).

Exploration of the diathesis identified four vulnerability factors. Two involved roles: lack of employment outside the home and presence of three or more children under fifteen rendered women more likely to respond to a provoking agent with depression. Two involved close relationships: lack of an intimate confiding relationship with someone at home (usually a partner), and childhood loss of mother through death or long-term separation. In speculating on how these might potentiate the effects of the stressors, we drew on Beck's (1967) influential cognitive perspective highlighting a triad of attitudes characterizing the symptoms of depression—the world appears pointless, the self worthless, and the future hopeless. Brown and Harris speculated that

(i)   the essence of vulnerability to depression might be an attitude resonating with this triad—a tendency to *generalise* the specific feelings of hopelessness likely to follow for anyone experiencing one of these losses;

(ii)   such a generalizing tendency was part of a wider low self-esteem and low mastery, which would link with the four vulnerability factors as in the diagram below;

(iii) social support tended to promote mastery, the support figure's sympathy reflecting an image of someone deserving of concern, thus raising self-esteem;

(iv)   following attachment theory (Bowlby, 1988) early loss of mother would mean the loss of such a supportive figure just when the foundations of the self-image were being laid and the subsequent mother-surrogate might not always be able to help the child compensate for this;

(v)   The concept of "role-identity" (McCall & Simmons, 1966) explained the other two vulnerability factors: women with a number of such role identities would be better able to resist the tendency to *generalize hopelessness* because of their wider range of alternative sources of self-validation. Thus, while most women were wives and mothers, those who also had identities involving work, friendship, neighbourhood or leisure activities would be better buffered against a loss in the domestic arena. The presence of three or more children requiring baby-sitting would be likely to prove a greater handicap to acquiring such alternative role identities than a smaller family. As one childless woman noted, "It was lucky I had just started that job in reception when my husband left me. They were all so complimentary to me there that it boosted my self-esteem [*sic*] and got me through".

The diagram below conveys this preliminary summary of the findings on stress and diathesis, with the capital letters conveying the verified links between factors we had actually measured and the lower case the variables we speculated were mediating these links.

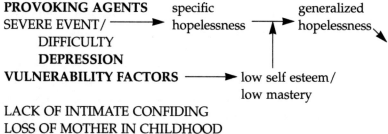

PROVOKING AGENTS   specific   generalized
SEVERE EVENT/ ⟶ hopelessness ⟶ hopelessness
     DIFFICULTY
     DEPRESSION
VULNERABILITY FACTORS ⟶ low self esteem/
                                          low mastery

LACK OF INTIMATE CONFIDING
LOSS OF MOTHER IN CHILDHOOD
THREE OR MORE CHILDREN UNDER 14
LACK OF OUTSIDE EMPLOYMENT

Subsequent work with a new longitudinal population sample with a new measure of negative evaluation of self (NES) turned some of the lower case into upper case, though it was not possible to monitor the follow-up period so closely as to be actually present when *generalization* of hopelessness took place. But women with NES at baseline interview and a provoking event during twelve-month follow-up were nearly three times more likely to have an onset of major depression than those with similar stress but no NES (Brown, Andrews, Harris, Adler, & Bridge, 1986). This study also measured coping style (Bifulco & Brown, 1996), rating not only proactive practical coping responses to stress, but also cognitive and emotional responses corresponding quite closely to some of the psychoanalytic defence mechanisms such as denial (Freud, A., 1936; Vaillant, 1976). Self-blame or denial increased the likelihood of depressive onset.

Another project pursued the manner in which early loss of mother might be contributing to adult depression. It became clear that it was the quality of the surrogate parental care rather than the loss *per se* which predisposed to depression in adulthood (Harris, Brown, & Bifulco, 1990). Even in samples where there was little loss of mother experiences of severe neglect or abuse in childhood later turned out to be related to current negative self evaluation and to predict depression in adult life (Bifulco, Brown, & Harris, 1994). This work identified two causal strands, one external/sociological like a conveyor belt from childhood severe life events to severe stressors in adulthood, often involving being trapped in the working class. The other strand was more internal/psychological, involving a similar link between childhood and adulthood, from lack of adequate parental care to negative evaluation of self and helplessness (Harris, Brown, & Bilfulco, 1990). Later work focusing in more detail on this link acknowledged the power of the psychoanalytic developmental model as extended by Bowlby, providing quantitative confirmation of associations between the supportiveness of a person's social network and their having a secure "attachment style" (Bifulco, Moran, Ball, & Bernazzani, 2002). There was something reassuring that starting from slightly different places the social psychiatry research had ended with a model so closely corresponding to a psychoanalytic developmental model (Bowlby, 1988, Chapter Nine).

Figure 1, an elaboration of the earlier stress/diathesis diagram, is an attempt to summarize this psychosocial model diagrammatically in terms of a framework familiar in psychotherapy parlance, that of inner and outer worlds. The key factors that stand out as needing consideration in any investigation of the impact of psychotherapy on outcome of depression must therefore be stressors, poor network emotional support, self evaluation, coping, and attachment styles.

Extending the model to incorporate remission/improvement from depression

The next step in thinking about the impact of any therapy for depression must be to extend the model by investigating the course of the disorder after onset. As much care must be taken to use valid and reliable ways of dating remission (a short-hand term covering either offset or improvement) as were followed in measuring onset.

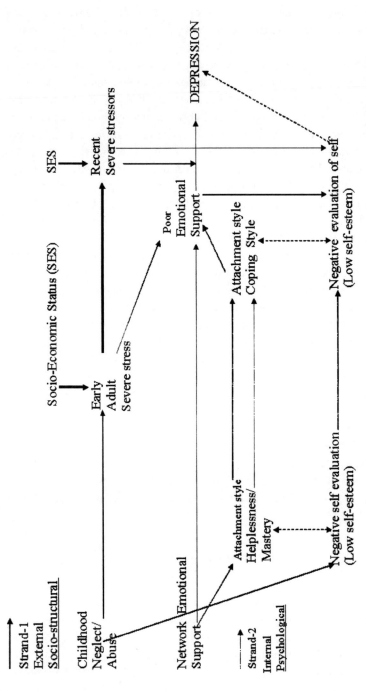

Figure 1. Key psychosocial factors in the aetiology of depression: a life-span model. Dotted lines represent impact of inner world (strand 2) on outer world (strand 1) and inner world. Continuous lines represent impact of outer world (strand 1) on inner world (strand 2).

The context of remission emerged as the mirror-image of that surrounding onset. For episodes lasting twenty weeks or more, remissions were more often than not preceded by reduction of the severity of a severe difficulty or by a fresh start event. The latter were defined not as *any* markedly positive event but as those which bring new hope, promising to end an ongoing state of deprivation (Brown, Adler, & Bifulco, 1988). Thus, marriage to a loved boyfriend by someone who had experienced a relatively trouble-free court-ship, or an examination distinction for someone who has always done well, would not be considered fresh starts, whereas becoming engaged after years of single parenthood, or starting full-time higher education after years in a poorly-paid job, would qualify.

Investigating the effectiveness of therapeutic interventions in the light of the model

As a final, more experimental, test of the model the team mounted a randomized controlled trial of an intervention for depression. Unfortunately, practical difficulties prevented the research team choosing psychotherapy as this intervention. Instead, volunteer befriending (for at least one hour at least once weekly) was selected on the grounds that it might provide an equivalent of the good emotional support identified as therapeutic in the causal model. Raising the funds themselves to finance social workers who would train volunteer befrienders and offer them backup support, Harris and Brown selected women who had been seriously depressed for at least twelve months and randomly allocated them to befriended or waiting-list-control status. They were followed up one year after being matched with the befriender (intervention group) or after first interview (control group).

There were six critical questions, among others less crucial, to ask of this dataset.

1. *Was there a positive impact of befriending upon depressive outcome?* The answer was yes. The percentage with remission among those forty-three allocated befriending in the first year was statistically significantly higher than among the forty-three in the first year control group.

2. *Were there other factors which also had an impact upon depressive outcome?* Again the answer was yes (see Table 1).

Table 1.   Percentage of women with remission from chronic depression by score on an index of (i) fresh start experience in follow-up; (ii) standard attachment style at baseline; (iii) absence of very poor coping at baseline; and (iv) allocation of befriending.

Index score	Percentage remission
All four factors present	100 (7/7)
Three factors present	83 (25/30)
Two factors present	47 (20/43)
One factor present	20 (7/35)
Nil	17 (1/6)
Total in sample	50 (60/121)

(N=121, including second-year befriendees who were first year controls)

3.   *After controlling for these other factors, does the association between befriending and depressive remission disappear?* That is, do any of these other factors explain away the simple link between befriending and remission? Fresh start experiences again featured as of key importance for remission, as did the absence of any new severe event during follow up. In addition secure attachment style and an absence of very poor coping were also predictors. In multivariate analyses including all four factors, befriending did not drop out of the best model, but was also required to model remission (Harris, Brown, & Robinson, 1999). In other words, the effect of befriending could not be explained away by the fact that, say, more of those receiving it had a standard attachment style.

4.   *Did any of these other factors act as mediators between befriending and remission? Did befriending have its positive impact by helping to bring about changes in the other key items?* This question can-not really apply to coping and attachment styles since those predictors were measured at baseline before the depressed women were matched with the befrienders. It could apply, however, to stressors occurring after the start of befriending: one of the pre-liminary hypotheses of the research team had been that the befrienders would help to bring about more fresh starts for their group of women than would occur in the control group. And indeed, one of the types of fresh start event that stood out in the qualitative descriptive records of these women was what we call

"fresh-start-reconcilations". In the extensive material collected about the relationship with the befriender it was often possible to discern evidence that their discussions together had encouraged the depressed woman to risk an attempt at reconciliation that at first interview she had described as "too risky". For example, one made up with her mother, whom she had not seen since her teenage pregnancy out of wedlock many years earlier, and another contacted a previous friend whose drift away had coincided with her failing to repay a loan to the befriendee. Thus, these reconciliations often involved forgiving as much as being forgiven. In these cases it did seem that the befrienders' encouragement had been crucial in allowing the depressed woman to take the risk of approaching the estranged person. However, overall the rate of fresh start experiences could not be explained by having a befriender. For fresh starts involving rehousing, starting new jobs, relationships, or training, the rate was the same in the control group, and these had their usual beneficial impact upon depressive remission in both groups. The same was true of experiencing new stressors. (There had also been a hypothesis that befriending might help to prevent new severe events.) So it was among those without a fresh start experience that the impact of befriending was most interesting to explore. And here it was possible to detect the role of changed appraisals: although severe difficulties were continuing, the befrienders seemed to have helped women feel less demeaned by them, with a consequent lessening of depressive symptoms.

5.   *Was there anything about the nature of the befriending received which made it more likely that befriendees with that particular experience would be more frequently remit than befriended women without it?* Looking at the impact of different aspects of befriending moves the research from a simple outcome investigation into a study of process. The answer was again yes: among the befriended those whose volunteer had given them not merely good, but markedly good, active emotional support did best of all. This confirmed the emphasis of the earlier causal model upon the protective role of a sensitively responsive care-giving close relationship. The befrienders who gave markedly good support had gone out of their way to be helpful, not merely talked sympathetically and regularly.

6. *Was there anything identifiable about those befrienders who gave markedly good, as opposed to merely good, support?* Contrary to expectation, having survived a major depression themselves was not such a characteristic. But it seemed that those who had experienced neglect and abuse in childhood, but who as adults currently did not score with negative self evaluation, poor coping, or insecure attachment styles, gave even better support than those without such adverse childhoods, whether or not they had been through a depression themselves in the past. (The few volunteers who gave poor support to their befriendees had often suffered childhood adversity but seemed not to have transcended its effects upon their adult self evaluation, coping, and attachment styles.)

Implications of this example for psychotherapy research

Befriending, of course, is not psychotherapy. On a continuum of different sorts of relationships it probably falls midway between the professional therapy service and ordinary friendship. However, the similarities of this befriending project and studies investigating psychotherapy mean that outlining this model of depression can set the scene for reflection on how we might be able to design and interpret studies of *psychotherapy* for depression. First, we might fit together two models by a process of terminological translation: the one already outlined for depressive onset and course (Figure 1) and one that portrays a more generic object relations model of psychotherapy (Figure 2). Both bring together the inner and outer worlds, suggesting how their interactions over the life-span—in Figure 2 via the representational imagos detailed in the box—have been, and will continue to be, critical for a person's future well-being. Both give prominence to the role of emotional support in reducing depression. However, the first pays more attention to the variety of other variables such as severe stressors, while the second tries to disentangle the elements of emotional support, particularly concerning the role of the psychotherapist in providing a secure base within the therapy sessions, since without this a therapeutic change is considered unlikely. And there is now considerable evidence confirming the role of this good therapeutic alliance in

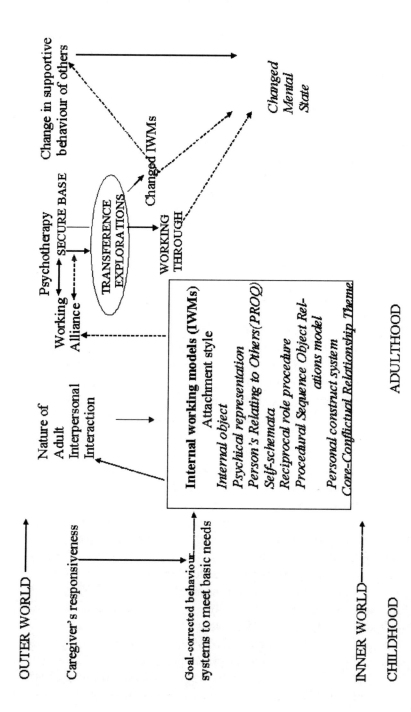

Figure 2. Model of psychological development and psychotherapy. Dotted lines represent impact of inner world on outer world. Continuous lines represent impact of outer world on inner world.

promoting positive psychotherapy outcomes for a range of distress (Horvath & Symonds, 1991; Piper, Azim, Joyce, & McCallum, 1991) even in the context of non-psychoanalytic (cognitive–behavioural) therapy (Burns & Nolen-Hoeksema, 1997).

If this parallel is accepted what has the work of Brown and colleagues to suggest about investigating psychotherapy for depression?

Perhaps the first lesson is methodological: no study has to be *either* quantitative *or* qualitative. It is possible to do both at once: with medium-sized samples, statistical and discourse analysis can be combined. With limited resources it is probably more cost-effective to do one study using both approaches than investigate two smaller samples using one of the two separate methods in each.

A second lesson concerns design: outcome research requires comparison of groups with and without the treatment. Here, randomized controlled trials have the advantage of reducing the likelihood of confounding (that is, when one group has a significantly higher proportion with a key predictive factor than the other group). But consent for randomization is difficult to achieve: only a small proportion of those with depression may be willing to be randomized and this raises the risk that any findings from the study will not be generalizable to other less amenable types of clients. However, if key factors such as severe stressors before onset, network emotional support, attachment, and coping style are measured before psychotherapy starts they will be able to act as control variables to reduce the likelihood that an effect on remission that is really due to one of these has wrongly been attributed to the therapy.

The third lesson is to look for mediators. Could psychotherapy be helping people to do something that those without therapy do much less often and which is itself the key therapeutic agent bringing about remission? For example, could it be helping to prevent new severe events or difficulties occurring, or to promote fresh start experiences? Another candidate as mediator would be coping style: and here cognitive-behavioural therapy explicitly targets self-blame as something to be worked on, as well as negative appraisal in the form of negative automatic thoughts. (Psychodynamic practice often reflects a similar, if less explicit, perspective.)

To some extent, charting the role of mediators involves the examination of "process", but the more usual meaning of "psychotherapy process research" would involve detailed exploration of what happens *within* sessions rather than whether changes *outside, but resulting from*, sessions have had a crucial impact on outcome. One such focus involves aspects of the therapeutic relationship, corresponding in many ways to the identification above of markedly good, as opposed to just good, emotional support offered by the befrienders. As already mentioned there are several measures of the working alliance that have been developed during the last decade.

Another aspect of process increasingly receiving attention is the increase in degree of reflectiveness of the client, as measured by the Narrative Process Coding System (NPCS, see Angus, Levitt, & Hardtke, 1999). There is a long tradition among psychotherapists that a client's "psychological-mindedness" (or reflectiveness) enhances the prospects of successful treatment (Coltart, 1988) as well as promoting security of attachment among cared-for children (Fonagy, 1991). However, this is an opinion about a *characteristic of the client at baseline* (that is before therapy starts).There is also a common understanding that the *process* of therapy, via interpretations producing insight, increases such reflective function (Fonagy, 1998).

Other aspects of psychotherapy process increasingly receiving attention are "significant events" in sessions (as identified by the clients themselves, see Hardy *et al.*, 1999), and emotion-abstraction patterns in verbatim protocols of sessions (Mergenthaler, 1996). As we listen more and more to what clients tell us has been helpful for them and in what way, it is hoped we will refine further important process measures.

Finally, as with the befrienders who had transcended their adverse childhoods to give especially good support, therapist characteristics can be explored to see if any relate to those process variables that have been identified as especially therapeutic (see Dozier, Cue, & Barnett, 1994).

To summarize in more general terms, we need to supplement the *process-outcome* focus of current discussions about psychotherapy research in order to include at least two other groups of factors in data collection and multivariate analysis; those concerning *relevant client characteristics at baseline* and those involving *absence of new stressors or presence of fresh starts during the period of psychotherapy.*

Before concluding it may be worth mentioning a recent study that follows this type of model (Godfrey, Chalder, Ogden, & Ridsdale, 2004). The authors compare two groups of patients, one receiving counselling and one cognitive–behaviour therapy for changes in symptoms (*outcome*) of chronic fatigue (CFS). They do not look at *stressors*, but do feed in *relevant baseline client characteristics* such as demographic and other predictors, like beliefs about the origins of CFS, as well as *process variables* such as the therapeutic alliance, and the therapist's encouragement of the patient's willingness to accept painful/uncomfortable feelings. Multivariate analysis identified this last, along with the client's initial willingness to attribute the fatigue to psychological sources, as accounting for 26% of the variance in outcome.

Concluding remarks

While some readers may feel that this chapter has pushed too far the similarities between psychotherapy research and the befriending intervention described, and others may feel that the detailed focus on a life-span developmental model of depression is not helpful in planning investigations of psychotherapy for other conditions, I hope that they will agree that it has been worth discussing at least some of the more general lessons of one field for the other. It is encouraging that the worlds of psychotherapy and research are now at last opening up dialogue, and it would be tragic if, despite this move to a more united perspective, new divisions were to emerge, say between proponents of qualitative and quantitative work, or between those who do not include comparison groups and those who reject anything but a randomized trial. In the end, however, it is the funding situation that constrains the quality of any proposed work. Psychotherapists, who often work in isolation from other colleagues with whom they could join to get funding, are thus particularly likely to settle for small sample research, if not for the single case study. Yet work with larger samples promises so many rewards, from the ability to look both qualitatively and quantitatively at the same material, that it seems incumbent on us all to join together and pool our ideas and ultimately our data. It is to be hoped that this conference will prove a first step in this direction.

References

Angus, L., Levitt, H., & Hardtke, K. (1999). The Narrative Process Coding System: research applications and implications for psychotherapy practice. *Journal of Clinical Psychology, 55*: 1255–1270.

Beck, A. T. (1967). *Depression: Clinical Experimental and Theoretical Aspects.* London: Staples.

Beck, A. T., Ward, C. H., & Mendelson, M. (1961). An inventory for measuring depression. *Archives of General Psychiatry, 4*: 561–571.

Benjamin, L. S. (1987). Use of structural analysis of social behaviour (SASB) to guide intervention in psychotherapy. In: J. C.Anchin & D. J.Kiesler (Eds.). *Handbook of Interpersonal Psychotherapy.* New York: Pergamon.

Bifulco, A., & Brown, G. W. (1996). Cognitive coping response to crises and onset of depression. *Journal of Social Psychiatry and Psychiatric Epidemiology, 31*: 163–172

Bifulco, A., Brown, G. W., & Harris, T. O. (1994). Childhood Experience of Care and Abuse (CECA): a retrospective interview measure. *Child Psychology and Psychiatry, 35*: 1419–1435.

Bifulco, A. T., Moran, P., Ball, C., & Bernazzani, O. (2002). Adult Attachment Style I: Its relationship to clinical depression. *Social Psychiatry and Psychiatric Epidemiology, 37*: 50–59.

Birtchnell, J. (1999). *Relating in Psychotherapy: The Application of a New Theory.* Westport, CT: Praeger.

Bowlby, J., (1988). *A Secure Base: Clinical Applications of Attachment Theory.* London: Routledge.

Brown, G. W., & Harris, T. O. (1978). *Social Origins of Depression: A Study of Psychiatric Disorder in Women.* London: Tavistock.

Brown, G. W., Adler, Z., & Bifulco, A. (1988). Life events, difficulties and recovery from chronic depression. *British Journal of Psychiatry, 152*: 487–498.

Brown, G. W., Andrews, B., Harris, T. O., Adler, Z., & Bridge, L. (1986). Social support, self-esteem and depression. *Psychological Medicine, 16*: 813–831.

Brown, G. W., Harris, T. O., & Hepworth, C. (1995). Loss, humiliation and entrapment among women developing depression: a patient and non-patient comparison. *Psychological Medicine, 25*: 7–21.

Burns, D., & Nolen-Hoeksema, S. (1997). Therapeutic empathy and recovery from depression in cognitive–behavioural therapy: a structural equation model. *Journal of Consulting & Clinical Psychology, 60*: 441–449.

Coltart, N. (1988). The assessment of psychological mindedness in the diagnostic interview. *British Journal of Psvchiatry*, 153: 819–820.

Dozier, M., Cue, K. L., & Barnett, L. (1994). Clinicians as caregivers: role of attachment organisation in treatment. *Journal of Consulting & Clinical Psychology*, 62: 793–800.

Evans, C., Connell, J., Barkham, M., Margison, F., McGrath G., Mellor-Clark, J. & Audin, K. (2002). Towards a standardised brief outcome measure: psychometric properties and utility of the CORE-OM. *British Journal of Psychiatry*, 180: 51–60.

Fonagy, P. (1998). An attachment theory approach to the treatment of difficult patients. *Bulletin of the Menninger Clinic*, 62: 147–169.

Freud, A. (1936). *The Ego and Mechanisms of Defence*. London: Hogarth.

George, C., Kaplan, N., & Main, M. (1985). The attachment interview for adults. Unpublished manuscript, University of California, Berkeley.

Glaser, B., & Strauss, A. (1967). *The Discovery of Grounded Theory: Strategies for Qualitative Research*. Chicago: Aldine.

Godfrey, E., Chalder, T., Seed, P., Ridsdale, L., & Ogden, J. (2004). Investigating the "active ingredients" of cognitive behaviour therapy and counselling for patients with chronic fatigue in primary care: an analysis of process and baseline predictors Submitted to *British Journal of Clinical Psychology*.

Hardy, G., Aldridge, J., Davidson, C., Rowe, C., Reilly, S., & Shapiro, D. (1999). Therapist responsiveness to client attachment styles and issues observed in client-identified significant events in psychodynamic-interpersonal therapy. *Psychotherapy Research*, 9: 36–53.

Harris, T. O. (1992). Some reflections on the process of social support: the nature of unsupportive behaviours. In: H. O. F. Veiel & U. Baumann (Eds.), *The Meaning and Measurement of Social Support* (pp. 171–189). Washington, DC: Hemisphere.

Harris, T., Brown, G. W., & Bifulco, A. (1990). Loss of parent in childhood and adult psychiatric disorder: a tentative overall model. *Development and Psychopathology*, 2: 311–328.

Harris, T. O., Brown, G. W., & Robinson, R. (1999). Befriending as an intervention for chronic depression among women in an inner city. I: Randomised Controlled Trial. *British Journal of Psychiatry*, 174: 219–225. II: Role of fresh-start experiences and baseline psychosocial factors in remission from depression. *British Journal of Psychiatry*, 174: 225–233.

Horowitz, L. M., Rosenberg, S. E., Baer, B. A., Ureno, G., & Villesenor, V. S. (1988). Inventory of interpersonal problems: psychometric properties and clinical applications. *Journal of Consulting and Clinical Psychology, 47*: 5–15.

Horvath, A. O., & Symonds, B. D. (1991). Relation between working alliance and outcome in psychotherapy: a meta-analysis. *Journal of Counselling Psychology, 38*: 139–149.

McCall, G. J., & Simmons, J. L. (1966). *Identities and Interactions.*New York: Free Press.

Mergenthaler, E. (1996). Emotion–abstraction patterns in verbatim protocols. A new way of describing psychotherapeutic processes. *Journal of Consulting & Clinical Psychology, 64*: 1306–1315.

Piper, W. E., Azim, H. F. A., Joyce, A. S., & McCallum, M. (1991). Transference interpretations, therapeutic alliance and outcome in short-term individual psychotherapy. *Archives General Psychiatry, 48*: 946–953.

Spielberger, C. D., Goruch, R. L., Luchese, R., Vagg, P. R., & Jacobs, G. A. (1983). *Manual for the State-Trait Anxiety Inventory*. Palo Alto, CA: Consulting Psychologies Press.

Vaillant, G. E. (1976). Natural history of male psychological health: V. The relation of choice of ego mechanisms of defence to adult adjustment, *Arch. Gen Psychiatry, 33*: 535–545.

CHAPTER TWENTY

Empirically supported treatments: recent developments in the cognitive–behavioural therapies, and implications for evidence-based psychotherapy

Keith and Deborah Dobson

Q uestions regarding the efficacy of psychotherapy and the relative merits of different types of therapeutic modalities have been asked for decades. In the first comprehensive review of the efficacy of different therapeutic models, Smith, Glass, and Miller (1980) conducted a meta-analysis of available outcome data. Their generally positive conclusions about the efficacy of psychotherapy none the less revealed serious limitations in the available evidence, and some disparity in the difference in outcomes comparing the most to the least successful of different therapy approaches. It is notable that Smith, Glass, and Miller (1980) have been followed by other meta-analyses of various treatment approaches, and with various clinical problems (e.g., Dobson, 1989; Miller & Berman, 1983). There is now ample evidence to support the claim that psychotherapy is effective in general, even while the research accumulates about the relative outcome of different therapy approaches for specific clinical disorders or conditions.

A different approach to examining the utility of psychotherapy was used by Seligman in his survey of treatment outcome (Seligman, 1995). This study used a mail-in questionnaire printed in *Consumer Reports*, which was completed by interested readers regarding their perceived usefulness of psychotherapy. This survey's results concluded that in general people who use psychotherapy find it to be of benefit. Although this method leads to concern about sampling bias, and the representativeness of the resulting findings, it does suggest that at least some members of the public that use psychotherapy find it to be useful.

The question behind both efficacy studies and consumer satisfaction surveys has been whether or not psychological treatments offer benefits to clients that can be reasonably seen as incremental to the non-specific therapeutic factors of social support and the passage of time. As psychotherapists have made claims about the efficacy of what they do, and as the field of psychotherapy has increasingly been recognized in mental health law and funding, health care systems and the public in many different countries are demanding evidence of positive therapeutic outcomes. While some of the basis for this emphasis has come from within the field of psychotherapy itself, it has been augmented by the continuing emphasis on evidence-based practice observed generally in medicine and health care (e.g., Hawley & Weisz, 2002; Strunk & DeRubeis, 2001). In the context of such pressures, the recent phenomenon of the movement towards empirically supported treatments (ESTs) in psychotherapy certainly bears scrutiny. This chapter therefore provides a history of this recent movement, and discusses the pertinent issues that have arisen as a consequence. In order to provide a focus within this broad field, the example of treatments for major depressive disorder will be used to demonstrate some of these points throughout this chapter.

Historical aspects of empirically supported treatments

In 1993, Dr David Barlow, as the President of the Clinical Psychology Division (Division 12) of the American Psychological Association (APA), struck a task force on the promotion and dissemination of psychological procedures. This task force was chaired by Dr Dianne Chambless, and a report was adopted by the Division 12 Board in October 1993. The report was published in 1995, with an updated version coming out only a year later in 1996. These reports have since generated a great deal of discussion, controversy, and awareness within and beyond the initial audience of APA. The original report defined and developed clear criteria for what constituted "empirically validated" treatments, and it provided examples of treatments that fulfilled these criteria. In the 1996 revision, the terms shifted somewhat from "empirically validated" to "empirically supported" treatments, taking a somewhat more moderate approach compared to the original document, and in recognition of the connotation that "validated" therapies might be seen as in need of no further validational evidence, which was certainly not the intention of the report. The report was further updated in 1998 (available at http://pantheon.yale.edu/~tat22/ est_docs/ValidatedTx.pdf), and the list of treatment manuals that were reflected in the list of empirically supported therapies was also published (available at http://pantheon.yale.edu/~tat22/ est_docs/TxManuals.pdf).

In 1996, the Executive of the Section on Clinical Psychology of the Canadian Psychological Association (CPA) passed a motion to constitute a task force charged with developing a position paper on Canadian psychology's response to the APA initiative. Dr John Hunsley chaired this task force and the report was submitted to the Clinical Section in 1998 (available at http://www.cpa.ca/clinical/ advancing/section.html). Also, in 1998, the child section of Division 12 of APA started to work on developing specific definitions, criteria, and examples for psychotherapies for children. Similar developments have occurred within the UK, as the Department of Health has published practice guidelines supporting the use of evidence based therapies in 2001 (available at http://www.doh.gov.uk/ mentalhealth/treatmentguideline/index.htm).

Developments related to evidence-based psychotherapy are not occurring only within the psychology community. The American Psychiatric Association has developed Expert Consensus Guidelines in the treatment of a number of disorders, all of which refer to psychotherapeutic interventions, as well as pharmaceutical treatments. These disorders include obsessive-compulsive, post-traumatic stress, panic, and mood disorders. Similarly, the Canadian Psychiatric Association has developed guidelines for additional problems, including schizophrenia. Clearly, the task force report (among other initiatives) has had a profound effect on the field of psychotherapy research and practice.

The initial Division 12 task force report reviewed the literature that was available in 1995–1996 on the efficacy of different psychotherapy approaches. The task force found that many studies predated the reliable categorization of clinical disorders as well as standardization of treatments. They refer to the Beck, Rush, Shaw, and Emery (1979) volume *Cognitive Therapy of Depression* as the first treatment manual for people with a specific problem. The criteria for empirically supported treatments that were developed by the task force include the following.

1.   At least two good between-group design experiments, demonstrating efficacy in one or more of the following ways:
     (a) the treatment is superior to pill or psychological placebo, or compared to another treatment;
     (b) the treatment is equivalent to an already established treatment in experiments with adequate statistical power (about thirty per group).
2.   A large series of single case design experiments must have been conducted ($n \geq 9$) demonstrating efficacy.

Regardless of the experimental paradigm used to conduct the research into the therapy, the experiments were required to have a good experimental design and a comparison between the intervention and another treatment. Further, and most important from the perspective of developing a replicable, consistent practice of evidence-based treatment, three other criteria were invoked:

1.   regardless of the type of experimental design, the outcome trials had to be conducted with written treatment manuals;
2.   characteristics of the client samples (typically including diagnostic assessment) had to be clearly specified; and
3.   treatment effects had to be demonstrated by at least two different investigators not working out of the same centre.

The criteria regarding written treatment manuals and the provision of a clear description of the sample utilized are included in order to encourage replication of results in independent clinics. The last criterion is intended to offset the tendency of the originators of new treatments to be aligned with the theory and be invested in demonstrating positive outcomes. Demonstrating positive results by different investigators provides more confidence in an approach. In order to prompt further research into newer or less well-developed treatments, a second category termed "probably efficacious" treatments was also included in the Task Force report. These treatments may be more effective compared to no treatment (e.g., wait-list control group), but may not yet have been compared to another treatment. They could be conducted by the same investigator or otherwise not be up to the standards of well-established treatments.

In terms of the breakdown of the currently included examples of empirically supported therapies, twenty-two meet the criteria for well established and twenty-five meet the criteria for probably efficacious therapies. When these therapies are assessed according to theoretical orientation, they are primarily behavioral (20/47) or cognitive or cognitive–behavioral (21/47). The six remaining therapies include interpersonal therapy for different disorders (e.g., Fairburn, Jones, Peveler, Hope, & O'Connor, 1993), emotionally focused couples therapy (James, 1991; Johnson & Greenberg, 1985) and family intervention for schizophrenia (Falloon et al., 1985; Randolph et al., 1994).

Using major depressive disorder as an example, the well-established treatments include cognitive therapy (Beck, Rush, Shaw, & Emery, 1979; Dobson, 1989) and interpersonal therapy (DiMascio et al., 1979; Elkin et al., 1989). The treatments that are considered to have met the criteria for being probably efficacious include: self-control therapy (Fuchs & Rehm, 1977; Rehm, Fuchs, Roth, Komblith, & Romano, 1979), psychoeducational treatment (Lewinsohn, Clarke, & Hoberman, 1989), and brief dynamic therapy (Gallagher-Thompson & Steffen, 1994). Further, there are two "probably efficacious" treatments that have been studied specifically in geriatric patients: cognitive therapy (Scogin & McElreath, 1994) and reminiscence therapy (Arean et al., 1993; Scogin & McElreath, 1994).

Issues related to ESTs

Despite the fact that ESTs represent one way to integrate science and practice in psychotherapy, which has long been espoused as a goal for the field (Dobson & Craig, 1998), the publication of the original papers has led to a great deal of discussion and debate within the field (cf. Chambless & Ollendick, 2000). In this section we review the major concerns, and the rebuttal that has been offered. The concerns can be roughly divided into those related to scientific methods versus application and dissemination.

Issues related to scientific methods

It has been argued that the EST criteria favour experimental designs and the qualitative tradition in psychology, and exclude valid data sources from quasi-experimental and qualitative studies. These arguments are manifestly true. The EST Task Force has endorsed the logico-empiricist tradition as the one on which psychotherapy should be based. Thus, while case studies, open trials, or uncontrolled research designs can be used to develop new treatments, they have taken the position that a true experimental design (either within or between participants) must be employed to derive scientifically valid results on which to develop an evidence-based practice of psychotherapy.

Another scientific concern that has been noted is that the methodologies encouraged tend to promote an adoption of the medical paradigm in psychotherapy practice. For example, the primary methodology encouraged in the EST Task Force is that of the randomized clinical trial (RCT). Because the RCT is the dominant research paradigm in medical research, and as it is highly consistent with the use of diagnosis as the basis for providing treatment, it has been argued that RCTs, in effect, "medicalize" psychotherapy research.

A third issue is that the EST Task Force criteria require that the nature of the sample on which the EST was developed must be clearly specified. This criterion was established so that when an EST is developed, it would be known what are both the appropriate and inappropriate client types and problems to apply the treatment to. In practice, this requirement has largely meant that the provision of a psychiatric diagnosis has become relatively standard in the research literature on psychological treatments. Further, as *DSM* criteria for diagnoses and standardized assessment methods are easily available, many psychotherapy researchers have relied upon them when developing ESTs (Chambless & Ollendick, 2000), which again has been cited as an increase in the medicalization of psychotherapy. It is important to note, though, that the need for a *DSM* diagnosis is not specifically noted anywhere in the Task Force criteria. Thus, while the use of diagnostic procedures has greatly enhanced communication in the field, it is possible for psychotherapy developers to derive non-*DSM* algorithms for identifying appropriate clients for their treatments. For example, the development of treatments for marital distress is not based on diagnostic criteria, but other operational criteria for relationship distress.

The RCT was primarily designed for use in efficacy research, and for addressing the question of what treatments "work" (i.e., have measurable outcomes) with specific, and typically well-defined, populations. It has been pointed out that RCTs may not be well equipped to address questions related to effectiveness of various treatments, or how well these treatments work in normative clinical practice, with patients with comorbid problems and treatments that may not be applied with as much purity or vigour as in the context of efficacy research (Nathan, Stuart, & Dolan, 2000). It has been suggested that as a result of an increasing emphasis on efficacy, the field of psychotherapy might become increasing technological (i.e., trying to find out how to treat disorders), rather than emphasizing the theoretical models and processes that underlie change in psychotherapy, and therefore contribute to its flexibility in clinical practice.

This criticism has merit, as RCT trials certainly do emphasize the measurement of outcomes for specific disorders. While RCTs can be used to design effectiveness research (for example, randomly assigning patients to strict protocols or to therapist-chosen treatment models and methods), such research is more difficult to fund. It is also often more difficult to interpret than efficacy research, as it explicitly and purposefully allows more "error variance" (e.g., patients with a wider variety of problems, more flexibility in the way that treatments are conducted) in the study.

The primary emphasis in most RCTs is the demonstration of treatment efficacy, especially at the completion of therapy, but in some studies also at various follow-up intervals. The concern that has been expressed is that the emphasis on outcomes with ESTs has had the unfortunate consequence of reduced research on mechanisms of change. Most ESTs have multiple components, which tend to be difficult to evaluate using the RCT methodology. Although examples of dismantling studies of empirically supported therapies do exist (e.g., Jacobson *et al.*, 1996) they also typically follow an RCT model and so have the same limitations expressed above. Typically, predictors of outcome are usually studied using regression, or other linear methods. As has been argued, though, such methods as random assignment and linear regression may not be the most appropriate ways to conceptualize and statistically model psychotherapy change (Krause & Howard, 2002, 2003).

Similar to the above points, critics have noted that ESTs are biased towards shorter-term and outcome-orientated therapies (e.g., those focusing upon symptom reduction or behavioural change). Other types of personal change that might also occur in the context of psychotherapy (e.g., the development of insight or change in personality structures) may be much more difficult to demonstrate by use of standardized and quantitative measures. Measurement of outcomes by comparing pre-test, post-test, and follow-up measures generally ignores the process of therapy. As a consequence, those psychotherapies that focus more upon the process of treatment than the outcome might be disadvantaged.

Much has been written about the impact of the therapeutic relationship in promoting client change (cf. Norcross, 2001, 2002). Most EST manuals, however, are either silent about the nature of the therapeutic relationship or report that a positive therapeutic relationship is a necessary, but insufficient, condition for change. Cognitive–behavioural therapists generally aim for a collaborative relationship with their clients, and the development of "collaborative empiricism" is seen as integral for change in cognitive therapy for depression (Beck, Rush, Shaw, & Emery, 1979; Beck, 1995). Therapies that use the therapeutic relationship as a primary mechanism of change are relatively more difficult to articulate in manualized form (Luborsky, 2001). Many of these treatments are based upon a theoretical approach, but are delivered in a non-standardized, individualized way. An interesting recent development regarding relationship characteristics has been the attempt to identify empirically supported relationship factors (Norcross, 2001). This movement, which has been promoted by the Division of

Psychotherapy (Division 29) of the APA, as well as the Society for Psychotherapy Research, has recently articulated criteria for these factors, and has begun to identify factors that have been demonstrably related to outcomes in psychotherapy. This list includes both "demonstrably effective" factors such as: Therapeutic Alliance, Cohesion in Group Therapy, Empathy, and Goal Consensus and Collaboration, as well as "promising and probably effective" factors, such as Positive Regard, Congruence/Genuineness, Feedback, Repair of Alliance Ruptures, Self-Disclosure, Management of Countertransference, and the Quality of Relational Interpretations. It remains unclear at present how the literatures on empirically supported treatments and empirically supported relationship factors will relate to each other in the future. It *is* fairly easy to predict, however, that future research will have to devoted to how these forces interact with each other; whether integrated treatments using both empirically supported relationship factors and treatment methods will emerge, remains an unknown issue at present.

Due to the requirement of specifying the nature of the clientele on which ESTs are developed, they encourage research in homogeneous samples. Although an emphasis on more homogeneous samples makes sense in treatment development, less is learned about the influences of client diversity upon outcomes. As such, the development of ESTs is really only the first step in the testing of treatments in real world settings. Benchmarking studies, in which the results of ESTs with "real world" clients are compared to results from more controlled RCTs, can be a very useful enterprise in this transfer of experience (Stuart, Treat, & Wade, 2000; Wade, Treat, & Stuart, 1998). The issue of comorbidity, in particular, is a difficult one. EST research often has significant exclusion criteria. For example, most depression trials exclude patients with extreme suicidality, current substance abuse, and lifetime psychotic features or bipolar disorder. Clinicians in non-research settings have argued that it is difficult to apply ESTs developed with client groups with such exclusion criteria to their clients, who often have one or more of the above characteristics. Put otherwise, the developers of ESTs often maximize the internal validity of their research trials, with the unfortunate consequence that the generalizability of their therapies to typical psychotherapy practice is tenuous. These comments lead to the next section's discussion.

Issues related to clinical applications and dissemination

Criticism has been levelled that the criteria for ESTs are biased towards short-term therapies. This criticism has some validity. By virtue of encouraging RCTs and quantitative measurement, it is the most practical and cost-effective to assess outcomes in short-term therapies. Consequently, there have been many more studies on relatively short-term as compared with longer-term therapies. Further, as a continuing emphasis within the health care system has been upon maximizing cost-efficiencies, short-term therapies are often an option favoured by funding sources.

As most behavioural and cognitive–behavioural therapies are shorter term than most psychodynamic or interpersonal therapies, critics have therefore noted that the former therapies have an unfair advantage in this regard. A related concern is that clients with more complex or serious problems who might require longer-term therapy might not be able to obtain these services if they are not recognized as empirically supported. There have been two responses to these criticisms. The first is that if shorter-term therapies can demonstrate adequate efficacy, then why should longer therapies be financially supported? Unless longer treatment models can provide evidence that they are associated with better outcomes (e.g., higher rates of recovery, lower relapse), they probably should not be as supported as more efficient models. The second response is that the criteria themselves do not bias against longer-term therapies that have been shown to be efficacious. It is rather funding policies, cost restrictions in the health care field, and the demand for short-term treatments by the public that are the problems with longer-term therapies being promoted.

Criticism has also been levelled towards the possible social, economic, and political consequences of ESTs. For example, if lists of ESTs are made available to the public (which they have been for some time) and to people with the power to provide or withhold funding (e.g., public health departments, HMOs), then the indiscriminate application of short-term therapies could be encouraged. In like measure, if ESTs are promoted, other types of treatment services that could be effective but have not yet been assessed, could be given only limited accessibility for clients. Researchers have also expressed concern that premature research and development closure could result. For example, if several effective treatments exist for depression, it might become more difficult to obtain funding support to develop additional treatments. Organizations that provide funding might be reluctant to provide financial backing for innovative new approaches if an efficient and effective treatment already exists.

Another issue related to application that has been discussed regarding ESTs, and that appears to be a major concern among practitioners (Addis & Krasnow, 2000), is the relative rigidity and flexibility of the treatments. Due to the requirement of a written treatment manual, ESTs encourage the specification of session-by-session methods and focus upon treatment techniques as opposed to the individual therapeutic relationship. There is considerable variability in manuals as to the degree of specificity provided. Some manuals delineate the therapist activities that are typical in each session (e.g,. Beck, Rush, Shaw, & Emery, 1979), whereas others are much more flexible (e.g., Beck, 1995). In practice, although ESTs are based on a theoretical model that has common or prototypical interventions, they are guided by individualized case conceptualizations (Persons, 1989) and applied in a relatively flexible manner.

Another important issue related to empirical outcome research in psychotherapy relates to the assessment of treatment fidelity (McGlinchey & Dobson, 2003). Critical components of treatment fidelity include *adherence* to the model and *competence* in the application of the model, the one building upon the other. The evaluation of ESTs demands adherence and encourages competence, but clinical practice requires competence and is silent about adherence. Indeed, many therapists maintain that their preferred method of conducting psychotherapy is to be eclectic, choosing those models and methods that they believe best suits the needs of their clients (Beutler, Consoli, & Williams, 1995; Garfield, 2000), rather than being adherent to a specific treatment model or manual. Consequently, the requirements of the research evaluation component are quite different from clinical practice and could be at odds with it.

The original EST Task Force report focused upon dissemination and delivery of ESTs to the public. Due to changes within public health systems towards more consumer involvement and public education, the demand for ESTs often outstrips the availability of services. Even though effective treatments exist within clinical research settings, many mental health and other programmes available to consumers either do not offer them or have very limited access to these therapies. The access problems include the time lag between the development and the widespread adoption of services, decreased funding to mental health services due to economic downturns, lack of communication between researchers and practitioners, and the lack of training opportunities for motivated practitioners. Increased consumer advocacy and media attention to treatments such as cognitive therapy for depression (e.g., the 20 January 2003 issue of *Time* magazine, in which it is questioned: "Can Freud get his job back?") have further increased consumer demand. Serious questions have arisen regarding methods by which these treatments can be efficiently and effectively disseminated to practitioners and delivered to consumers. In British Columbia, Canada, a Provincial Anxiety Disorders Strategy has been recently developed (2002) utilizing the principles of ESTs within a publicly funded health care system. Strategies such as prevention are included, as are a range of interventions from web-based education and support to community-based self-help therapy, and all of the way to specialized day programmes for anxiety disorders. These services are organized using a stepped-care approach, in which the most intensive and costly services are targeted to those needing them most, but that assessment of client needs is then matched with an appropriate level of intervention. This initiative is an example of cost-effective dissemination of ESTs for anxiety disorders.

Several other concerns arise with respect to the overall issue of dissemination. Research is required in order to determine the level of fidelity to treatment required in general clinical practice to maintain efficacy. It is unknown whether or not using only portions of an approach or some particular techniques are helpful in terms of resolving problems or enhancing outcomes. In addition, we do not currently know the importance of other aspects of effectiveness as opposed to efficacy in clinical practice. The impact of factors such as demand characteristics or therapist and client expectations upon ESTs is largely unknown. In pharmaceutical research, the public perception of a new effective drug often enhances outcome due to these factors, but only for limited periods of time. The same effect could occur for psychotherapies.

One of the ways in which the issues of fidelity and dissemination have been addressed has been through training and credentialling of service providers. Questions remain about the optimal way to train, as well as the optimal time to train providers. Many training and internship programmes require some training in ESTs. While this change is positive in many respects, it potentially creates increased demands for time during training; as such, the emphasis placed upon other aspects of training (e.g., theoretical underpinning of approaches, experimental research, other therapy models) may decline.

Training and the provision of credentials also have the prospect of becoming guild issues. While adherence and competency are likely to lead to consistent and high quality services, the negative concern of limiting access to clients is an important one. Controlling access to who is able to claim expertise in, and therefore provide, ESTs has sometimes been negatively perceived as limiting availability to clients who need treatment in order to gain market control. Several therapies have worked towards credentialling within North America. These include Eye Movement Desensitization and Reprocessing (EMDR) (Shapiro, 1995), Dialectic Behaviour Therapy (Linehan, Cochran, & Kehrer, 2000), and Panic Control Therapy (Klosko, Barlow, Tassinari, & Cerny, 2000). The Academy of Cognitive Therapy was formed in 2000, in order to provide a consistent credentialling system for cognitive therapy (Dobson, Beck, & Beck, 2003). These credentialling systems all list qualified providers and promote their credentialling system to the general public. For example, referral services are an active part of the Academy of Cognitive Therapy web site. It is a research evaluation question at present to determine whether or not such credentialling systems improve the quality of psychotherapy provided. Are outcomes better when the services are provided by practitioners who meet the credentialling criteria? At present, we do not have a database on which to answer these questions. Hopefully, as these systems develop, they will endeavour to provide evidence of additional benefit to other training systems and models.

The future of ESTs

This chapter has highlighted the emergence of the recent movement towards empirically supported treatments, and the broad implications that this movement has for the field of psychotherapy. Although the general emphasis of this movement has been to bridge the gap between science and practice, it has adopted a particular approach to the scientific process that is not without criticism. In this chapter we have tried to summarize these criticisms, and have addressed those that have merit. Our attempt has been to promote a healthy discussion within the field of psychotherapy research and practice, related to both the strengths and limitation of the EST movement.

Advocates of the EST approach have argued that the providers of treatments should be held accountable and provide documentation of positive outcomes for their therapies. As the public has become better informed regarding health care and treatment options, it often demands demonstration of research outcomes. In those countries where mental health treatment is publicly funded, it appears that policy makers are also increasingly wanting to see the evidence that supports the use and funding of certain treatment methods (cf., Miller & Magruder, 1999). Psychotherapy has become more open and transparent through these processes, with clients actively participating in treatment choices.

The movement towards ESTs has the long hoped for, but often undelivered, prospect of unifying science and practice within the field of psychotherapy. Certain risks and opportunities are part of this prospect. In our opinion, most of the risks lie in the over-zealous applications of ESTs rather than anything inherent in the methods or techniques themselves. For example, there is a risk of private-for-profit interest in ESTs (e.g., HMOs, insurance), which should be resisted so that the profession maintains responsibility for them. Certainly, continued innovation and research are essential for the development of the field. Many clinical problems do not currently have an available empirically supported treatment choice. For many clinical problems where ESTs exist, it is not clear which individual difference variables in clients (e.g., age, severity, personality features) make these treatments more or less appropriate as treatment options. We know little about how evidence-based psychotherapy relationships factors interact with empirically supported treatment techniques. We know little about how to effectively disseminate ESTs to the community of clinical psychotherapists. We know little about how ESTs can be utilized in different countries and cultures (Hamilton & Dobson, 2001). In short, many questions remain. Thus, while the attempt here has been to communicate some of the enthusiasm that may be appropriate for the movement to ESTs, appropriate caution needs to be exercised as this movement continues.

Author notes

This chapter is based upon a presentation at the UK Council for Psychotherapy 1st Annual Research Conference, University of Surrey, 29 May 2002. Please address requests for reprints to the first author at the Department of Psychology, University of Calgary, Calgary, Alberta, Canada T2N 1N4, or by e-mail to keith.dobson @ucalgary.ca.

References

Addis, M. E., & Krasnow, A. D. (2000). A national survey of practicing psychologists' attitudes toward psychotherapy treatment manuals. *Journal of Consulting & Clinical Psychology, 68*: 331–339.

Arean, P., Perri, M., Nezu, A., Schein, R., Christopher, F., & Joseph, T. (1993). Comparative effectiveness of social problem-solving therapy and reminiscence therapy as treatments for depression in older adults. *Journal of Consulting and Clinical Psychology, 61*: 1003–1010.

Beck, A., Rush, J., Shaw, B., & Emery, G. (1979). *The Cognitive Therapy of Depression.* New York: Guilford Press.

Beck, J. (1995). *Cognitive Therapy: Basics and Beyond.* New York: Guilford Press.

Beutler, L. E., Consoli, A. J., & Williams, R. E. (1995). Integrative and eclectic therapies in practice. In: B. M. Bongar & L. E. Beutler (Eds.), *Comprehensive Textbook of Psychotherapy: Theory and Practice. Oxford textbooks in Clinical Psychology, Vol. 1.* (pp. 274–292). New York, NY: Oxford University Press.

Chambless, D., & Ollendick, T. (2000). Empirically supported psychological interventions: controversies and evidence. *Annual Review of Psychology, 52*: 685–716.

DiMascio, A., Weissman, M. M., Prusoff, B., Neu, C., Zwilling, M., & Klerman, G. (1979). Differential symptom reduction by drugs and psychotherapy in acute depression. *Archives of General Psychiatry*, 36: 1450–1456.

Dobson, K. S. (1989). A meta-analysis of the efficiency of cognitive therapy for depression. *Journal of Consulting and Clinical Psychology*, 57: 414–419.

Dobson, K. S., & Craig, K. (Eds.) (1998). *Empirically Supported Therapies: Best Practice in Professional Psychology*. Thousand Oaks, CA: Sage.

Dobson, K. S., Beck, J., & Beck, A. T. (2003). Credentialing processes in cognitive therapy: The Academy of Cognitive Therapy. Unpublished manuscript, University of Calgary.

Elkin, I., Shea, M., Watkins, J., Imber, S., Sotsky, S., Collins, J., Glass, D., Pilkonis, P., Leber, W., Docherty, J., Fiester, S., & Parloff, M. (1989). National Institute of Mental Health Treatment of Depression Collaborative Research Program: General effectiveness of treatments. *Archives of General Psychiatry*, 46: 971–982.

Fairburn, C., Jones, R., Peveler, R., Hope, R., & O'Connor, M. (1993). Psychotherapy and bulimia nervosa: longer-term effects of interpersonal psychotherapy, behavior therapy, and cognitive behavior therapy. *Archives of General Psychiatry*, 50: 419–428.

Falloon, R., Boyd, J., McGill, C., Williamson, M., Razani, A., Moss, H., Giulderman, A., & Simpson, G. (1985). Family management in the prevention of morbidity of schizophrenia: clinical outcome of a two-year longitudinal study. *Archives of General Psychiatry*, 42: 887–896.

Fuchs, C., & Rehm, L., (1977). A self-control behavior therapy program for depression. *Journal of Consulting and Clinical Psychology*, 45: 206–215.

Gallagher-Thompson, D., & Steffen, A. (1994). Comparative effects of cognitive behavioral and brief dynamic therapy for depressed family caregivers. *Journal of Consulting and Clinical Psychology*, 62: 543–549.

Garfield, S. L. (2000). Eclecticism and integration: A personal retrospective view. *Journal of Psychotherapy Integration*, 10: 341–355.

Hamilton, K. E., & Dobson, K. S. (2001). Empirically supported treatments in psychology: implications for international promotion and dissemination. *Revista Internacional de Psicologia Clinica y de la Salud/International Journal of Clinical and Health Psychology*, 1: 35–51

Hawley, K. M., & Weisz, J. R. (2002). Increasing the relevance of evidence-based treatment review to practitioners and consumers. *Clinical Psychology-Science & Practice*, 9: 225–230.

Jacobson, N. S., Dobson, K. S., Truax, P. A., Addis, M. E., Koerner, K., Gollan, J. K., Gortner, E., & Prince, S. E. (1996). A component analysis of cognitive-behavioral treatment for depression. *Journal of Consulting and Clinical Psychology*, *64*: 295–304.

James, P. (1991). Effects of a communication training component added to an emotionally focused couples therapy. *Journal of Marital and Family Therapy*, *17*: 263–275.

Johnson, S., & Greenberg, L. (1985). Differential effects of experiential and problem solving interventions in resolving marital conflict. *Journal of Consulting and Clinical Psychology*, *58*: 77–84.

Klosko, J. S., Barlow, D. H., Tassinari, R., & Cerny, J. A. (1990). A comparison of alprazolam and behavior therapy in treatment of panic disorder. *Journal of Consulting and Clinical Psychology*, *58*: 77–84.

Krause, M. S., & Howard, K. I., (2002). The linear model is a very special case: how to explore data for their full clinical implications. *Psychotherapy Research*, *12*: 475–490.

Krause, M. S., & Howard, K. I. (2003). What random assignment does and does not do. *Journal of Clinical Psychology*, *59*: 751–766.

Lewinsohn, P. M., Clarke, G. N., & Hoberman, H. M. (1989). The Coping with Depression Course: review and future directions. *Canadian Journal of Behavioral Science*, *21*: 470–493.

Linehan, M. M., Cochran, B. N., & Kehrer, C. A. (2001). Dialectical behavior therapy for borderline personality disorder. In: D. H. Barlow (Ed.) *Clinical Handbook of Psychological Disorders: A Step-by-step Treatment Manual* (3rd edn) (pp. 470–522). New York: Guilford Press.

Luborsky, L. (2001). The meaning of empirically supported treatment research for psychoanalytic and other long-term therapies. *Psychoanalytic Dialogues*, *11*: 583–604.

McGlinchey, J. B., & Dobson, K. S. (2003) Treatment integrity concerns in cognitive therapy for depression. *Journal of Cognitive Psychotherapy*, *17*: 299–318.

Miller, C., & Berman, J. S. (1983). The efficacy of cognitive behaviour therapists: a quantitative review of the research evidence. *Psychological Bulletin*, *94*: 39–54.

Miller, N. E., & Magruder, K. M. (Eds.) (1999). *Cost-effectiveness of Psychotherapy: A Guide for Practitioners, Researchers and Policymakers*. Bethesda, MA: National Institutes of Health, Office of Director.

Nathan, P. E., Stuart, S. P., & Dolan, S. L. (2000). Research on psychotherapy efficacy and effectiveness: Between Scylla and Charybdis? *Psychological Bulletin*, *126*: 964–981.

Norcross, J. C. (2001). Purposes, processes and products of the task force on empirically supported therapy relationship. *Psychotherapy: Theory, Research, Practice, and Training*, *38*: 345–356.

Norcross, J. C. (2002). Empirically supported therapy relationships. In: J. C. Norcross (Ed.), *Psychotherapy Relationships that Work: Therapist Contributions and Responsiveness to Patients* (pp. 3–16). London: Oxford University Press.

Persons, J. (1989). Cognitive Therapy in Practice: A Case Formulation Approach. New York: W. W. Norton.

Randolph, E. T., Eth, S., Glynn, S. M., Paz, G. G., Leong, G. B., Shaner, A. L., Strachan, A., Van Vort, W., Escobar, J. I., & Liberman, R. P. (1994). Behavioural family management in schiophrenia: outcome of a clinic-based intervention. *British Journal of Psychiatry, 164*: 501–506.

Rehm, L., Fuchs, C., Roth, D., Komblith, S., & Romano, J. (1979). A comparison of self-control and assertion skills treatments of depression. *Behavior Therapy, 10*: 429–442.

Scogin, F., & McElreath, L. (1994). Efficacy of psychosocial treatments for geriatric depression: a quantitative review. *Journal of Consulting and Clinical Psychology, 62*: 69–74.

Seligman, M. (1995). The effectiveness of psychotherapy: The Consumer Reports study. *American Psychologist, 50*, 965–974.

Shapiro, F. (1995). *Eye Movement Desensitization and Reprocessing: Basic Principles, Protocols and Procedures*. New York: Guilford Press.

Smith, M., Glass, G., & Miller, T. (1980). *The Benefits of Psychotherapy*. Baltimore: Johns Hopkins University Press.

Stuart, G. L., Treat, T. A., & Wade, W. A. (2000). Effectiveness of an empirically based treatment for panic disorder delivered in a service clinic setting: 1-year follow-up. *Journal of Consulting and Clinical Psychology, 68*: 506–512.

Strunk, D. R., & DeRubeis, R. J. (2001). Cognitive therapy for depression: a review of its efficacy. *Journal of Cognitive Psychotherapy, 15*: 289–297.

The Provincial Strategy Advisory Committee for Anxiety Disorders (April 11, 2002). *A Provincial Anxiety Disorders Strategy*. B.C. Provincial Plan: Author.

Wade, W. A., Treat, T. A., & Stuart, G. L. (1998). Transporting an empirically supported treatment for panic disorder to a service clinic setting: a benchmarking strategy. *Journal of Consulting & Clinical Psychology, 66*: 231–239.

CHAPTER TWENTY-ONE

Psychoanalytically informed research on obesity

Julia Buckroyd

I n the past two decades psychological therapies have developed from a niche product for the financially secure to a provision widely available through primary care settings and in numerous agencies with charitable status at no or low cost. These therapies are increasingly seen as the treatment of choice, with or without complementary drug regimes, for a wide variety of common conditions, including depression, traumatic experience of every kind, chronic and terminal illness, and a wide range of addictions and phobias.

This much more generous provision of psychological help is available, in a way that private practice never has been, to those many people without the resources to pay. Inevitably this situation has and will give power to those who fund the treatments to enquire "What works?" in terms both of clinical effectiveness and cost–benefit analysis (Maynard, 2000) and to require that therapies back their claims to efficacy with research findings. Certainly the avowed aim of recent NHS policy documents is to fund "evidence based practice" (Department of Health, 1999; Ferguson & Russell, 2000; Parry, 2000).

This requirement finds the psychoanalytically based therapies at a grave disadvantage. Since the time of Freud, practitioners of this persuasion have very largely conducted their researches in a mode that would now be called reflective practice. Therapists have mused upon their experience with individual clients and have published those musings for the benefit of other practitioners. *The International Journal of Psychoanalysis* and other journals of psychoanalytic psychotherapy, including, for example, *the British Journal of Psychotherapy* and *Psychoanalytic Psychotherapy*, have published thousands of these accounts. Senior figures in this world have published books in the same style: Christopher Bollas is a good example; Neville Symington, Valerie Sinason, and many others have gathered together their clinical experience and presented their reflections upon it. There can be no doubt that this manner of proceeding has developed the theory and practice of psychoanalytic therapies out of all recognition. It is as a result a discipline progressively better equipped to struggle with the variety of human experience and human response. This style of writing follows a long-standing tradition of minimal reference to other thinkers. However, as standards of proof and referencing have developed in other disciplines, psychoanalytic writing has remained largely unchanged.

There are difficulties about this manner of proceeding in relation to the need to persuade funders of the clinical value of the work. The first difficulty is that it is rare (although less rare than it used to be) for practitioners to set their work in the context of other disciplines and a tendency to denigrate work in related fields. The most conspicuous example is that of John Bowlby, whose attempt to integrate ethnographic and other data into the psychoanalytic discourse was met with a response from the Institute of Psychoanalysis which eventually drove him to relinquish his membership (Holmes, 1993). Belatedly attachment theory has been adopted by the psychoanalytic world and in some quarters enthusiastically embraced (Cortina & Marrone, 2003; Fonagy & Target, 2003). Unfortunately, this failure to integrate psychoanalytic therapies into wider discourse has made it more difficult than it might otherwise have been for the world of medicine, psychology, and psychiatry to take appropriate notice of psychoanalytic understandings. It has also deprived psychoanalytic thinking of the stimulus and advantages of advances in other fields.

This intellectual isolation is not necessary (and certainly not desirable). Recent attempts to integrate neuro-science and psychotherapy have proved both possible and fruitful (Kaplan-Solms & Solms, 2000). However, it appears that there survives a strong tradition within psychoanalytic thinking of wishing to talk only to each other. The highly technical language of psychoanalysis compounds this tendency. Almost any review of psychoanalytic work in the general press will refer to it as "jargon laden". Other disciplines with technical language, most obviously medicine, have found a way to communicate with the general public. It seems that the psychoanalytic community makes little attempt to render itself comprehensible either to other disciplines or to the general public.

The direct result of this has been the frequent failure to carry out research in a form that is convincing to those who are accustomed to having the results of research presented in a format that generally includes comparison, percentage and statistic, that describes a methodology and that analyses results according to widely understood conventions (Kvale, 1999). Practitioners may wish to believe that they can stand outside these demands, or even be implacably hostile towards them, but such attitudes are likely to be very destructive:

> Generally speaking [types of therapy which have been extensively researched] . . . have been the briefer more structured and focal therapies, particularly (but not exclusively) cognitive behaviour therapy. Where research evidence is lacking for other approaches—for example, longer-term psychoanalytic work—it is easy to jump to the conclusion that such approaches are not supported by evidence. This could have disastrous consequences for these services, where funding could be withdrawn and potentially valuable and effective therapies lost to the NHS. [Parry, 2000, p. 68]

My particular concern about these tendencies with psychoanalysis is the effect that they have on the ability of psychoanalytic therapy to win the confidence of funders who are in the position to ensure that the insights of the psychoanalysis are made available to as wide a user group as possible. The particular topic with which I wish to illustrate my concern is that of obesity.

It seems to me perfectly possible to carry out therapeutic interventions informed by psychoanalytic ideas that will meet the criteria for research that are required in other disciplines without betraying psychoanalytic conviction. Clearly, a practitioner working alone with a succession of patients seen several times a week and focusing on the transference relationship will find it impossible to carry out anything that can, in common understanding, be called research (Kvale, 1999) (although it might be called reflective practice). But psychoanalysis is both a theory and a method. It is possible to conduct therapeutic interventions that respect the values and theories of psychoanalysis but at the same time respect the values of social science research. In what follows I describe an intervention with obese women that illustrates the point I wish to make.

Obesity is a serious problem in our time that constitutes a worldwide epidemic (James, 2002; Seidell & Tijhuis, 2000). It has serious and psychological consequences (Rosen, 2002). It is a significant economic drain on resources (National Audit Office 2000–2001; Wolf, 2002). The vast majority of work done on obesity totally ignores the psychological meaning of eating behaviour and focuses on underlying physiological processes and desirable lifestyles. Unsurprisingly to anyone from a psychoanalytic background, interventions based on these factors have consistently failed to demonstrate sustained weight loss.

Over the years, psychoanalytic writers have had a good deal to say about obesity. We examined a range of papers dating from 1979 to 2003 that reported individual treatments of obese patients in psychoanalytic therapies. These papers identified possible causal factors in obesity; for example, Shainess (1979) emphasizes the importance of the early mother–child interaction during early feeding and the consequent effect of this interaction on separation and individuation. Rodriguez-Rendo (1984) focused on body image; Glucksman (1989) emphasized developmental phases and transference phenomena, as did Greenberg (1998). Glennon (2001) returned to the meaning of fat as protection and Rose (2003) again emphasized development. These authors between them identify a number of interesting approaches to the problem of obesity, which probably cover most of the psychoanalytic understandings of the problem. However, the status of these reflections in research terms can only be that of hypothesis. None of the authors reported on weight loss. The authors are proposing understandings of obesity that have relevance for treatment but none of them could claim that their understanding had been tested in any formal manner or in a way which could be replicated.

We considered a similar range of group psychoanalytic treatments for obesity dating from 1960 to 2002. The authors of these papers, like their colleagues in individual work, developed hypotheses about the causes of the group members' obesity. Becker (1960) identified difficulties in relating to others and oneself; Holt and Winnick (1961) were more generally focused on the adaptation and emotional well-being of group members. Kaplan (1966) addressed emotional maladjustment; Slawson (1965) linked obesity with sexual difficulties and an equation of food and love. All of these early papers differed from the reports of individual therapy in that the group therapies were explicitly undertaken as research projects, and of them all but Becker attempted some kind of quantitative evaluation. These characteristics of a group therapy undertaken exclusively as a research project and an attempt at quantitative evaluation we have found in one modern paper (Ciano, Rocco, Angarano, Biasin, & Balestrini, 2002). These researchers compared different therapies including psychodynamic therapy for binge eating disorder but reported that no weight was lost.

In the field of feminist psychoanalytic writing, especially, a huge amount of work has been carried out and, moreover, explored in an unusually accessible form. Susie Orbach's book *Fat is a Feminist Issue* (1978) was a remarkable tour de force. Other authors, including Kim Chernin (1985) and Geneen Roth (1982) have done similarly important work. More recently, writers in this tradition, including Burgard and Lyons (1994), Ball and Norman (1996) and Wooley and Wooley (1984) have continued in this area. These authors have been as clear as their mainstream psychoanalytic colleagues that obesity is a sign of internal conflicts, although they lay much greater weight on the cultural context in which those conflicts have developed. Again, none of these authors is concerned with weight loss. The earlier work by feminists can only be called reflective practice, although their insights and case material are extremely interesting. More recently, feminist researchers have incorporated qualitative methods that have reported shifts in attitude that may well dispose to weight loss.

Our review of a range of psychoanalytically informed work done on obesity, with the sole exception of that done by Ciano and colleagues (2002), concludes that the work is strongly suggestive of common themes relevant to the development of obesity in the emotional lives of obese people. However, no systematic evaluation of a treatment based on those themes in respect of its effect on weight loss has yet taken place. We find ourselves bound to agree with Foster (2002) and Ogden (2003) that these hypotheses remain to be tested. In other words, our colleagues in other psychological therapies are interested in our theorizing but await our research findings. We note also that Ciano and colleagues (2002) were unable to report weight loss. We consider that those investigators who have explicitly denied the importance of weight loss and focused on the emotional well-being of group members are developing therapies that are most unlikely to be funded with public money, are insufficiently concerned with the serious consequences of obesity, and (in our experience) the desire of obese people themselves to lose weight. If we make an analogy with smoking, we would hardly expect public funding for a smoking cessation programme that left the participants feeling a lot happier, but did nothing to change their smoking behaviour.

The point we are making is that, as far as we are aware, the huge volume of work on obesity in the psychoanalytic tradition has failed to influence current approaches to the treatment of obesity in the British National Health Service. What is particularly disappointing is that ordinary people will readily agree that their eating behaviour is influenced by emotional factors. Psychoanalysis is pushing at an open door in terms of a popular willingness to accept its premises in relation to eating. The only possible conclusion is that the insights of psychoanalysis will remain in the private domain unless they can be presented in a way that meets the preoccupations of funders (Kvale, 1999; Parry, 2000).

In what follows we would like to describe an intervention carried out with obese women in a community setting that has resulted in weight loss and that may indicate a possible way forward for psychoanalytically informed researchers who wish to work in the field of obesity. (This study, and another that preceded it, will be reported in more detail elsewhere.)

The theoretical basis for the intervention was not exclusively psychoanalytic. It drew from a wide range of theoretical approaches. We have been strongly influenced by the implications of the examples quoted earlier of attachment theory and neuroscience in their fruitfulness for the development of effective therapies. The element from other understandings of obesity, which we have incorporated in our research groups, has been that of cognitive–behavioural therapy. We are both interested in and impressed by the work done on obesity by cognitive–behaviour therapists especially the work done by Fairburn and his associates (e.g., Cooper, Fairburn, & Hawker, 2003; Fairburn & Brownell, 2002). However, our theoretical commitment has been to the central psychoanalytic idea that all behaviour has meaning and can be understood in terms of that meaning. Our central focus was the exploration of the meanings for our participants of their behaviour.

The study was carried out in a community setting and recruited participants via advertisements in community agencies. Participants were therefore self-referred. The participants were all female and the intervention took place in a group. We have been convinced by the psychoanalytic writing on groups for obese people, which stresses the value of group support and the opportunity it offers for the development of the capacity for relationship; e.g., Ball and Norman (1996). Hayaki and Brownell (1996) urged the further investigation of groups in the treatment of obesity.

Twelve women attended group meetings in a community-counselling agency. Each participant provided a self-report of her weight and height and participated in a semi-structured interview. This interview was tape-recorded. These measures were all repeated at the end of each "term" of the intervention and at nine months' follow-up. Conventional research methods in the social sciences urge that the research is kept separate from the intervention as far as possible, to protect against bias. However, psychoanalytic groups also wish to protect the integrity of the group leader–participants' relationship. For these reasons we did our best to separate these functions, although lack of resources meant that a complete separation was not achieved. In future projects this separation will be more rigorously enforced.

The interview asked the participants what sense they made of their eating behaviour as well as a history of their emotional lives. This information was sought as a means of creating a baseline against which development could be measured, but it also started participants on a process of reflecting upon the meaning of their eating disorder that was congruent with the process of the group. McLeod (2003) notes the need to "find ways of gathering data which are consistent with the underlying psychodynamic theory" (p. 160). The nature of our interview processes was designed to meet this objective. In this initial interview it was also explained that the group would attempt to explore the reasons why the participants ate more than they needed or wanted and that the group itself would be useful for the participants.

The group met on thirty-six occasions for two hours over a period of fifteen months. The meetings took place in three "terms" each of approximately twelve weeks each. This extended spacing of the intervention was to allow for school holidays. Interventions in other traditions are frequently much shorter in duration. Our psychoanalytic background led us to believe that the sort of change that would lead to spontaneous alterations to eating behaviour would take a considerable amount of time. We have been influenced by Malan (1981), whose researches suggested that significant change required a minimum of between twenty and thirty sessions.

This group was given a self-help book (Fairburn, 1995). This book provided the cognitive element within the intervention. Its use was based on the widely accepted belief within the field of eating disorders that a cognitive element to address current eating behaviour is valuable (Roth & Fonagy, 1996). At each meeting the first half-hour was spent reviewing participants' progress with that programme. The rest of the time (one and a half hours) in each meeting was taken up by psychoanalytically informed work.

The first "term" of twelve weeks was structured by experiential exercises derived from psychodynamic, feminist, and self-psychological understandings of eating disorders.

The work of the therapeutic intervention included exercises to explore:

1. The relationship of weight changes to life events.
2. The use of food in the family of origin.
3. Attitudes to the body over the life span.
4. A self-portrait.
5. The expression of feelings in the family.
6. The identification of feelings.
7. The relationship with the mother.
8. The identification of concerned adults in the past.
9. The issue of trust.
10. The meaning of relationship.

It will be seen, from our earlier review of the literature, that the psychoanalytic influence on the choice of these subjects was very strong. Participants were seeking to understand the origins, meaning, and function of that eating behaviour. The consistent theme of the group leaders' interventions was the recognition of the value and purpose of the eating behaviour to the participants.

Since this was not a conventional psychoanalytic group, participants were asked to continue the work of the group between meetings, in three different ways:

1. By following the programme in Fairburn's book, which included monitoring their food use, meal planning, and working through the successive chapters. This programme was not directed at weight loss but at increasing awareness of psychological triggers.
2. Reflecting further on the themes addressed in the group meetings and carrying out related tasks (e.g., talking to family members about their experience, observing and recording their emotional reactions, etc.).
3. Contacting at least one other member of the group to share progress.

The requirement to contact another group member between sessions was intended to develop the participants' capacity to interact with others. We were astonished by the degree of resistance to this requirement and are uncertain how it can be interpreted. From an analytic viewpoint it may be that contact between the group members outside the group sessions was experienced as unsafe. On the other hand, the reluctance to make these contacts brought into sharp focus participants' reliance on food and rejection of other people in the management of their day-to-day lives. We are not yet certain whether we will include this as an element in future work.

The group was conducted in a "work-shop" mode rather than a group therapy mode. Strategies such as brain-storming, individual reflection, pair work, and small group work were used more than whole group discussion. These strategies were intended to allow participants who might be shy or anxious a more protected environment than that of whole group discussion. It was not thought possible, or appropriate, to create unstructured time or to encourage the disclosure of very difficult material. Nevertheless, the difficult histories and current circumstances of many of the participants meant that painful memories were sometimes activated. We became very much aware of the limitations of what a group can do for people with serious difficulties. We are interested in Kaplan's (1996) suggestion that group and individual therapy for this client group might well be conducted in tandem. Yalom (1985) makes the same suggestion, but it is, of course, a solution that is very expensive in resource terms.

The second term continued the discussion of the themes indicated above (as well as continuing with Fairburn's book). No exercises were provided since we considered that by this time the group would be able to engage with these themes without the support of greater structure.

The third term was more like a conventional psychoanalytic group. There was no further explicit work on Fairburn's book and group members themselves determined what should be discussed. Interestingly, in the evaluation of the group that was carried out at the end of the entire intervention, opinion was divided among participants as to whether the decreased structure was beneficial or not. We are familiar as trainers with a similar ambivalence among student participants in psychoanalytic groups. Our feeling is that the maintenance of the focus that was originally identified would be more beneficial than completely unstructured work and we will incorporate this modification into future interventions.

We should remind the reader that none of the work described was focused on weight loss. Nevertheless, of the twelve participants, six lost five per cent or more of their baseline weight by nine-month follow-up. This is the figure that is now agreed to produce significant health benefits (Blackburn, 2002). A further three participants had maintained a weight loss less than five per cent. Three participants gained weight.

These results show that a therapeutic group that is not focused on weight loss can produce changes in behaviour which lead to weight loss. Remarkably, weight loss at the end of the intervention continued over the period to the latest follow-up we have conducted at nine months. We will continue our monitoring for a further period. We have not found other research showing that weight loss can continue after the intervention is complete. It may well be that other psychoanalytically informed researchers who have conducted broadly similar interventions, e.g. Ball and Norman (1996), would have found similar results. Our point is that they did not, in fact, measure weight loss and therefore were unable to say whether the group was effective in this respect or not.

The series of interviews that were carried out showed a progressive development of understanding in the participants of the meaning of their use of food. This qualitative data also showed improvements in relationships and self-esteem, similar to those which have been reported by other psychoanalytically informed researchers.

This material demonstrates two features of our research, which we consider important. The first is that we came to conclusions about the emotional meanings of obesity that replicate reports by other psychoanalytic researchers and that therefore may be of value for practitioners (to be reported more fully elsewhere). We think that this conclusion demonstrates the value of conducting fresh research on old hypotheses and thereby consolidating earlier research. This process of replication, common in the social sciences and in positivist research generally, is very unusual in psychoanalytically informed research. Second, we consider that our combined qualitative and quantitative research methodology offers a way forward for psychoanalytically informed research. We were able to produce numerical data but, in addition, qualitative information that both enabled us to refine our design for future work and greatly enriched the account of the intervention.

As researchers we may be in danger of falling between the two stools of positivist experimental research design and purist psychoanalytic practice. In conventional research terms our methodology was very soft; we had no controls, our criteria for inclusion and exclusion were rather broad, we relied upon self-report, and we conducted no psychological assessments at the beginning or end of our intervention. Our wish was to explore whether psychoanalytically informed groups for obese women would lead to weight loss. This group did (which may be as much as we can say for now). Our psychoanalytic colleagues may feel that our methodologies, including cognitive–behavioural elements and the use of a semi-structured format, are so far from what is generally understood as psychoanalytic that our work does not deserve that name. However, we can find no other name for work that explicitly honoured the symptom as a coping mechanism, that recognized the impact of the past on the present, that looked for unconscious meanings, and that, above all, sought to enable relationship and connection between people.

We think that we may have negotiated these twin dangers well enough to present our results to funders and continue our researches. At the time of writing we have been approached by one primary care trust that wishes to commission us to run a group, and we have applied for funding to run three further groups. In addition, a psychoanalytic colleague has approached us wishing to run our group in her own PCT. We will be more than delighted if our aim to extend psychoanalytically informed work on obesity in the National Health Service begins to be achieved through these endeavours.

The development in our participants and their enthusiasm and commitment to the project has been inspiring. At the time of writing, three and a half years from the inception of the project, we are still receiving complete returns on the follow-up questionnaires. Even those three participants who chose to complete only the first term of the intervention have continued to send us their returns. This response, together with the results in relation to weight, have encouraged us in our conviction that psychoanalytic thinking has much to offer the field of research in obesity and deserves public funding and wider application.

Acknowledgements

I would like to acknowledge the help of Sharon Rother, MA, in the preparation of this paper.

References

Ball, J., & Norman, A. (1996). Without the group I'd still be eating half the co-op. An example of groupwork with women who use food. *Groupwork*. **9.** (1): 48–61.

Becker, B. (1960). The obese patient in group psychoanalysis. *American Journal of Psychotherapy*, 14: 323–337.

Blackburn, G. L. (2002). Weight loss and risk factors. In: C. G. Fairburn & K. D. Brownell (Eds.), *Eating Disorders and Obesity*. New York, NY: Guilford Press.

Burgard, D., & Lyons, P. (1994). Alternatives in obesity treatment: focusing on health for fat women. In: P. Fallon, M. A. Katzman, & S. C. Wooley (Eds.), *Feminist Perspectives on Eating Disorders*. New York, NY: Guilford Press.

Chernin, K. (1985). *The Hungry Self: Women, Eating and Identity*. London: Virago.

Ciano, R., Rocco, P. L., Angarano, A., Biasin, E., & Balestrini, M. (2002). Group-analytic and psychoeducational therapies for binge eating disorder: an exploratory study on efficacy and persistence of effects. *Psychotherapy Research*, 12(2): 231–239.

Cooper, Z., Fairburn, C. G., & Hawker, D. M. (2003). *Cognitive–Behavioral Treatment of Obesity: A Clinicians Guide*. New York, NY: Guilford Press.

Cortina, M., & Marrone, M. (Eds.) (2003). *Attatchment Theory and the Psychoanalytic Process*. London: Whurr.

Department of Health (1999). *National Service Framework for Mental Health*. London: HMSO.

Fairburn, C. (1995). *Overcoming Binge Eating*. New York, NY: Guilford Press.

Fairburn, C. G., & Brownell, K. D. (Eds). (2002). *Eating Disorders and Obesity*. New York, NY: Guilford Press.

Ferguson, B., & Russell, I. (2000). Towards evidence-based health care. In: N. Rowland & S. Goss (Eds.), *Evidence Based Counselling and Psychological Therapies: Research and Application*. New York, NY: Routledge.

Fonagy, P., & Target, M. (2003). *Psychoanalytic Theories*. London: Whurr.

Foster, G. D. (2002). Nondieting approaches. In: C. G. Fairburn & K. D. Brownell, (Eds.), *Eating Disorders and Obesity*. New York, NY: Guilford Press.

Glennon, S. S. (2001). The armored self: the symbolic significance of obesity. In: . Petrucelli & C. Stuart (Eds.), *Hungers and Compulsions: The Psychodynamic Treatment of Eating Disorders and Addictions*. Northvale, NJ: Jason Aronson.

Glucksman, M. L. (1989). Obesity: a psychoanalytic challenge. *Journal of the American Academy of Psychoanalysis*, 17(1): 151–171.

Greenberg, J. (1998). A clinical moment. *Psychoanalytic Dialogues, 8*(2): 217–224.

Hayaki, J., & Brownell, K. (1996). Behaviour change in practice: group approaches. *International Journal of Obesity, 20*(1): s27–30.

Holmes, J. (1993). *John Bowlby and Attachment Theory.* London: Routledge.

Holt, H., & Winnick, C. (1961). Group psychotherapy with obese women. *Archives of General Psychiatry, 5*: 64–76.

James, W. P. T. (2002). A world view of the obesity problem. In: C. G. Fairburn & K. D. Brownell (Eds.), *Eating Disorders and Obesity.* New York, NY: Guilford Press.

Kaplan, L. P. (1966). Some observations from conjoint individual and group therapy with obese women. *International Journal of Group Psychotherapy, 16*: 357–366.

Kaplan-Solms, K., & Solms, M. (2000). *Clinical Studies in Neuro-Psychoanalysis: Introduction to a Depth Neuropsychology.* London: Karnac.

Kvale, S. (1999). The psychoanalytic interview as qualitative research. *Qualitative Inquiry, 5*(1): 87–113.

Malan, D. H. (1981). *The Frontier of Brief Psychotherapy.* New York, NY: Plenum.

Maynard, A. (2000). Economic issues. In: N. Rowland & S. Goss (Eds.), *Evidence Based Counselling and Psychological Therapies: Research and Application.* New York, NY: Routledge.

McLeod, J. (2003). *Doing Counselling Research.* London: Sage.

National Audit Office (2000–2001) *Tackling Obesity in England.*

Ogden, J. (2003). *The Psychology of Eating.* Oxford: Blackwell.

Orbach, S. (1978). *Fat is a Feminist Issue.* London: Arrow.

Parry, G. (2000). Evidence-based psychotherapy: an overview. In: N. Rowland & S. Goss (Eds.), *Evidence Based Counselling and Psychological Therapies: Research and Application.* New York: Routledge.

Rodriguez-Rendo, M. C. (1984). There once was a body: history of the psychoanalysis of Marianne. *Topique: Revue Freudienne. 14*(33): 111–120.

Rose, M. (2003). The body doesn't lie: five tales of superobesity as somatic language. *Psychoanalytic Inquiry, 21*(3): 337–355.

Rosen, J. C. (2002). Obesity and body image. In: C. G. Fairburn & K. D. Brownell (Eds.), *Eating Disorders and Obesity.* New York: Guilford Press.

Roth, G. (1982). *Feeding the Hungry Heart: The Experience of Compulsive Eating.* New York, NY: Signet.

Roth, A., & Fonagy, P. (1996). *What Works for Whom? A Critical Review of Psychotherapy Research.* New York, NY: Guilford Press.

Seidell, J. C., & Tijhuis, M. A. R. (2002). Obesity and quality of life. In: C. G. Fairburn & K. D. Brownell (Eds.), *Eating Disorders and Obesity.* New York, NY: Guilford Press.

Shainess, N. (1979). The swing of the pendulum: from anorexia to obesity. *American Journal of Psychoanalysis, 39*(3): 225–234.

Slawson, P. F. (1965). Group psychotherapy with obese women. *Psychosomatics, 6*: 206–209.

Wolf, A. M. (2002). The health economics of obesity and weight loss. In: C. G. Fairburn & K. D. Brownell (Eds.), *Eating Disorders and Obesity.* New York, NY: Guilford Press.

Wooley, S. C., & Wooley, O. W. (1984). Should obesity be treated at all? In: A. J. Stunkard & E. J. Stellar (Eds.), *Eating and its Disorders.* New York, NY: Raven.

Yalom, I. D. (1985). *The Theory and Practice of Group Psychotherapy.* New York: Basic Books.

PART V

RESEARCHING THE THERAPIST AND THE THERAPEUTIC CONTEXT

Who do you think you are? A study of how psychotherapists' thinking styles affect orientation choice and practice

Andrew R. Arthur

Introduction

Why did Freud not develop cognitive–behavioural psychotherapy and Aaron Beck psychoanalysis; why cannot differently orientated psychotherapists respect each other's clinical and research work; and why do some patients not receive the "best" treatment for their problem? Is it possible that the personal epistemologies (theories of knowledge) or thinking styles of psychotherapists prevent it? Psychotherapists believe they make rational choices about their theoretical orientation, the type of treatment offered to patients, and the type of "evidence" they will attend to, but there is little thought given to how thinking styles or epistemological biases affect these decisions. Understanding more about the influence of these factors is important, because it explains why there is often prejudice, hostility, or ignorance when it come to valuing different research and treatment methods. There is another important reason; the underlying philosophy or epistemological view of the world contained in a psychotherapeutic approach will be communicated, and probably accepted and internalized by clients without their awareness or consent. Therefore, clients may not realize that along with their therapeutic treatment comes an epistemology and philosophical worldview; for example, that emotions derive from thoughts in cognitive–behaviour therapy (CBT), that there is an unconscious that may be in conflict in psychodynamic psychotherapy, or that psychological disturbance is a social construction. This may have profound effects on their philosophical and psychological worldview, sense of identity, and their own theories of knowledge.

The research and study presented here will show how different patterns of cognitive style and epistemology are significant influencing factors in psychotherapists' choice of theoretical orientation and treatment modality. In addition, it will also show how this affects the ability to fairly evaluate the strengths and weaknesses of other psychotherapeutic treatments, biases practitioners to learn and advocate for a particular therapy, and can lead to therapeutic failure and dissatisfaction when therapist and patient epistemologies do not match. We begin with a dichotomy.

The grand epistemic dichotomy

CBT and psychodynamic practitioners are particularly good examples of two orientations that appear to have two very different types of practice, ways of thinking about evidence, and theories of knowledge. This is not unique to psychotherapists or psychotherapists of these two schools; it also exists between, and within, other professional/academic groups. Indeed, a review of the literature found evidence suggesting the presence of what some authors call a "grand epistemological dichotomy" with two distinct patterns of personality traits among many professions (Johnson, Germer, Efran, & Overton, 1988; Royce & Moss, 1980). Notably the writer and scientist C. P. Snow (1964), in his 1959 Rede lecture at Cambridge University, described the existence of two competing value and philosophical systems, which he called "the two cultures". As a result of spending time with scientists and literary colleagues, Snow found that he was constantly

> ... moving among two groups—comparable in intelligence, identical in race, not grossly different in social origin, earning about the

same incomes who had almost ceased to communicate at all, who in intellectual, moral and psychological climate had so little in common . . . [*ibid.*, p. 2]

In a similar vein, John Conway (1992), in his Presidential Address to the Canadian Psychological Association, described a grand philosophical dichotomy (*science* versus *humanism*), like C. P. Snow's, along which he fitted the metatheoretical values of psychologists. His extensive and comprehensive review of the research strongly supports the idea of a metatheoretical, metapsychological and metaphysical dichotomy that has received many different labels, e.g., *subjectivism* versus *objectivism*, *elementarism* versus *holism*, *organicism* versus *mechanism*, and *metaphorism* versus *empiricism*.

Table 1 shows Conway's "grand epistemic dichotomy of worldviews" (Johnson & Miller, 1990). It reviews psychological epistemology from the past ninety years and evidence from twenty-three publications that supports the existence of two distinctly different theories of knowledge: a linear, analytic style versus a holistic, intuitive style. Empirical support came from a factor analysis of the seven major psychometric measures of epistemological style (noted by an asterisk in Table 1), which found two different factors that resembled and gave support to the existence of Conway's grand epistemic dichotomy.

Conway's (1992) review shows that a psychologist's position on the epistemic dichotomy can be associated with belief in particular psychological models and suggests that, in a similar fashion, a psychotherapist's epistemological position on this dichotomy should be associated with particular orientation choices.

Further evidence for the epistemic dichotomy comes from a large study of psychologists' orientation choice. It employed psychometric instruments and factor analytic techniques, and found that *objectivism–subjectivism* was the main factor that accounted for most of the variance between orientations (Coan, 1979). This dichotomy (Table 2) has a marked resemblance to Johnson and Miller's (1990).

Coan also found that personality traits correlated with *objectivism–subjectivism*. He added that it was reasonable to assume individual temperament and life history will make an individual receptive to different theories.

Table 1. Summary of the proposed epistemic dichotomy. Reproduced from Johnson and Miller (1990).

Linear, analytic style	Holistic, intuitive style	Source
Lockean	Leibnizean	Allport (1955)
Non-creative	Creative	Barron & Harrington (1981)
Analytical	Intuitive	Bruner (1960)
Objective	Subjective	Brunswick (1952)
Restrictive	Fluid	Coan (1979)
Objectivist	Subjectivist	Coan (1987)*
Mechanism	Systems philosophy	Holt *et al.* (1984)*
Modern, scientific	Primitive, magical	Horton (1975)
Tough-minded	Tender-minded	James (1907)
Mechanistic	Organicismic	Johnson *et al.* (1988)*
Thinking, sensing	Feeling, intuiting	Jung (1923)
Science	Humanism	Kimble (1984)*
Apollonian, Pythagorean	Donysian	Knapp (1964)
Formism, mechanism	Relativism, dialectism	Kramer *et al.* (1987)*
Generic	Particular	Maslow (1957)
Peripheralists	Centralists	Murray (1938)
Left brain	Right brain	Ornstein (1972)
Rational, empirical	Metaphorical	Royce (1964)*
Scientists	Humanists	Snow (1964)
Rightist ideoaffect	Leftist ideoaffect	Tomkins (1965)
Geometrical–technical	Physiognomic	Werner (1955)
Field dependent	Field indepdendent	Witkin & Goodenough (1977)
Dispositional, causal	Precausal	Young (1975)*

*Indicates that a psychometric measure was used and factor analysed in Johnson and Miller's (1990) study.

Table 2. Coan's Objectivism–subjectivism dichotomy.

Objectivism	Subjectivism
Factual orientation	Theoretical orientation
Impersonal causality	Personal will
Behavioural content emphasis	Experiential content emphasis
Elementarism	Holism
Physicalism	A rejection of physicalism
Quantitative orientation	Qualitative orientation

The first study to employ psychometric measures of epistemology examined 119 psychotherapists from two orientation groups, behaviour therapists and psychoanalysts (Schacht & Black, 1985). The Psycho-Epistemological Profile (PEP) (Royce & Mos, 1980) measured their epistemological beliefs. The PEP describes three epistemological styles; *metaphorism, empiricism,* and *rationalism.* The three styles are not mutually exclusive but arranged in a profile with the predominant style (highest score) first. The predicted predominant style for psychoanalysts was *metaphorism* as the highest scale, followed by *rationalism* and *empiricism.* For behaviourists, the prediction was *empiricism* as the highest scale, followed by *rationalism* and *metaphorism.* The results were that for 86% of psychoanalysts the predominant style was indeed *metaphorism,* followed by *rationalism* and *empiricism.* For behaviourists there was no predominant style and none of the PEP profile possibilities occurred at a frequency greater than chance. However, a separate comparison of just the mean scores for *metaphorism* and *empiricism* showed both differed in the predicted direction; the psychoanalysts' mean score for *metaphorism* was significantly higher than behaviourists', and the behaviourists' mean score for *empiricism* was significantly higher than psychoanalysts'. They explained this anomaly by pointing out it reflected the psychoanalytic group's homogeneousness and the behaviourists' heterogeneousness.

A large-scale investigation (*n* = 622) into link between the epistemological beliefs and personalities of scientists, including psychologists of different orientations, used the Organicism–Mechanism Paradigm Inventory (OMPI) to measure participants on a dichotomy of metaphysical belief from *mechanism* to *organicism.* The OMPI measure of philosophical worldviews correlated pervasively but not consistently with a variety of personality variables (Johnson, Germer, Efran, & Overton, 1988). The authors concluded, "In short, individuals' personalities mirror their overall philosophical worldviews" (*ibid.,* p. 833). The findings from Johnson's study describe two types of scientist; the *mechanistically* versus *organismically* inclined.

Mechanistically inclined

Mechanistically oriented persons (e.g. behaviourists) tend to be orderly, stable, conventional and conforming, objective, and realistic in their cognitive style. Interpersonally they are passive, obedient and reactive. This personality description is consistent with the *mechanistic* worldview, which assumes an ontology of stability and elementarism, an epistemology of objectivism and realism, and a view of persons as reactive, passive, and estranged from yet determined by their environments, who fail to develop progressively.

Organismically inclined

In contrast *organismically* inclined individuals (e.g. developmental psychologists) tend to be fluid, changing, creative, and non-conforming. They tend to be participative and imaginative in their cognitive style. They are active, purposeful, autonomous and individualistic, yet integrated into their interpersonal environment. This personality portrait is consistent with the *organicismic* world view, which assumes an ontology of change and holism, an epistemology that is interactive and constructivistic, and a view of persons as active, purposeful, autonomous, creative, integrated into the social matrix, who progressively develop toward goals. [*ibid.*, p. 833]

In a related study, and as part of an investigation into the effects of discrepancies between therapists' and their therapeutic models, the epistemological styles of 140 Portuguese psychotherapists from five different orientations were assessed using the PEP & OMPI (Vasco, Garcia-Marques, & Dryden, 1993). Data from the study supplied by private communication (Vasco, 1997) showed there was a significant difference between orientations for *organicism* and *mechanicism* on the OMPI and for *rationalism* on the PEP. Table 3

Table 3.   Mean scores for the OMPI and PEP scales for different therapist orientations.

	Behavioural	Cognitive	Eclectic	Humanist	Psycho-dynamic	Systems	F
	$n = 12$	$n = 59$	$n = 21$	$n = 14$	$n = 32$	$n = 16$	
Organicism	17.17	21.49	20.9	21.86	21.03	21.25	4.4**
Metaphorism	3.58	3.6	3.77	3.74	3.81	3.71	1.4 NS
Rationalism	3.31	3.37	3.23	3.06	3.28	3.36	2.1*
Empircism	3.32	3.19	3.19	3.04	3,13	3.25	0.8 NS

**$p < 0.001$; *$p < 0.07$
Source: Vasco, 1997.

shows behaviourists scoring in the *mechanistic* direction (the lowest *organicism* score = 17.17). For *rationalism,* the biggest difference in scores is between the humanistic/existentialists (lowest score = 3.06) and the system/communication group (highest score = 3.36). No significant difference between analysts and behaviourists was found on the PEP for *metaphorism* and *empiricism,* as had been found by Schacht and Black (1985). This may because of the very unequal group sizes, which ranged from 12 to 59.

The present study

Method

This study examined the cognitive styles and epistemological beliefs of cognitive–behavioural and psychoanalytic psychothera-pists as part of a larger study into the factors influencing orienta-tion choice among psychotherapists (Arthur, 1998, 2001, 2000a,b).

Cognitive-behavioural and psychoanalytic psychotherapists completed standardized paper and pencil personality (Millon Index of Personality Styles (MIPS), Millon, 1994) and epistemological inventories (Organicism–Mechanism Paradigm Inventory (OMPI) Johnson, Germer, Efran, & Overton, 1988; Psycho-Epistemological Profile (PEP), Royce and Mos, 1980) and their results compared.

A large number (247) of cognitive–behavioural (113) and regis-tered psychoanalytic psychotherapists (134) participated in this postal study from an invited sample of 544 (response rate 45%). Convenience and random sampling methods and were employed and participants selected from the appropriate section of the United Kingdom Council for Psychotherapists and British Confederation of Psychotherapists registers. Participants completed the personal-ity inventory (MIPS), the two epistemological inventories (OMPI and PEP) and a questionnaire to ensure that they actually practised within their professed orientation, and were committed and satis-fied with it. Results suggested almost all participants practised within their registered orientation.

Personality and cognitive–epistemological traits are the result of lifelong developmental processes, and not likely to be easily affected by temporary environmental influences such as life events.

They are the result of early experience, education, genetics, mother–infant bonding, and family relations. Therefore, if these traits had originally been involved in orientation choice, then on inventories measuring these variables participants should differ significantly. A review of trait stability involving major personality inventories (Cattel 16PF, MMPI, NEO Five Factor Personality Inventory) demonstrates that basic personality traits (*neuroticism, extraversion, openness to experience, conscientiousness,* and *agreeableness*) are stable over very long periods (Costa and McCrae, 1994). It is likely that because epistemological traits have been shown to correlate pervasively, albeit not consistently, with a wide variety of personality inventories they will also be stable over very long periods (Johnson, Germer, Efran, & Overton, 1988); "In short, individuals' personalities mirror their overall philosophical worldviews" (*ibid.*, p. 833).

Analysis and results

This investigation compared two independent groups of participants (psychoanalytic and cognitive–behavioural psychotherapists) on a personality inventory that contained scales for cognitive styles and two epistemological measures.

The main factor (the independent variable) was the therapeutic orientation of the participants. The data on two additional factors, gender and years of experience, were examined for any possible interaction effects. All data from the dependent variables (personality, cognitive–epistemological style, commitment questions) were analysed initially by analysis of variance (ANOVAs) for the three factors (orientation, gender, experience) and the three factor interactions (orientation by gender by experience). Where a between-subjects effect was found, a follow up ANOVA was performed and, if appropriate, follow up *post hoc* statistical tests.

The results of the ANOVA found participants differed significantly ($p < 0.05$ to $p < 0.001$) by orientation on twelve out of twenty-four traits on the personality inventory; cognitive traits were the most significant differentiating factor (six of the eight cognitive subscales). On the two epistemological inventories, the OMPI differentiated participants by orientation ($F(1,238 = 7.41, p = < 0.007$) and the PEP found a significant difference ($F(1,163 = 10.63, p = < 0.001$) for one of three epistemological traits. Results indicate, therefore,

that the orientation of the psychotherapist consistently and pervasively affected scores on all the measures. This strongly suggests
that the theoretical orientation of psychotherapists reflects certain
characteristic personality traits and cognitive–epistemological
styles.

Personality and cognitive–epistemological factors clearly distin-
guish psychoanalytic from cognitive–behavioural psychotherapists.
They have distinctly different motivational aims (MIPS), cognitive
styles (MIPS), epistemological beliefs (OMPI and PEP), interpersonal behaviours (MIPS), and levels of commitment to their chosen
orientation—as measured by their questionnaire responses. It is
likely that these personality and cognitive–epistemological factors
play an important role in the psychotherapist's choice and practice
of therapeutic orientation.

The interactions between psychotherapeutic orientation and the
gender and experience of therapists for the cognitive–epistemological traits revealed that gender made no difference but experience
did. Analysis of variance (ANOVA) indicated there was an interaction between orientation and experience for two of the MIPS
cognitive traits and the OMPI. These results suggested novice
psychoanalytic psychotherapists are less *systematizing* and *sensing*,
and more *organismic* than their novice cognitive–behaviourist coun-
terparts and that the novice psychoanalytic psychotherapists are
more *organismic* than their own senior psychoanalytic colleagues.
With greater experience, these cognitive–epistemological differences disappear and there are no significant interaction effects at
the intermediate or senior levels. Overall, the personality and
cognitive–epistemological trait patterns are consistent with those
derived from a previous meta-analysis of personality and cognitive–epistemological trait differences found in a review of the literature (Arthur, 2000a).

Discussion

The findings from this study suggest important differences exist in
styles of thinking between cognitive–behavioural and psychoanalytic psychotherapists and that this affects orientation choice, and
has implications for clinical practice. In this investigation, thinking

style was considered from two perspectives: (1) the structure and functional style of the cognitive apparatus itself (cognition) and (2) the beliefs, theories of knowledge, and philosophical worldview that originate from that apparatus (epistemology). Discussion begins with an evaluation of the cognitive style differences followed by the epistemological findings and the implications of this research are then considered.

Cognitive style

There are four bipolar pairs of traits that constitute the cognitive modes and their operation according to Millon's model and as measured by the MIPS:

MIPS COGNITIVE MODES	DESCRIPTION
Extraversing–Introversing	Source of information gathering
Sensing–Intuiting	Style of information gathering
Thinking–Feeling	Style of information processing
Systematizing–Innovating	How information is organized

The first cognitive dimension, *extraversing–introversing*, relates to the sources used to gather knowledge. It is concerned with whether individuals characteristically seek knowledge outside themselves (*extraversing*), having regard to the environment and others, or whether they seek it within themselves (*introversing*) having regard to internal thoughts and feelings. Analysts and behaviourists did not differ on this *extraversing–introversing* dimension.

This is a surprising finding, because empirical observation and theory suggest the behaviourist is primarily concerned with the external interpsychic world of consciousness and the analyst is primarily concerned with the internal intrapsychic world of unconsciousness. There is evidence from the literature reviewed to support these observations (Angelos, 1977; Caine & Smail, 1969a,b; Kreitman, 1962; Walton, 1966). The explanation is that Millon understood *extraversing–introversing* as a cognitive trait from his reading of Jung:

> What did Jung mean by "Extraversion" and "Introversion"? The view commonly held by Jung's interpreters is that these terms refer to behavioural aspects of sociability . . . It is the author's view that

Jung intended something appreciably different. His was essentially a cognitive orientation, so that Extroversion and Introversion signified not a person's social style but the question of his or her attentions and interests. [Millon, 1994, p. 22]

The evidence from this investigation therefore suggests that analysts and behaviourists do not differ in their primary source of information. They use a similar pattern of internal and external sources. What then happens to that knowledge? Examination of the scores from the other cognitive modes shows there are differences in how it is gathered, processed and organised. According to Millon, two traits measure the gathering of knowledge; *sensing* and *intuiting*. *Sensing* is seen by Millon as describing the type of person who relies on their physical senses for tangible, structured, and well-defined information-gathering, while the *intuiting* person is seen as preferring thoughts of an abstract, complex, connotative, symbolic, and metaphysical nature.

Novice behaviourists scored significantly higher on *sensing* than analysts. This difference disappeared after eleven years of practice and orientations are then similar on this trait. An examination of the pattern of scores for *sensing* shows that behaviourists decreased on this trait with experience. Then, at the intermediate experience level, the analysts' score increases until there is no longer any significant difference. This trend continues into the senior level.

Processing and organizing knowledge

After being gathered, knowledge is processed by either *thinking* or *feeling* and later organized in either a *systematic* or an *innovative* manner, according to Millon. The *thinking* trait emphasizes the use of reason, logic, reduction of emotional input, and objectivity, *feeling* emphasizes the primacy of affect to transform information, use of introspective analysis, and empathic response. The MIPS results showed analysts scored significantly higher for *feeling* than behaviourists did, and behaviourists scored significantly higher for *thinking* than analysts. Clinically, this suggests behaviourists probably rely more on reason and logic to transform information concerning the patient (e.g., observation, measures of observable behaviours, environmental cues) and analysts rely more on their feelings to understand and assess the patient's responses.

The final step in cognitive transformation concerns how information and knowledge are organized by the person, whether the person fits new information into their pre-existing cognitive systems (*systematizing*) or whether they allow imagination and creativity to suggest a unique understanding (*innovating*). Analysts scored significantly higher for *innovating* than behaviourists. For *systematizing*, there was a difference at the novice level, with behaviourists scoring significantly higher. The analysts' score then increased and the behaviourists' decreased in the other experience levels, until they were similar for this trait.

It is possible that the analysts' *innovative* cognitive style fits more closely to the less systematically structured analytic model and the novice behaviourists' *systematizing* style fits their primarily cognitive–behavioural clinical psychology training. It is important, in this connection, to recall that the psychoanalytic movement was and still is characterized by revolution, splitting, fragmentation, diversity, and strong personalities, as reflected by the founders of the movement. Peter Gay (1988) in his book, *Freud, A Life for our Time*, described how Freud's psychoanalytic theory was an innovation and how Freud experimented and changed his own theories. By contrast, the history and development of early behaviourism into cognitive–behaviour therapy appears scientific, orderly, sequential, and systematic.

These differences in historical development and training may help to explain the finding that *systematizing* is the predominant cognitive–organizational style for behaviourists, and *innovating* for analysts. There may have been a resonance or fit between the participants' perception of the orientations' apparent cognitive style and their own that "tempts" the potential therapist towards their appropriate orientation;

> Psychotherapists' attitudes toward the theoretical and metatheoretical assumptions of different orientations are the result of personal perspectives, philosophical stances, worldviews, and values. All these variables combine to make a particular orientation more tantalising than others, contributing to an eventual goodness of fit between a therapist's personality and a particular orientation. [Vasco, Garcia-Marques, & Dryden, 1993, p. 183]

It is to be hoped that the orientation of most therapists fits with their cognitive style, but what happens if it doesn't? For example, what might happen if a person who is highly *systematizing* misperceives an analytical training as structured, systematic, and consistent? An investigation into the consequence of dissonance between the therapist's personal philosophy and values and the metatheoretical assumptions of their selected orientation found that when dissonance was present there was dissatisfaction (Vasco, Garcia-Marques, & Dryden, 1993). This may cause therapists to abandon their work, select eclecticism, "retreat to commitment", and feel dissatisfied and become less effective.

The epistemological measures

Findings from the MIPS cognitive scales should correlate with the epistemological scales (OMPI & PEP). Predictions concerning the expected correlations between all the cognitive and epistemological scales suggested that the MIPS *sensing, thinking,* and *systematizing* scales should fit with OMPI *mechanism* and PEP *empiricism–rationalism,* and be called the "objective" dimension. Behaviourists, in fact, were found to score significantly higher than analysts on all those scales, except PEP *empiricism–rationalism.* Likewise, the MIPS *intuiting, feeling,* and *innovating* scales should fit with OMPI *organicism* and PEP *metaphorism* and be called the "subjective" dimension. Analysts were found to score significantly higher than behaviourists on all those traits. However, some of these differences disappear with experience and were really only observed consistently and clearly with less experienced practitioners.

On the two measures of epistemological styles (OMPI and PEP) both orientations differed significantly. This suggests that analysts and behaviourists have different epistemological styles, which further confirms the differences found on the cognitive modes component of the MIPS. The findings from the two epistemological inventories will now be explored in depth.

The Organicism Mechanism Paradigm Inventory

The scores for the OMPI went entirely in the predicted direction with the behaviourists predominantly *mechanistic* and the analysts *organismic*. This result suggests that the philosophical worldview of analysts tends to the *organicism* direction and of behaviourists to the *mechanicism* direction.

Novice analysts scored significantly toward the *organicism* direction and novice behaviourists toward the *mechanicism* direction. At the intermediate and senior levels the OMPI scores moved closer and were no longer significantly different. This could suggest that analysts and behaviourists may have begun their practices with significantly dissimilar epistemological beliefs but through experience came to share similar views. However, an alternative explanation is that over the years analysts with more *organismic* and behaviourists with more *mechanistic* epistemologies are being attracted to their orientations.

Psycho-epistemological profile

A second measure of epistemological beliefs, the Psycho-Epistemological Profile (PEP) was offered to those participants (*n*=247) who had completed the original questionnaire packs containing the OMPI and MIPS. Two-thirds (165 of 247) of participants returned useable PEPs in similar orientation proportions to the main study: 55% (90 of 165) were analysts, and 45% (75 of 165) were behaviourists.

The PEP determines predominant epistemological style from three subscales; *metaphorism, empiricism,* or *rationalism*. Results from previous research suggest that the analysts' predominant epistemology should be *metaphorism* and behaviourists' *empiricism* (Johnson & Miller, 1990; Royce & Mos, 1980; Schacht & Black, 1985). In this investigation, analysts scored significantly higher than behaviourists did on *metaphorism* but there was no difference for *empiricism*. The hierarchical pattern for analysts was *metaphorism* followed by *rationalism* and *empiricism*, which was also the pattern for the behaviourists. So, the expected epistemological prediction was found for analysts but not for behaviourists. One possible explanation for this finding is that behaviourists may have a greater range of epistemological beliefs but be less consistently committed to them. They may be a more heterogeneous group as a previous investigation found (Schacht & Black, 1985). This could reflect a greater epistemological flexibility or perhaps uncertainty concerning the nature of evidence they require. When asked about their commitment to their orientation, behaviourists responded that they would be more likely to step outside their cognitive–behavioural orientation than analysts.

Seniors from both orientations showed significantly higher *empiricism* scores than novices. This suggests, like the findings from the cognitive scales, that there is a tendency to develop a more objective attitude with experience.

Implications of the research

This research, and the review of previous investigations, suggests that it may be important for persons considering their orientation as a psychotherapist to assess their own personalities and cognitive–epistemological styles. Research has shown that when there is dissonance between a particular orientation's metatheoretical assumptions and a person's own personal values and epistemological style there can be dissatisfaction. This may result three common reactions:

> (a) re-entrenchment, by allowing their theory to influence even further their practice (psychodynamics); (b) changing and revising by diminishing the influence of selected theory in practice (cognitive and behaviourists), or by selecting eclectic as secondary theoretical orientation (cognitive); or (c) abandoning career (psychodynamics and systemics). A fourth way is also conceivable, though not yet empirically supported—prevalent crisis" [Vasco, Garcia-Marques, & Dryden, 1993, p. 193]

It is possible that within each individual's particular pattern of personality traits and cognitive–epistemological styles, there lies embedded an orientation fit that may take time and development to realize. This may be why some therapists go through various theoretical and paradigm shifts until they reach the position that feels correct. What may be happening is that through development and insight they are finding their embedded orientation.

This research also suggests that the different cognitive–epistemological styles make dialogue extremely difficult between these two major psychotherapeutic orientations and possibly others as well. As Lyddon (1989) concludes after a discussion of the philosophical differences between orientations

> ... differences across philosophical positions cannot be resolved at the level of competing facts and theories. A more comprehensive understanding needs to include a deeper level of analysis—that is, an exploration of the fundamental philosophical assumptions upon which different counselling theories and approaches are based. [*ibid.*, p. 446]

Without this fundamental exploration, such attempts are fruitless and lead to confusion and misunderstanding. Attempts to integrate psychoanalysis with cognitive therapy without an awareness of their different epistemologies should be treated with extreme caution in order to avoid possible theoretical and methodological confusion (Liotti & Reda, 1981). Although such an integration should be favourably considered because of the practical value, both approaches are of ". . . equal scientific legitimacy but of incompatible philosophical natures. As a consequence . . . we must approach this integration with extreme caution in order to avoid the possible theoretical and methodological confusion" (*ibid.*, p. 235).

In a paper describing a "posteclectic" approach to integrative psychotherapy Millon (author of the MIPS used in this study) admits that the integration of different therapeutic methods must contend with ". . . differing 'worldviews' concerning the essential nature of psychological experience" (Millon, 1988, p. 210), but sees no problem in encouraging active dialectic amongst the different theorists and practitioners. However, although the differences can be creative and challenging, as previous research suggests, if they are not acknowledged and properly understood they may lead to re-entrenchment, isolation, conflict and lack of communication (Vasco, Garcia-Marques, & Dryden, 1993).

Conclusions

This study and review of the literature on cognitive–epistemological styles compares differently orientated psychotherapists and finds that significant differences in personality, particularly cognitive–epistemological style, exist. This has implications for communicating, evaluating, and processing psychotherapeutic knowledge; the ability to consider the validity of other approaches; the choice and practice of therapy for clients; training selection and satisfaction for practitioners; and therapeutic outcome—especially when therapist and client may not share the same cognitive–epistemology. Finally, psychotherapists from different orientation experience, understand, and process knowledge differently—they do not just differ theoretically. This makes it very important that we become aware and make attempts to overcome the restrictions of our own cognitive–epistemological styles.

Acknowledgement

The late Timothy Arthur for his help with this study.

References

Arthur, A. R. (1998). An investigation into the personality traits and cognitive-epistemological styles of cognitive-behavioural and psychoanalytic psychotherapists. Unpublished doctoral dissertation. City University, London.

Arthur, A. R. (2001). Personality, epistemology and psychotherapists' choice of theoretical model: a review and analysis. *The European Journal of Psychotherapy, Counselling and Health*, 4(1): 45–64.

Arthur, A. R. (2000a). The personality and cognitive-epistemological traits of cognitive-behavioural and psychoanalytic psychotherapists. *The British Journal of Medical Psychology*, 73(2), 243–258).

Arthur, A. R. (2000b). Do I choose my orientation or does it choose me? *The Psychotherapist*, 14(Spring): 24–27.

Angelos, C. A. (1977). Relationships of psychotherapists' personality and therapy methods (Doctoral Dissertation, University of Michigan, 1977). *Dissertation Abstracts International*, 38: 1392B.

Caine, T. M., & Smail, D. J. (1969a). The effects of personality and training on attitudes to treatment: preliminary investigations. *British Journal of Medical Psychology*, 42: 277–282.

Caine, T. M., & Smail, D. J. (1969b). *The Treatment of Mental Illness: Science, Faith, and the Therapeutic Personality.* London: University of London Press.

Coan, R. W. (1979). *Psychologists—Personal and Theoretical Pathways.* New York: John Wiley.

Conway, J. B. (1992). A world of differences among psychologists. *Canadian Psychology, 33*(1): 1–23.

Costa, P. T., & McCrae, R. R. (1994). Set like plaster? Evidence for the stability of adult personality. In: T. F. Hetherton & J. L. Weinberger (Eds.), *Can Personality Change?* Washington, DC: American Psychological Association.

Gay, P. (1988). *Freud, A Life for Our Time.* London: MacMillan.

Johnson, J. A., Germer, C. K., Efran, J. S., & Overton, W. F. (1988). Personality as the basis for theoretical predilections. *Journal of Personality and Social Psychology, 55*(5): 824–835.

Johnson, J. A., & Miller, M. L. (1990). Factor analysis of worldview inventories suggest two fundamental ways of knowing. Unpublished manuscript, Pennsylvania State University.

Kreitman, N. (1962). Psychiatric orientation: a study of attitudes among psychiatrists. *Journal of Mental Science, 108*: 317–328.

Liotti, G., & Reda, M. (1981). Some epistemological remarks on behavior therapy, cognitive therapy and psychoanalysis. *Cognitive Therapy and Research, 5*(3): 231–236.

Lyddon, W. J. (1989). Root metaphor theory: a philosophical framework for counselling and psychotherapy. *Journal of Counseling and Development, 67*: 442–448.

Millon, T. (1994). *Millon Index of Personality Styles-Manual.* San Antonio, TX: The Psychological Corporation/Harcourt, Brace.

Millon, T. (1988). Personolgic psychotherapy: Ten commandments for a posteclectic approach to integrative treatment. *Psychotherapy, 25*(2): 209–219.

Royce, J. R., & Mos, L. P. (1980). *Manual, Psycho-Epistemological Profile.* (Center for Advanced Study in Theoretical Psychology). University of Alberta, Canada.

Schacht, T. E., & Black, D. A. (1985). Epistemological commitments of behavioral and psychoanalytic therapists. *Professional Psychology: Research and Practice, 16*(2): 316–323.

Snow, C. P. (1964). *The Two Cultures and a Second Look.* London: Cambridge University Press.

Vasco, A. B. (1997). Mean OMPI and PEP scores for different therapist orientations. Unpublished raw data.

Vasco, A. B., Garcia-Marques, L., & Dryden, W. (1993). "Psycho-therapist know thyself!": Dissonance between metatheoretical and personal values in psychotherapists of different theoretical orienta-tions. *Psychology Research*, 3(3): 181–196.

Walton, H. J. (1966). Difference between physically-minded and psychologically-minded medical practitioners. *British Journal of Psychiatry*, 112: 1097–1102.

CHAPTER TWENTY-THREE

Psychotherapists' "personal styles": construing and preferred theoretical orientations

David Winter, Finn Tschudi and Nicholas Gilbert

Introduction

Disagreements between psychotherapists of different orientations are often characterized more by emotional intensity than by cool scientific argument. Why is this? And how do budding psychotherapists, and indeed clients, select their preferred approaches from the 500 or so therapies that are now available (Karasu, 1986), given that there is little to choose between them in terms of research evidence of their effectiveness (Wampole *et al.*, 1997)? Some answers to these questions have been provided by a research programme that commenced over thirty years ago, initially to explore resistance to the introduction of a therapeutic community in a traditional psychiatric hospital, Claybury Hospital. This provided consistent evidence that the attitudes and preferences of both staff and clients concerning psychiatric and psychological treatment reflect individuals' "personal styles" (Caine & Smail, 1969; Caine, Wijesinghe, & Winter, 1981; Caine & Winter, 1993; Winter, 1990). Specifically, staff who favour, or choose to practise, more structured, directive treatment approaches have been found to be more outer-directed and conservative than those who favour less directive, more interpersonally-focused approaches. There have been similar findings with clients, whose personal styles (as assessed by measures of direction of interest and conservatism) have also been found to be reflected in features of their personal construct systems, scores on measures of openness to experience and convergent/divergent thinking, the nature of their presenting symptoms, and their response to different forms of therapy.

A further body of research has demonstrated that in clients (Lyddon & Adamson, 1992; Neimeyer, Prichard, Lyddon, & Sherrard, 1993), behavioural scientists (Johnson, Germer, Efran, & Overton, 1988), and psychotherapists (Arthur, 1999; Schacht & Black, 1985), individuals' "worldview" reflects their preferences for theoretical orientations, those with a mechanistic worldview preferring a behavioural, and those with an organicist worldview a constructivist, developmental, or psychodynamic, approach. Arthur's study also found differences on various other aspects of epistemological style and personality between cognitive–behavioural and psychodynamic therapists. In addition, the therapeutic preferences of students and psychotherapists have been found to reflect the extent to which their epistemological orientation is constructivist or rationalist (Neimeyer & Morton, 1997).

The present study examined differences between therapists of different orientations using measures of both personal styles and philosophical beliefs, allowing investigation of the relationship between these domains. The use of repertory grid technique (Kelly, 1955) also allowed exploration of therapists' constructions of their own and other therapeutic approaches, and examination of the extent of commonality of their construing within and between orientations. Specifically, the hypotheses investigated were as follows:

(i)   that outer-directedness is related to rationalist philosophical beliefs;

(ii)   that therapists of different theoretical orientations differ in inner-directedness, personal construct, humanistic, and psychodynamic therapists being the most inner-directed and cognitive–behavioural therapists the least;

(iii) that therapists of different orientations differ in philosophical beliefs, personal construct, systemic, and humanistic therapists

being the most constructivist and cognitive–behavioural therapists the most rationalist;

(iv) that there is greater commonality of construing of therapists
within therapeutic orientations than between therapists of
different orientations.

Method

Participants

Invitations to participate were sent to the following psychotherapists on the National Register of the United Kingdom Council for
Psychotherapy (numbers agreeing to participate are indicated in
parentheses):

118 analytical psychologists (11);
 42 cognitive-analytic therapists (5);
160 randomly selected cognitive-behavioural therapists (13);
281 humanistic therapists, stratified to include each particular
 humanistic orientation (33);
150 hypno-psychotherapists (15);
 63 neurolinguistic psychotherapists (8);
 37 personal construct psychotherapists (9);
150 randomly selected psychodynamic psychotherapists (11);
152 randomly selected systemic therapists (12).

The overall response rate was 9.9%.

Measures

Participants were asked to complete:

a questionnaire requesting demographic information and
details of the respondent's therapeutic orientation and experience;
the Direction of Interest Questionnaire (DIQ) (Caine, Smail,
Wijesinghe, & Winter, 1982), high scores on which indicate
inner-directedness;

the Therapist Attitude Questionnaire-Short Form (TAQ) (Neimeyer & Morton, 1997), which includes rationalism and constructivism scales;

a repertory grid in which, as listed below, sixteen therapeutic approaches and an ideal approach were rated on eighteen supplied constructs drawn from the literature on psychotherapy and optional elicited constructs. Grids were analysed by FLEXIGRID (Tschudi, 1998), from which various measures were extracted, and the MULTIGRID package (Tschudi, 2001) was employed to examine the mean grids of therapists of different orientations and to provide various other calculations.

Elements and constructs in the repertory grid

Elements
Behaviour therapy
Cognitive therapy
Psychoanalytic psychotherapy
Analytical psychology
Gestalt psychotherapy
Transactional analysis
Psychosynthesis
Existential psychotherapy
Cognitive analytic therapy
Psychodrama
Personal construct psychotherapy
Neurolinguistic programming
Systemic therapy
Client centred therapy
Hypno-psychotherapy
Group analysis
Your own preferred approach (if not included in the above list)
An ideal treatment approach
Constructs
Deterministic—indeterministic
Elementaristic—holistic
Apersonal—individually focused
Realistic—idealistic

Extraspective—introspective
Aims for corrective treatment goals—aims for creative treatment goals
Focuses on conscious awareness—focuses on unconscious awareness
Objective—subjective
Mechanistic—contextualist
Unstructured treatment sessions—highly structured treatment sessions
Authoritarian therapeutic relationship—democratic
Impersonal—personal
Concerned with the past—concerned with the present and future
Has a weak evidence base—has a strong evidence base
Ineffective—effective
Unlikely to be harmful—potentially harmful
Would feel uncomfortable to employ—would feel comfortable
Would not wish to be treated by—would be happy to be treated by.

Results

Relationships between measures

As predicted in hypothesis (i), inner direction of interest was, as expected, found to be significantly inversely correlated with rationalist philosophical beliefs ($r = -0.45$; $p<0.01$). Its lack of correlation with the measure of constructivist beliefs ($r = -0.06$) is consistent with the lack of evidence of the predictive validity of the TAQ Constructivism scale in previous research.

Various significant correlations were also found between grid measures and other variables. Of most interest were:

the relationship between outer direction of interest and a more unidimensional construct system, as indicated in a low percentage of variance accounted for by the second principal component of the grid ($r = 0.29$; $p < 0.05$);

a relationship between number of years since the completion of training and degree of satisfaction with the therapist's own treatment orientation, as reflected in a low distance between

the grid element referring to this orientation and the "ideal
treatment approach" element ($r = -0.44$; $p < 0.01$);
a relationship between rationalist beliefs and favourable
constructions of behaviour therapy and cognitive therapy, as
reflected in the distances between these elements and the
"ideal treatment approach" element (both $rs = -0.42$; $p < 0.01$);
a relationship between constructivist beliefs and a favourable
construction of existential therapy ($r = -0.31$; $p < 0.05$).

Differences between orientations on questionnaire measures

As indicated in Table 1, cognitive–behavioural therapists were
found to be significantly more outer-directed than therapists of all
other orientations. Psychodynamic therapists were the most inner-
directed, and significantly more so than hypno-psychotherapists. A
similar pattern emerged on the Rationalism Scale (see Table 2),
cognitive–behaviour therapists being more rationalist than all other
groups except hypno-psychotherapists, who in turn were were
more rationalist than all the remaining groups except neurolinguistic psychotherapists. Perhaps surprisingly, in that they are classified
within the UK Council for Psychotherapy as constructivists,
neurolinguistic psychotherapists were more rationalist than

Table 1.   Differences between therapists on the direction of interest
questionnaire.

Orientation	N	Mean	SD
Cognitive–behavioural	13	14.69	4.66
Hypno-psychotherapy	14	19.00	5.84
Systemic	12	19.67	4.27
Analytical psychology	11	20.73	4.17
Neurolinguistic	8	20.75	4.53
Cognitive–analytic	6	20.83	5.53
Humanistic	32	21.09	4.45
Personal construct	8	22.50	4.11
Psychodynamic	10	23.50	4.09

Analysis of variance revealed a significant difference between
orientations: $F(8, 105) = 3.50$, $p = 0.001$
LSD tests indicated the following significant differences:
cognitive–behavioural therapy < all other orientations
psychodynamic psychotherapy > hypno-psychotherapy

Table 2.   Differences between therapists on the therapist attitude
questionnaire.

Orientation	N	Mean	SD
Rationalism scale			
Cognitive–behavioural	13	27.08	3.97
Hypno-psychotherapy	15	26.03	3.65
Neurolinguistic	8	22.19	3.16
Systemic	12	19.71	4.61
Analytical psychology	11	18.95	4.50
Cognitive–analytic	5	18.60	5.55
Humanistic	33	17.39	4.75
Personal construct	9	16.22	6.02
Psychodynamic	11	15.27	3.55

Constructivism scale
No significant differences between therapists were observed.

Analysis of variance revealed a significant difference between
orientations: $F(8,108) = 11.70$; $p < 0.001$
LSD tests revealed the following significant differences:
cognitive–behavioural > all orientations except hypno-psychotherapy
hypno-psychotherapy > all orientations except CBT and NLP
neurolinguistic > psychodynamic, personal construct and humanistic
systemic > psychodynamic

psychodynamic, personal construct, and humanistic therapists.
Systemic therapists were also more rationalist than psychodynamic
therapists. No significant differences between the groups emerged
on the TAQ Constructivism Scale.

Differences between groups on repertory grids

As expected, on the repertory grid most therapists tended to view
their own approach more positively (i.e., as more similar to an ideal
treatment approach) than did therapists of other orientations.

Differences and commonalities between the grids of therapists of
different orientations were examined further by the use of Tschudi's
(2001) MULTIGRID package. This allowed the construction of a
mean grid for the therapists as a whole as well as for therapists
within each orientation. The plot derived from principal component
analysis of the mean grid of the whole group is shown in Figure 1. In
the plot, the greater the distance between two therapies, the less
similarity was perceived by the group as a whole. The first principal

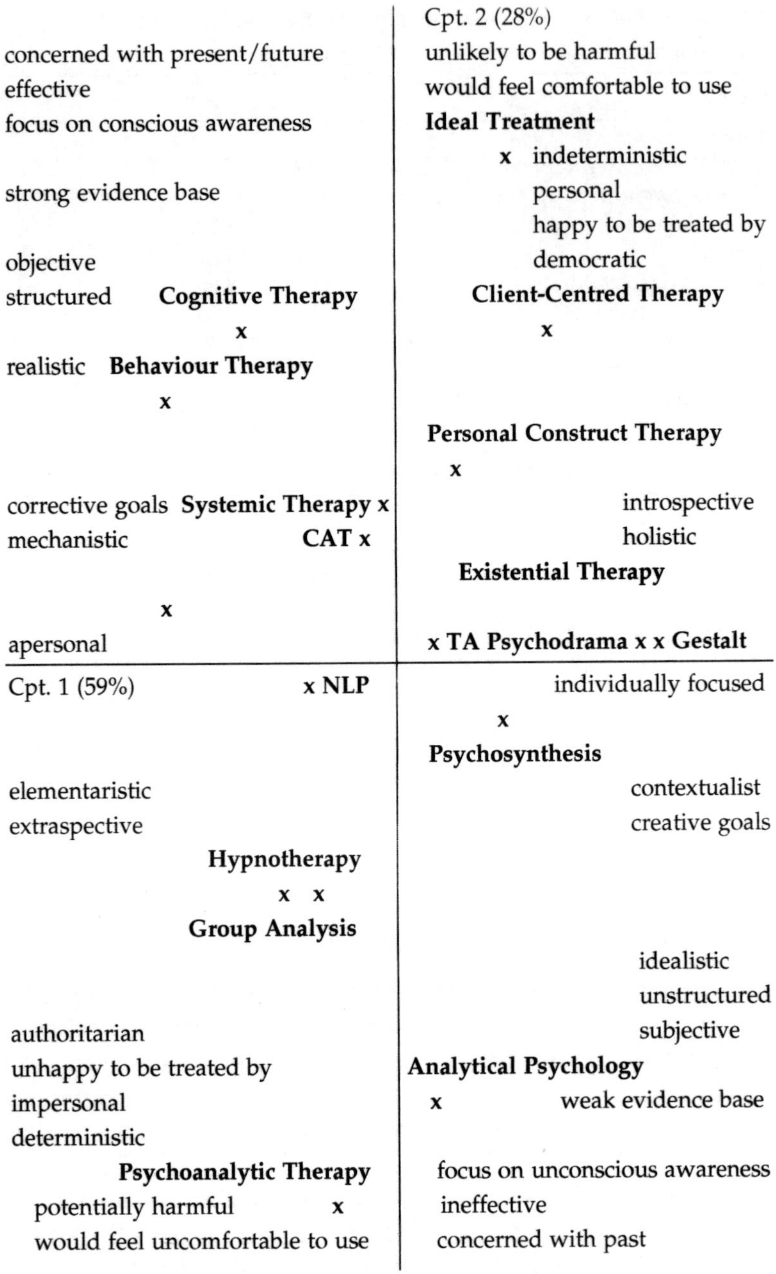

Cpt. 2 (28%)

concerned with present/future   unlikely to be harmful

effective   would feel comfortable to use

focus on conscious awareness   **Ideal Treatment**

                                          x   indeterministic

strong evidence base   personal

                                        happy to be treated by

objective   democratic

structured   **Cognitive Therapy**   **Client-Centred Therapy**

                     x   x

realistic   **Behaviour Therapy**

                x

                                    Personal Construct Therapy

                                      x

corrective goals **Systemic Therapy** x   introspective

mechanistic   **CAT** x   holistic

                                 Existential Therapy

                   x

apersonal   x TA Psychodrama x x Gestalt

Cpt. 1 (59%)   x **NLP**   individually focused

                                       x

                                 Psychosynthesis

elementaristic   contextualist

extraspective   creative goals

                      Hypnotherapy

                        x   x

                     Group Analysis

                                      idealistic

                                      unstructured

authoritarian   subjective

unhappy to be treated by   **Analytical Psychology**

impersonal   x   weak evidence base

deterministic

                   Psychoanalytic Therapy

potentially harmful   x   focus on unconscious awareness

would feel uncomfortable to use   ineffective

                                concerned with past

Figure 1. Plot of elements in construct space from principal component analysis of therapists' mean grid.

component (horizontal axis) of this grid differentiated therapies in terms of whether they were introspective, holistic, individually focused, contextualist, and had creative treatment goals or extra-spective, elementaristic, apersonal, mechanistic, and corrective. The placement of the therapies indicated that this could be regarded as a "humanistic" versus "cognitive–behavioural" dimension. The second component was concerned with whether therapies were effective, had a low potential to harm, felt comfortable to use, and were more concerned with the present and future and with conscious awareness. Client-centred and cognitive therapies were viewed in these terms and contrasted with analytic therapies.

Table 3 provides the mean correlations between the groups of grids and, in the diagonal, the mean within group correlations. It can be seen that the former correlations tended to be lower than the latter, indicating that, as predicted, there was greater commonality of construing within than between orientations. If those orienta-tions where less than four grids were available are excluded, personal construct psychotherapy is the most homogeneous group in terms of commonality of construing and cognitive–behaviour therapy the least.

Analysis of elicited constructs

The previous grid analyses all focused upon participants' ratings of therapies on the supplied constructs. In addition, two approaches were adopted in analysing the constructs elicited from participants. In the first of these, a grid was created of different participants' ratings of the elements on their elicited constructs. One hundred and

Table 3.   Correlations between mean grids

	NLP	PCP	Hyp	CBT	Sys	Hum	CAT	Psy
PCP	0.69							
Hypnotherapy	0.58	0.63						
CBT	0.44	0.61	0.63					
Systemic	0.55	0.66	0.62	0.63				
Humanistic	0.58	0.69	0.67	0.60	0.70			
CAT	0.47	0.53	0.53	0.55	0.49	0.66		
Psychodynamic	0.47	0.51	0.54	0.47	0.58	0.78	0.62	
Analytical	0.32	0.39	0.44	0.48	0.53	0.67	0.60	0.71

twenty-three constructs were included in this grid, which was analysed in two halves. In both of these grids the first principal components essentially contrasted cognitive–behavioural approaches, described by such construct poles as "symptom focused" and "technique focused", with analytic approaches, described by construct poles such as "very time consuming" and "trains via apostolic succession". In both grids, cognitive–behavioural and analytic approaches were similarly placed on the second component, and contrasted with constructivist and some humanistic approaches. The constructs loading highly on this component largely concerned humanistic issues, such as the importance accorded to the individual client, as well as issues related to the breadth of the approach. The similarity between the results of the analyses of the two grids provides some indication of the reliability of the procedure.

The other approach adopted to the analysis of the elicited construct poles was that two of the authors of the paper independently divided them into a number of categories. They then discussed their classifications, and agreed upon a taxonomy which, as listed below, consisted of sixteen categories, all except one of which were divided into subcategories.

1. Usefulness
2. Structure
3. Focus on aspect of the client's functioning
4. Concern with the therapeutic relationship
5. Concern with psychodynamic structure and process
6. Concern with personal meaning
7. Concern with treatment goals
8. Concern with personal growth, wholeness, and choice
9. Concern with social context
10. Technical approach
11. Concern with theory
12. Temporal focus
13. Reflexivity
14. Value judgements
15. Self reference
16. Other

Definitions were written for each category and subcategory (these may be obtained from the first author on request). The two authors concerned then reclassified all of the construct poles in terms of this category system. Examination of the reliability of the coding of the first 1298 construct poles elicited revealed a very respectable kappa of 0.67 for the sixteen superordinate categories. The codings of the senior author of all the 2087 construct poles elicited, which were made blind to the therapeutic orientation of the respondent, were used in the subsequent analysis. This revealed a highly significant difference in the content of the constructs used by therapists of different orientations (chi square = 410; p < 0.001). As can be seen in Table 4, over a quarter of construct poles concerned either focus on an aspect of the client's functioning or the therapeutic relationship. Although most groups of therapists differentiated approaches highly on the basis of these two construct categories, other categories revealed more distinctive, and predictable, preoccupations of particular orientations. For example, the cognitive–behaviour therapists used a large number of constructs concerning technical aspects of therapy, the psychodynamic therapists showed a particular concern with psychodynamic structure and processes, the

Table 4. Percentage of construct poles in each category

| | THERAPISTS | | | | | | | | |
	Total	CBT	Psy	Hum	CAT	PCP	NLP	Sys	Hyp
Usefulness	4.6	7.9	5.9	3.4	3.3	1.8	6.7	1.3	7.9
Structure	8.5	15.0	9.5	7.0	**12.3**	5.0	7.5	5.2	**16.1**
Focus	**13.6**	**15.4**	10.5	13.9	13.9	**15.8**	10.2	**22.7**	6.9
Relationship	**13.5**	**16.6**	**18.8**	**14.5**	9.0	7.7	**12.9**	10.4	10.1
Psychodynamics	**10.3**	6.3	**20.4**	8.6	10.7	7.2	10.2	9.7	10.1
Meaning	6.0	2.8	2.3	6.6	4.9	**13.5**	4.1	7.8	6.3
Goals	3.5	5.1	1.0	4.2	0.8	3.2	6.8	5.8	0.5
Growth	4.7	0.0	2.3	7.3	5.7	5.0	8.8	1.3	4.2
Social	9.9	7.5	6.9	**11.1**	8.2	**15.3**	6.8	**20.8**	2.1
Technical	6.4	**15.7**	4.9	7.6	2.5	7.2	4.1	3.2	7.9
Theory	3.4	3.2	4.6	2.7	2.5	5.0	2.7	1.3	4.8
Temporal	4.9	3.6	4.6	5.3	5.7	5.9	1.4	1.9	9.0
Reflexivity	0.1	0.0	0.0	0.0	0.0	0.5	0.7	0.6	0.0
Value	5.8	5.9	5.6	3.7	9.0	6.8	**10.9**	4.5	7.4
Self Reference	4.0	1.6	1.0	3.2	**11.5**	0.5	5.4	3.2	**13.8**
Other	0.7	0.8	1.6	0.7	0.0	0.0	2.0	0.0	0.0

The three categories used with most frequency by each group are highlighted in bold type.

personal construct psychotherapists were concerned with personal meaning, and the systemic therapists, not unpredictably, focused on the social context of therapy. Despite the current climate of evidence-based practice, the therapists were relatively unconcerned with the usefulness of therapy, and neither did they show any great concern with theoretical issues. Several of them were not averse to making value judgements concerning other approaches, often seeing these in less than complimentary terms, as reflected in such construct poles as "crap therapy", "ineffective claptrap", "long-winded, old-fashioned", "Procrustean", "heavy on waffle, light on outcome data", "loony theory", and "ineffective claptrap". The reader may wish to guess which therapies were described in these terms by therapists of which orientations.

Therapeutic preferences

A further indication of respondents' evaluation of other therapies was provided by examining their responses to questions asking them to which therapies they would never refer a client and which they would opt for if they were a client. Table 5 indicates the mean number of times therapists in each orientation mentioned a therapy to which they would never refer. If this can be regarded as a measure of intolerance of other approaches, it can be seen that the psychodynamic psychotherapists were the most intolerant and the Jungians, neurolinguistic, and personal construct psychotherapists the most tolerant. As can also be seen in Table 5, nearly a third of the approaches to which respondents would never refer fell within the humanistic spectrum.

However, a somewhat different picture is presented when considering which approaches these therapists would choose if they were clients. Although previous research has indicated that therapists generally seek personal therapy within their own orientation (Norcross et al., 1988; Norcross, 1990), in this sample, as can be seen from Table 6, nearly half of the therapists (46.93 per cent) would have opted for another orientation. In this regard, humanistic approaches were particularly popular, being chosen by a quarter of the therapists who would seek therapy within an orientation other than their own. Not unpredictably, the constructivist therapists, namely neurolinguistic and personal construct psychotherapists,

Table 5. Mean number of therapies to which therapists in each orientation would never refer.

Psychodynamic	2.20
Cognitive–analytic	1.83
Cognitive–behavioural	1.62
Humanistic	1.28
Hypno-psychotherapy	1.14
Systemic	1.08
Personal construct	0.50
Neurolinguistic	0.25
Analytical psychology	0.00

THERAPIES TO WHICH RESPONDENTS WOULD NOT REFER

Humanistic	31.75	(expressed as percentages of total of therapies to which they would not refer)
Neurolinguistic	15.08	
Hypno-psychotherapy	14.29	
Psychodynamic	13.49	
Cognitive–behavioural	10.32	
Personal construct	5.56	
Group analysis	3.97	
Analytical psychology	3.17	
Cognitive–analytic	1.59	
Systemic	0.79	

were most likely to experiment with alternative orientations. More surprising was the willingness of some cognitive–behaviour therapists to undergo therapies that might be considered to contrast markedly with their own orientation, three opting for a Jungian approach, one for psychodynamic psychotherapy, five for a humanistic therapy, and three for cognitive analytic therapy.

Conclusions

Our findings provide further support for all of the hypotheses. They have implications in three main areas.

Communication difficulties between therapists

The findings would suggest that heated disputes between therapists may occur because any challenge to a therapist's preferred

Table 6.   Percentage of therapists who would choose personal therapy of an alternative orientation.

Neurolinguistic	66.67
Personal construct	62.50
Hypno-psychotherapy	60.87
Systemic	50.00
Analytical psychology	50.00
Cognitive–behavioural	48.00
Psychodynamic	46.67
Humanistic	33.87
Cognitive–analytic	33.33
TOTAL	46.93
THERAPIES CHOSEN FROM OTHER ORIENTATIONS (as %)	
Humanistic	25.00
Analytical psychology	17.86
Psychodynamic	11.90
Group analysis	10.71
Cognitive–behavioural	8.33
Neurolinguistic	8.33
Cognitive–analytic	7.14
Systemic	4.76
Hypno-psychotherapy	3.57
Personal construct	2.38

theoretical orientation is likely to imply a challenge to their personal style and fundamental philosophical beliefs, or in personal construct theory terms their core constructs. As Kelly (1955) has indicated, people feel threatened when they anticipate invalidation of their core constructs.

Treatment selection

The findings also imply that personal styles, philosophical beliefs, and personal constructs could usefully be taken into consideration not only in selecting trainee therapists but also in matching therapists with clients.

Research methodology

The study has provided further evidence of the value of the Direction of Interest Questionnaire, the Therapist Attitude

Questionnaire Rationalism Scale, and the repertory grid in research in this area.

References

Arthur, A. (1999). Clinical psychologists, psychotherapists and orientation choice: does personality matter? *Clinical Psychology Forum, 125*: 33–37.

Caine, T. M., & Smail, D. J. (1969). *The Treatment of Mental illness: Science, Faith and the Therapeutic Personality*. London: University of London Press.

Caine, T. M., Smail, D. J., Wijesinghe, O. B. A., & Winter, D. A. (1982). *The Claybury Selection Battery Manual*. Windsor: NFER-Nelson.

Caine, T. M., Wijesinghe, O. B. A., & Winter, D. A. (1981). *Personal Styles in Neurosis: Implications for Small Group Psychotherapy and Behaviour Therapy*. London: Routledge and Kegan Paul.

Caine, T. M., & Winter, D. A. (1993). Personal styles and universal polarities: implications for therapeutic practice. *Therapeutic Communities, 14*: 91–102.

Johnson, J. A., Germer, C. K., Efran, J. S., & Overton, W. F. (1988). Personality as the basis for theoretical predilections. *Journal of Personality and Social Psychology, 55*: 824–835.

Karasu, T. B. (1986). The psychotherapies: benefits and limitations. *American Journal of Psychotherapy, 40*: 324–343.

Kelly, G. A. (1955). *The Psychology of Personal Constructs*. New York: Norton.

Lyddon, W. J. & Adamson, L. A. (1992). Worldview and counseling preference: an analogue study. *Journal of Counseling and Development, 71*: 41–47.

Neimeyer, G. J., & Morton, R. J. (1997). Personal epistemologies and preferences for rationalist versus constructivist psychotherapies. *Journal of Constructivist Psychology, 10*: 109–123.

Neimeyer, G. J., Prichard, S., Lyddon, W. J., & Sherrard, P. A. D. (1993). The role of epistemic style in counseling preference and orientation. *Journal of Counseling and Development, 71*: 515–523.

Norcross, J. C. (1990). Eclecticism misrepresented and integration misunderstood—commentary. *Psychotherapy, 27*(2): 297–300.

Norcross, J. C., Strausser, D. J., & Faltus, F. J. (1988). The therapist's therapist. *American Journal of Psychotherapy, 42*(1): 53–66.

Schacht, T. E., & Black, D. A. (1985). Epistemological commitments of behavioral and psychoanalytic therapists. *Professional Psychology: Research and Practice, 16*: 316–323.

Tschudi, F. (1998). *Flexigrid*. Oslo: Tschudi Systems Sales.

Tschudi, F. (2001). *Multigrid*. Oslo: Tschudi Systems Sales.

Wampole, B. E., Mondin, G. W., Moody, M., Stich, F., Benson, K., & Ahn, H. (1997). A meta-analysis of outcome studies comparing bona fide psychotherapies: Empirically, "All must have prizes". *Psychological Bulletin, 122*: 203–215.

Winter, D. A. (1990). Therapeutic alternatives for psychological disorder: personal construct psychology investigations in a health service setting. In: G. J. Neimeyer & R. A. Neimeyer (Eds.), *Advances in Personal Construct Psychology*, Volume 1. New York: JAI Press.

SUGGESTIONS FOR FURTHER READING ON PSYCHOTHERAPEUTIC RESEARCH

These references are organized in a three-by-three matrix according to (a) levels of complexity/complication, (b) whether concerning outcome, process or both. In terms of the UKCP committee's "top ten" papers, we recommend the first ten below.

Level 1 Basic

(i) Outcome

Evans, C., Mellor-Clark, J., & Margison, F. *et al.* (2000). CORE: Clinical Outcomes in Routine Evaluation. *Journal of Mental Health, 9*: 247–255.

Inventory of Interpersonal Problems (IIP), Horowitz , L. M, Rosenberg, S. E., Baer, B. A., Ureno, G., & Villesenor, V. S. (1988). Inventory of Interpersonal problems: psychometric properties and clinical applications, *Journal of Consulting and Clinical Psychology, 47*: 5–15.

(ii) Process

Frosh, S., Burck, C., Strickland-Clark, L., *et al.* (1996). Engaging with change: a process study of family therapy. *Journal of Family Therapy, 18*: 141–161 *and then:*

Guthrie, *et al.* (1998). Brief Dynamic/Interpersonal Therapy for patients with severe psychiatric illness which is unresponsive to treatment *British Journal of Psychotherapy*, 15(2).

Hardy, G., Aldridge, J., Davidson, C., Rowe, C., Reilly, S., & Shapiro, D. (1999). therapist responsiveness to client attachment styles and issues observed in client-identified significant events in psychodynamic-interpersonal therapy. *Psychotherapy Research*, 9: 36–53.

Llewelyn, S., & Hardy, G. (2001). Process research in understanding and applying psychological therapies. *British Journal of Clinical Psychology*, 40: 1–21.

Stancombe, J., & White, S. (1997). Notes on the tenacity of therapeutic presuppositions in process research: examining the artfulness of blamings in family therapy. *Journal of Family Therapy*, 19: 21–41 *which gives a different analysis of the same therapy.*

(iii) Both process and outcome

Burland, J. A. (1997). The role of working through in bringing about psychic change. *International Journal of Psychoanalysis*, 78: 469–484.

Ogrodniczuk, J. S., Piper, W. E., Joyce, A. S., & McCallum, M. (1999). Transference interpretations in short-term dynamic psychotherapy. *Journal of Nervous & Mental Disease*, 187: 572–579.

Persons, J. B., Silberschatz, G. (1998). Are results of randomized controlled trials useful to psychotherapists? *Journal of Consulting & Clinical Psychology*, 66(1).

Luborsky, L. (1994) Therapeutic alliances as predictors of psychotherapy outcomes: Factors explaining the predictive success. In: A. O. Horvath & L. S. Greenberg (Eds.), *The Working Alliance: Theory, Research, and Practice*. Wiley series on personality processes.

Level 2: more advanced

(i) Outcome

Bateman, A., & Fonagy, P. (1999). Effectiveness of partial hospitalization in the treatment of borderline personality disorder: a randomized controlled trial. *American Journal of Psychiatry*, 156: 1563–1969, and the follow-up paper to that: Bateman, A., & Fonagy, P. (2001).

Treatment of borderline personality disorder with psychoanalytically informed partial hospitalization: an 18-month follow-up. *American Journal of Psychiatry, 158*: 36–42.

Hansen, N. B., & Lambert, M. J. (1996). Clinical significance: an overview of methods. *Journal of Mental Health, 5*: 17–24.

Relating: Birtchnell, J. (1999). The Person's Relating to Others Questionnaire (PROQ2) in *Relating in Psychotherapy: The Application of a New Theory.* Westport, CT: Praeger.

Repertory Grid Technique (RGT), in D. Winter (2003), Repertory Grid Technique as a psychotherapy research measure. *Psychotherapy Research, 13*: 25–42.

(ii) Process

Brief Structured Recall (BSR): Elliott, R., & Shapiro, D. A. (1988). Brief structured recall: a more efficient method for studying significant therapy events. *British Journal of Medical Psychology, 61*: 141–153.

Stern, D. *et al.* (1998). Non-interpretative mechanisms in psychoanalytic psychotherapy. *International Journal of Psychoanalysis, 79*: 3.

Triangle of person (current figures, transference and childhood relationships) and triangle of conflict (impulses/feelings, defences and anxiety): Malan (1976). *The Frontier of Brief Psychotherapy.* New York: Plenum.

(iii) Both process and outcome

Horvath, A. O., & Symonds, B. D. (1991). Relation between working alliance and outcome in psychotherapy: a meta-analysis. *Journal of Counselling Psychology, 38*: 139–149.

Margison, F. R. Barkham, M., Evans, C., McGrath, G., Clark, J. M., Audin, K., & Connell, J. (2000). Measurement and psychotherapy. Evidence-based practice and practice-based evidence. *British Journal of Psychiatry, 177*: 123–30.

Safran, J., & Muran, J. C. (1996). Resolution of ruptures in the therapeutic alliance. *Journal of Consulting and Clinical Psychology, 64*: 447–458.

Level 3: Complex

(i) Outcome

Guthrie, E. (2000). Psychotherapy for patients with complex disorders and chronic symptoms the need for a new research paradigm. *British Journal of Psychiatry, 177*: 131–137.

(ii) Process

Angus, L., Levitt, H., & Hardtke, K. (1999). The narrative Process Coding system: Research applications and implications for psychotherapy practice. *Journal of Clinical Psychology*, *55*(10): 1255–1270.

Levitt, H. (2001). Sounds of silence in psychotherapy: the categorization of patients' pauses. *Psychotherapy Research*, *11*(3): 295–311.

Tamura, T., & Lau, A. (1992). Connectedness versus separateness: applicability of family therapy to Japanese families. *Family Process*, *31*: 319–340.

(iii) Both process and outcome

Burns, D., & Nolen-Hoeksma, S. (1997). Therapeutic empathy and recovery from depression in cognitive–behavioural therapy: a structural equation model, *Journal of Consulting & Clinical Psychology*, *60*: 441–449.

Hatcher, R. L., Barends, A., Hansell, J., & Gutfreund, M. J. (1995). Patients' and therapists' shared and unique views of the therapeutic alliance: an investigation using confirmatory factor analysis in a nested design. *Journal of Consulting & Clinical Psychology*, *63*(4): 636–643.

Teasdale, J. D., Moore, R. G., Hayhurst, H., Pope, M., Williams, S., & Segal, Z. V. (20002). Metacognitive awareness and prevention of relapse in depression: Empirical evidence. *Journal of Consulting & Clinical Psychology*, *70*(2): 275–287.

INDEX